SCIENCE, METAPHYSICS, AND THE CHANCE OF SALVATION:
An Interpretation of the Thought of
William James

AMERICAN ACADEMY OF RELIGION
DISSERTATION SERIES

edited by
H. Ganse Little, Jr.

Number 24

SCIENCE, METAPHYSICS, AND THE CHANCE OF SALVATION:
An Interpretation of the Thought of William James

by
Henry S. Levinson

SCHOLARS PRESS
Missoula, Montana

SCIENCE, METAPHYSICS, AND THE CHANCE OF SALVATION:
An Interpretation of the Thought of
William James

by

Henry S. Levinson

Published by
SCHOLARS PRESS
for
The American Academy of Religion

Distributed by

SCHOLARS PRESS
P.O. Box 5207
Missoula, Montana 59806

SCIENCE, METAPHYSICS, AND THE CHANCE OF SALVATION:
An Interpretation of the Thought of William James

by

Henry S. Levinson
Stanford University

Library of Congress Cataloging in Publication Data
Levinson, Henry S.
    Science, metaphysics, and the chance of salva-
tion.

    (Dissertation series – American Academy of
Religon ; no. 24)
    Originally presented as the author's thesis,
Princeton University, 1976.
    Bibliography: p.
    1. James, William, 1842–1910. 2. Salvation.
I. Title. II. Series: American Academy of
Religion. Dissertation series – American Academy
of Religion ; no. 24.
B945.J24L44   1978   191   78–7383
ISBN 0–89130–234–4

                Printed in the United States of America
                    1   2   3   4   5   6

TABLE OF CONTENTS

FOR CATHY AND MOLLY

CHAPTER I
INTRODUCTION: JAMES'S CENTER OF VISION

This dissertation presents an essay about the thought of
William James. In it, I address some of the issues about
thought and action, belief and knowledge, personhood and
experience that James raised in his published work. My essay
is hardly the first of its kind. James has been the subject
of debate, interpretation, and reformulation since before his
death. His work has inspired criticism across the globe and
particularly in Anglo-American academies. Indeed, there are
so many William Jameses that it becomes appropriate to ask
why we need yet another one. If we take the major interpretations of James alone, we have James the pragmatic realist
(Perry);[1] James the existential phenomenologist (Wild);[2] James
the proto-transcendental phenomenologist (Wilshire);[3] and
James the forerunner of logical empiricism (Ayer).[4]

Why do we need yet another interpretation of the thought
of William James? In my opinion, a crucial error in method
has been committed by the interpreters noted above and many
others. Each has arranged his interpretation of James
according to claims about *how* James asks and answers questions
of philosophical import. To determine James's philosophical
method, of course, is necessary for an adequate understanding
of his work. But no major James scholar has centered his
arguments and claims about James either on *what* questions
James asked or on what James construed to be the sorts of
circumstance and conditions that generate those questions.
It will be my intention to interpret James from these latter
points of view.

I will, of course, detail, analyze, and criticize James's
philosophical psychology, epistemology, metaphysics, and
religious thought, because I take these to be the fundamental
conceptual frames in which he moves and positions himself
intellectually. But I will do so, not primarily in order to
place James in one philosophical camp or another. I will do
so in order to locate and clarify what he referred to as his

1

center of vision.

    By focussing on James's "center of vision," I will hope-
fully spare myself from the deserved and fundamental criticism
that James addressed to a youthful contemporary who had
recently completed a thesis about his thought. His remarkable
letter to "Miss S" must be quoted at length:

> Dear Miss S_____, I am a caitiff! I have left
> your essay on my poor self unanswered. . . .
> It is a great compliment to me to be taken so
> philologically and importantly; and I must say
> that from a technical point of view you may be
> proud of your production. I like greatly the
> objective and dispassionate key in which you
> keep everything, and the number of subdivisions
> and articulations which you make gives me ver-
> tiginous admiration. Nevertheless, the tragic
> fact remains that I don't feel wounded at all
> by all that output of ability, and for reasons
> which I think I can set down briefly enough.
> It all comes, in my eyes, from too much philo-
> logical method--as a Ph.D. thesis your essay is
> supreme, but why don't you go farther. You take
> utterances of mine written at different dates,
> for different audiences belonging to different
> universes of discourse, and string them together
> as the abstract elements of a total philosophy
> which you then show to be inwardly incoherent.
> This is splendid philology, but is it live
> criticism of anyone's *Weltanschauung*? Your use
> of the method only strengthens the impression I
> have got from reading criticisms of my "pragmatic"
> account of "truth," that the whole Ph.D. industry
> of building up an author's meaning out of separate
> texts leads nowhere, unless you have first grasped
> his centre of vision, by an act of imagination.
> That, it seems to me, you lack in my case. . . .
>   Now if I may presume to give a word of advice
> to one so much more accomplished than myself in
> dialectic technique, may I urge, since you have
> shown what a superb mistress you are in that
> difficult art of discriminating abstractions and
> opposing them to each other one by one, since in
> short there is no university extant that wouldn't
> give you its *summa cum laude*--I should certainly
> so reward your thesis at Harvard--may I urge, I
> say, that you should turn your back on that aca-
> demic sort of thing altogether, and devote your
> great talents to reality in its concreteness?
> In other words, do some *positive* work at the
> problem of what truth signifies, substitute a
> definite alternative to the humanism which I
> present, as the latter's substitute. Not by
> proving their inward incoherence does one refute
> philosophies--every human being is incoherent--
> but only by superseding them by other philosophies
> more satisfactory. Your wonderful technical skill

ought to serve you in good stead if you would
exchange the philological kind of criticism
for constructive work. I fear however that
you won't--the iron may have bitten too deeply
into your soul !!
       . . . Well! There! that is all! But dear
Madam, I should like to know where you come from,
who you are, what your present "situation" is.
etc., etc.--It is natural to have some personal
curiosity about a lady who has taken such an
extraordinary amount of pains for me!
       Believe me, dear Miss S____, with renewed
apologies for the extreme tardiness of this
acknowledgment, yours with mingled admiration
and abhorence,

W. James.[5]

Now we can cull both a warning and a warrant from
James's letter to dear Miss S. The warning: If we are in the
business of interpreting the thought of a particular thinker,
we must not employ conceptual analysis as an end in itself.
Rather, we must analyze that thought in order to reconstruct
the vision of things articulated through it. The warrant:
If we are to take the thought of a thinker seriously, we are
bound to point out, but not dote upon, its measure of
coherence or incoherence. We must be prepared to show that
and why and how the positions a thinker takes and the moves
that he makes are adequate or inadequate. But we must also
be prepared to readdress ourselves to his questions when we
think that his answers fail in some respect or other. In
other words, we must be prepared both to interpret justly and
to reformulate more adequately. The former marks service to
historical justice while the latter demonstrates submission to
philosophical demand. As a philosopher who has chosen to
consider James's thought, I am committed to both sorts of
service. As a philosopher, I am bound to James by the
questions that he raises, but neither the method that he uses
to answer those questions nor his particular answers.

But without further ado, I must share my "act of
imagination" concerning the center of James's vision. I
claim that the possibility of salvation or what James calls
"the chance of salvation"[6] stands at the center of his vision.
I propose to argue to the thesis that James's work must be
taken as that of a *religious thinker*; that is, a thinker whose
fundamental questions have to do most precisely with the

problem of salvation.

James's work is informed by three key questions. Is life
worth living? Can people effect changes they intend? Are
there gods, or unseen powers that cooperate with us as agents
and patients of communities? While his psychological,
epistemological, metaphysical, and phenomenological inquiries
enable him to *answer* these questions, they do not generate
them. The questions are generated from a soteric frame. They
are things that James thinks he must ask if he is to resolve
*the issue whether our outstanding problems as persons are
solvable problems*. He asks whether life is worth living
because the soteric issue is defused if it is not. He asks
whether people can effect changes they intend inasmuch as he
thinks that doing so is a necessary condition for the solution
of our problems. And he asks whether there are gods because
his inquiries lead him to believe that the efforts of people
alone probably will not result in the solution of their own
outstanding problems.

Now when I claim that James is a religious thinker, I
implicitly claim that *he is not a theologian*. As I see it,[7]
a religious thinker asks soteric questions and tries to
determine their answers. But he has no such answers in store
and, indeed, is open to the possibility that there simply are
none to be found. A theologian, to the contrary, asks
"secular questions"--ethical, epistemological, metaphysical
questions--and provides theological answers according to
theological methods developed within a particular religious
tradition based on some particular revelation or other.

So take note: By claiming that James is a religious
thinker, I do not preclude him from using a variety of methods
both to consider the meaningfulness of the questions he asks
and to generate answers to those that he claims are, in fact,
meaningful. Indeed, as a philosopher, I hold him responsible
for doing these things.

As a matter of fact, James is so far from construing
himself as issuing theological information, and so perspicacious a philosopher, that I need to qualify his stance as a
religious thinker. I need to admit from the outset that, *as a
thinker* at least, James demonstrates no interest in defending

either the necessity or actuality of salvation. Indeed, he
precludes both options by argument. James intends to consider
and defend the possibility of salvation. In other words, he
will argue that people are such, and the universe is such, as
to allow for a chance of salvation. In support of his conten-
tion that things generally may admit to solutions, he will
generate a synoptic philosophy equally critical of those who
claim, on the one hand, either the necessity or actuality of
salvation, and of those on the other who claim the impossibility of salvation.

Thus, for instance, he argues against post-Hegelian
absolute idealists inasmuch as they insist on the necessity
and/or ineluctability of salvation. He argues against the
claims of the mystics, insofar as they insist on the actuality
of salvation. And he argues against "scientific naturalists"
and materialists because they preclude the possibility of
salvation. To the contrary, he argues that salvation is not
impossible and that, indeed, there is a kind of human
experience--the kind he construes to be religious experience--
that supports its plausibility.

Perhaps most significantly, James is convinced that any
argument for the possibility of salvation hangs on a claim
about the conditions of persons. As James sees it, salvation
simply does not make sense unless the differences people
apparently make are really made. As he sees it, salvation or
the solution of our outstanding problems is an absurd notion
unless people are able to *serve* the interests they *bring* to
things. Quite simply, people must have the power to intend
both to do things they desire and to bring about states of
affairs that complement those desires.

James sees intentionality as crucial, *not* because he
thinks that if salvation is possible it is because persons can
mastermind it, but because he takes it as *evidence* for the
claim that things in general may be such as to allow for the
satisfaction of interests and the fulfilment of purposes. In
this light, much of his work can be taken as an attempt to
specify the conditions and circumstances surrounding the
behavior of persons, as well as an attempt to isolate and
describe the sorts of human experience in which significant

and demonstrable changes seem to occur.

Now I have titled my dissertation *Science, Metaphysics, and the Chance of Salvation* because James sees the need to turn to (what he considers) science, metaphysics, and religious experience to support his central vision. He turns to science to specify what is *describable as* human experience. He turns to metaphysics to determine *the sorts of conditions that must hold* if human experience is really what it seems to be. And he turns to the varieties of religious experience to isolate *events in which human interests are apparently fully served despite the apparent inability of humans to serve them fully*.

To the extent that James attempts to specify what persons can know about themselves and things generally, what persons can and should do, and what persons might hope, his philosophical anthropology is, of course, remarkably Kantian. But where Kant turned first and foremost to the specification of reason or the logical conditions of knowledge in order to answer his questions about persons, James turned to the specification of human behavior to draw up his agenda. Kant saw himself as effecting a Copernican revolution in philosophy by insisting that

> Hitherto it has been assumed that all our knowledge must conform to objects. But all attempts to extend our knowledge of objects by establishing something in regard to them *a priori*, by means of concepts, have, on this assumption, ended in failure. We must therefore . . . suppose that objects must conform to our knowledge.[8]

But James saw himself as part of a movement that was effecting what he called a "protestant revolution" in critical philosophy by insisting that the notion of correspondence or "conformation" between knowledge and matters of fact was itself vague and obscure, no matter which side of the correspondence was stipulated as primitive or foundational. Asserting that knowledge and reality were both parts of experience which, by definition, could only be specified *a posteriori*, James (along with other classical pragmatists) turned from foundations to consequences, from epistemology as *the* logically prior science to epistemology as a social process, from a search for the infallible to a search for the verifiable, from claims about apodictic truth to claims about adequate accounts, to determine the conditions of men in the universe.

Like Kant, James guided his philosophical vessel between the *Charybdis* of introspective rationalism and the *Scylla* of sense-data empiricism. But unlike Kant, he did not seek to find a mechanism of *rapprochement* between them. Instead he claimed the "vicious intellectualism" of both rationalism and sense-data empiricism. He attempted to unmask the fact that both rely on fallacious myths of the given. He attempted to show that no idea is known to be true simply because it is clear and distinct, inasmuch as all ideas are set in inferential contexts. He attempted to show that the "sensations" of the British empiricists are hardly given as matters of fact; but rather, that "sensations" are abstractions based on lines of inference from and about experience.

All in all, he points to the hollowness of "correspondence" as a useful philosophical term. He applauds Kant for curbing both the pretensions of sense and the fanciful flights of the intellect. He accepts Kant's reflexive or critical turn as crucial preparation for anyone interested in returning to first-order questions. But he literally derides Kant for merely turning the tables on the question of the foundations of human experience. According to James, reality is not the foundation of human experience; knowledge is not the foundation of human experience. Human experience, the logical space in which we say and do what we say and do, is the place, *in medias res*, where people know and take things to be real; where people desire, intend to fulfil desires, and enact intentions; and where people suffer and hope for salvation-- in each and all, where people are able to make a difference.

Kant, of course, is not characteristically inimical to James. Hegel is. More accurately, those of James's contemporaries who invoke "Hegel's method" serve the office of *bête noire* in James's work. To begin with, James construes the likes of Royce and Bradley to be more apt opponents than Kant. He realizes that they, like himself, are promulgating a philosophical position meant to overcome the Cartesian dualism between mind and body on which Kant's bifurcation of reason

ultimately rested. He realizes that what bothers him about
Kant bothers them as well: the rigid distinction between
theoretical and practical reason, the sharp division between
knowing that x is the case and intending that x be the case,
the bifurcation of conditions for thought and conditions for
action. But he also realizes that they celebrate what he
takes to be Kant's grossest error: he sees them celebrating
the transcendental ego or self; and he sees them deploying it
as a mechanism in terms of which the specifications of
apodictic truth or the foundations for human experience may
be established.

If and when James argues that philosophy would have been
better off detouring around Kant,[9] it is because he believes
that philosophy took the reflexive or critical turn before
Kant, with Locke, and because he believes that Kant's introduction of the notion of the transcendental ego has had
disastrous consequences for the critical tradition. Within
the context of Kant's own work, of course, the transcendental
ego makes little if any difference. If it is a ghost in the
machine, it does not frighten anybody. It has the officious
duty of somehow holding together the impressions of sense and
the expressions of mind, which remain bifurcated in any case.
Nevertheless, the notion places critical philosophy in
jeopardy by generating an occasion for Hegel, who makes
awesome, and as far as James is concerned, awful claims for
and about it.[10]   Enter Hegel's *Geist* or Absolute, in which,
he claims, we live and move and have our being.

The crucial mistake that Hegel makes, from James's point
of view, is a matter of philosophical method and strategy.
Both James and Hegel seek radical reform of Kant's critical
position, and for basically the same reason. They think that
it rests on Cartesian dualism, and they do not think Cartesian
dualism makes sense. They both finally attempt to resolve the
distinction between subject and object, as that distinction is
drawn and supposed by Kant. They both gear their philosophies
to generate primitive terms that will collapse, overcome, or
in some way make fictive the distinction between mind and body

and all that the distinction entails.

But Hegel's method for reform is one of *ascent*, while James's method is one of *descent*. Hegel's response to Kant's problems is to take yet another reflexive turn. His aim is to offer a philosophical perspective *higher* than the perspective given in Kant's critiques. Indeed, his aim (as James sees it) is to offer a philosophical perspective so high that there could be no higher. To this end, Hegel will claim that from the vantage point of his dialectical science, the ills of critical philosophy can be diagnosed and cured. What are those ills, according to Hegel? Kant suffers from nothing less than the *cure* he was administering to naive rationalists and sense-data empiricists. The *form* of Kant's argument is diseased. The discrete determinations of the understanding inevitably result in the contradictions of the antinomies, because of Kant's formal dependence on the subject/object bifurcation, or in Hegel's terms, the supposition that "there is a difference between ourselves and . . . knowledge."[11]

Hegel's cure for Kant's disease is a further and, he claims, complete specification of thought. The key term in that specification is *consciousness*, because as Hegel sees it, that notion overcomes Kant's formal problems. It relocates knowledge. For Kant, knowledge consisted in a set of determinations which, as a matter of principle, was endless. Hegel, to the contrary, was able to construe knowledge as the *medium* in which persons think and act. But Hegel's medium is no ordinary medium. It is *Geist* or Spirit or independent, intentional subjectivity coming to recognize itself. In other words, it is Kant's transcendental ego transformed into an incontestable being ineluctably expressing itself in word and deed: an awesome ghost indeed.

Of course, it matters little how Hegel--the 'real' Hegel--actually employed *Geist*, as far as our understanding of James is concerned. In my opinion, James often turned Hegel and his admirers into straw men. But so far as this dissertation is concerned, I will not attempt to correct James's misapprehensions of Hegel, Royce, Bradley or others. What will be significant for us is how these and other thinkers were taken by James.

James construed Hegel's method of ascent as a strategy of retreat. He believed that instead of facing the problems of experience head-on, Hegel chose to establish even more abstract criteria for thought and action than the criteria proposed by Kant.[12] He took Hegel to be claiming that there is a transcendental being which serves as the foundation for both true thought and right action, and which defines or delimits the way in which things have been, are now, and could be. He took Hegel to be asserting that we are bound to have thought and acted the way we have, inasmuch as we articulate the intentions of *Geist*, which has but one interest--self-recognition--and which is incapable of making a mistake in satisfying that interest. He thought the acceptance of the notion of *Geist* entailed the acceptance of the notion of a world that has already been determined, a world in which things could not have been different, a world in which people are precluded from making a difference.

Where James saw Hegel opting to reformulate thought and action in terms of forms of consciousness generated from *Geist*, or the conditions of independent, intentional, subjectivity transcendental to experience, he saw himself opting to reformulate thought and action in terms of human behavior generated from human interests and desires, in the course of human experience. He commandeered the historio-graphic methodology of Charles Darwin in an attempt to delineate a method of descent, or a strategy of return to experience, in which human theories and practices are construed as diversely as the interests that generate them, and are measured in terms of the satisfactions their conse-quences bring.

Indeed, if the possibility of salvation lies at the center of James's vision, and the key argument in its favor has to do with how it is to be a person, the primitive term --stipulated and left undefined--is *interest*. Interest is as fundamental to James as consciousness is to Hegel, because James construes interest to be the integrating factor in human experience. As James sees it, there simply is no sort of knowledge or activity (or, obviously, expectation or hope) that is disinterested or indifferent. Every specifiable

aspect of human behavior attends to some need, responds to
some problematic situation, is committed to some tendency or
other: in sum, holds some interest. Indeed, as I have
indicated, the chance of salvation for James is the chance
that our outstanding problems will be solved, and the chance
that our outstanding problems will be solved is the chance
that our interests will be adequately served.

James will argue, therefore, that any philosophical
position that precludes the effects of human interests *in
their variety*, whether by strategy of absorption or by
strategy of reduction, is simply inadequate. Philosophers
who hold such positions, James will say, are guilty of the
grossest sort of neglect: They are guilty of forgetting, or
of obfuscating, or of hiding from their own experience.
Insofar as Hegel absorbs the variety of human interests into
the one interest of self-recognition, he is masking just how
complicated--just how "gothic," James would say--human
patterns of behavior really are.

But if Hegel is mistaken in attempting to distil an
essential human interest from the apparent variety at hand, at
least interest plays a crucial role in his account of man in
the universe. James holds others accountable for "derealiz-
ing" human interests altogether. In particular, he construes
the position of some "scientific naturalists" and sense-data
empiricists to be inadequate, inasmuch as they reduce all talk
of interest to talk about states of atomic-energy interaction
and/or to talk about brain states.

Indeed, if James spars with absolute idealists in one
arena, he combats some varieties of "Victorian Scientific
Naturalism"[13] in several others. His friend and philosophical
correspondent James Ward summed up the core position of these
opponents in his Gifford Lectures of 1896 and 1898, as
follows:

> This naturalistic philosophy consists in the
> union of 3 fundamental theories: (1) the
> theory that nature is ultimately resolvable
> into a single vast mechanism; (2) the theory
> of evolution as the working of this mechanism;
> (3) the theory of psychophysical parallelism,
> or conscious automatism, according to which
> theory mental phenomena occasionally accompany

but never determine the movements and inter-
actions of the material world.[14]

Like the post-Hegelian idealists, these scientific
realists claimed to be specifying the way things have necessarily been, necessarily are, and necessarily will be. But
instead of transforming Kant's transcendental ego into a
ruling *Geist*, they reduced all experience to the workings of
a machine. They specified the conditions of the universe in
purely physical terms; conceived of evolution not in biological and/or ecological terms but in material ones; and claimed
that all animate behavior is reducible to a kind of associa-
tive performance which is epiphenomenal to brain-states.

If Hegel's system claimed the necessity of salvation,
these materialists claimed its impossibility, by construing
the world (in James's terms) as a "purposeless configuration"
of atomic particles. If Hegel transformed the world into one
logically independent, intentional subject, these materialists
transformed it into one logically independent nonintentional
object. *Both* (according to James) precluded persons from
having any formative role in their world, by claiming, as
James put it, that "our mind comes upon a world complete in
itself, and has the duty of ascertaining its content; but has
no power of redetermining its character, for that is already
given."[15] Both precluded the chance of salvation simply by
denying that probability plays any part in the way things hang
together. The optimistic Hegelian claimed that his "world is
certain to be saved, yes, is saved already, unconditionally
and from eternity, in spite of all the phenomenal appearances
of risk."[16] The pessimistic scientific realist claimed that
our interests are bound to "shipwreck":

> The world's history . . . signifies only the 're-
> distribution' of the unchanged atoms of the
> primal firemist, parting and merging so as to
> appear to us spectators in the infinitely diversi-
> fied configurations which we name as processes
> and things.[17]

Both the Hegelian and the scientific realist of James's day
insisted that "your way is blocked in all directions save
one."[18]

But James was convinced that "possibility, as distinguished from necessity on the one hand and from impossibility

on the other, is an essential category of human thinking."[19] And he was also convinced that "genuine novelty can occur," or in other words that "from the point of view of what is already given, what comes may have to be treated as a matter of chance."[20] So, unlike the Hegelian, he was not optimistic; and unlike the materialist, he was not pessimistic. The world, he thought, "may be saved, on condition that all its parts shall do their best. But shipwreck in detail, or even on the whole, is among the open possibilities."[21] In other words, as he saw it, things could have been different, things are now ambiguous, i.e., "possibly this, but also possibly that,"[22] and the future of things *may* just depend on what we persons do and how we do it.

To convince others of the possibility of salvation, then, James turned to the experience of persons, or, as he says, to men living in their biographies, and he did so for considered reasons. He did so because he believed that no matter how we specify the conditions of the universe when we deliberately theorize, "it is when we come to human lives that our point of view changes." "Men of science and philosophy, the moment they forget their theoretic abstractions, live in their biographies as much as anyone else, and believe as naively that fact even now is making, and that they themselves, by doing 'original work,' help to determine what the future shall become."[23]

James, of course, has been criticized over and over again, for confusing questions of philosophy with questions of biography, and for conflating matters having to do with thought and action with matters concerning feeling and temperament. He has been called a subjectivist. He has been labelled an irrationalist. Some have found him guilty of the fallacy of psychologism. I myself will argue that James does support the notion that philosophies are proposed by philosophers whose biographies have something to do with why and how and about what they theorize. Then too, I will argue that James insists that chance (but *not* irrationality) plays a significant role in the universe. And I will argue that, once he has leveled his pragmatic attack on the myth of epistemic givens, James is bound to ask genetic-epistemological

questions in conjunction with epistemological and logical
ones, if he is to describe adequately the process we call
knowing.

As William James Earle points out, if James's philosophy
is subjective, it is because "it is philosophy, not because it
is James's philosophy."[24] If James's philosophy is partly
psychological, it is because epistemology as the prior science
has been displaced by him and other pragmatists. But if
James's philosophy is construed as supporting irrationalism,
it is misconstrued. For his project is launched to allow for
more adequate theory and better action on the part of people
who are trying to find their way around the places where they
live. And to argue as well as assert that this is the case,
I must detail, analyze, and criticize James's scientific
method and his various scientific investigations.

[1] See Ralph Barton Perry, *The Thought and Character of William James*, 2 vols. (Boston: Little, Brown and Co., 1935), hereafter cited as *TC*; and *In the Spirit of William James* (Bloomington: Indiana University Press, 1958), hereafter cited as *Spirit*.

[2] See John Wild, *The Radical Empiricism of William James* (Garden City: Doubleday & Co., 1969).

[3] See Bruce Wilshire, *William James and Phenomenology* (Bloomington: Indiana University Press, 1968).

[4] See A. J. Ayer, *The Origins of Pragmatism* (San Francisco: Freeman, Cooper and Co., 1968).

[5] Henry James, ed., *The Letters of William James* (Boston: The Atlantic Monthly Press, 1920), vol. 2, pp. 354-356.

[6] See, in particular, William James, *The Varieties of Religious Experience: A Study in Human Nature* (New York: The Modern Library, n.d.), pp. 515-516. Hereafter cited as *Varieties*.

[7] I owe this distinction to William A. Clebsch, *American Religious Thought* (Chicago: University of Chicago Press, 1973); in particular, pp. 1-4. I am not certain I use the distinction in precisely the same way Professor Clebsch does.

[8] Immanuel Kant, *Critique of Pure Reason*, trans. Norman Kemp Smith (New York: St. Martin's Press, 1965), p. 22.

[9] See William James, "Philosophical Conceptions and Practical Results," in *Collected Essays and Reviews* (New York: Longmans, Green and Co., 1920), ed. Ralph Barton Perry, pp. 435-437; as well as *Some Problems of Philosophy* (New York: Longmans, Green and Co., 1911), pp. 14-15. These references will hereafter be cited as "Philosophical Conceptions," and *Problems*.

[10] See in particular William James, "On Some Hegelisms," in *The Will to Believe and Other Essays* (New York: Dover Publications, 1956), pp. 263-298, as well as "Hegel and his Method," in *A Pluralistic Universe* (New York: Longmans, Green, and Co., 1909), pp. 85-129. The books from which these references are taken will hereafter be cited respectively as *Will* and *Universe*.

[11]The characterization of Hegel's method in terms of diagnosis and cure was suggested to me by Jeffrey Stout, Princeton University.

[12]One case in point concerning James's misconstrual of thinkers: Hegel goes out of his way to criticize the abstractions of critical philosophy and to underscore the need to return to first-order questions about human experience. See particularly the "Introduction," in *The Phenomenology of Mind*, trans. J. B. Baillie (New York: Harper and Row, 1967).

[13]For a lucid, fascinating account of Victorian Scientific Naturalism and its major British opponents, see Frank Miller Turner, *Between Science and Religion: The Reaction to Scientific Naturalism in Late Victorian England* (New Haven: Yale University Press, 1974).

[14]James Ward, *Naturalism and Agnosticism*, 2 vols. (London: Macmillan and Co., 1899), vol. 1, p. 186.

[15]*Problems*, p. 221.

[16]*Ibid.*, p. 141.

[17]*Ibid.*, p. 149.

[18]*Ibid.*, p. 62.

[19]*Ibid.*, p. 139.

[20]*Ibid.*, p. 145.

[21]*Ibid.*, p. 142.

[22]*Ibid.*, p. 140.

[23]*Ibid.*, p. 152.

[24]William James Earle, "William James," in *The Encyclopedia of Philosophy*, 8 vols., ed. Paul Edwards (New York: Collier-Macmillan, 1967), vol. 4, p. 241. Hereafter cited as *Encyclopedia of Philosophy*.

CHAPTER II
SCIENCE

Data, Selection, and the Long Run of Experience

The greatest scientific influence on James was the work of Charles Darwin. Both Perry and Wiener pointed this out long ago;[1] and significant interpretations of James continue to refer to the fact. Perry remarked that the "influence of Darwin was both early and profound, and its effects crop up in diverse and unexpected quarters."[2] Wiener identified some of those quarters, and claimed generally that James revolutionized "American psychology and philosophy by carrying evolution as far as he could in both fields."[3] In support of his broad claim, Wiener pinpointed the places at which Darwinian assumptions and/or assertions appear in *The Principles* as well as in various essays. The impact that the Darwinian notion of evolution had on James and other pragmatists was traumatic scientifically and philosophically, because it expelled "from nature the last fixity, that of species";[4] and because it forced "the consideration of a biological view of man's intelligence itself."[5]

But while Perry, Wiener and others have underscored the part *evolution* played in James's thought, there has been no adequate consideration of the part Darwin's *method of analysis* played in it. This is unfortunate, because the method of analysis that James used to describe all the sorts of human phenomena he investigated was basically Darwinian.[6] By this I mean three things: it was historiographic; it was populational; and it was formed around two analytic variables, variation and selection.

When I say that James's analytic method was historiographic, I simply mean that it was descriptive of changes that take place in things that are *assumed* to be historical; or, as Toulmin has put it, things that have "transient identity" because they maintain their identity not in spite of, but in light of, their vicissitudes.[7] When I say that it was populational (a word James hardly, if ever, used), I mean that

17

the sorts of things James investigated were *assumed* to be
composite things the constituents of which behave *like* the
constituents in biological populations in certain key
respects. And when I say that it was formed around two
analytic variables, variation and selection, I mean to
identify those 'certain key respects.' According to James
(*pace* Darwin), each historical entity, *like* a biological
population, is constituted of two sorts of factors, variant
ones and selective ones. The variant factors in any
historical entity delimit the boundaries of it; they comprise
the *variety of data* describable as *that* particular historical
entity. The selective factors in any historical entity are
the factors according to which variants are maintained or
abandoned, remain vital or die. Historiographic description,
on these grounds, depends on a depiction of the interaction
between variant and selective factors in any given historical
thing. The art involved in this 'science' is to make the
correct identification of variant and selective factors as well
as the forms of their interaction.

If I am right in claiming that James's *scientific method*
is broadly but specifically Darwinian, then the method of
analysis that he articulates explicitly in "Great Men and
Their Environment,"[8] and in its subsequent appendage, "The
Importance of Individuals,"[9] will be recognized as decisive
for his psychological, ethical, epistemological, metaphysical,
and religious studies. So let me turn to these two essays.

Now the manifest problem that James investigates in
"Great Men and Their Environment" is not methodological but
substantive. The question before him is, "What are the causes
that make communities change from generation to generation?"[10]
The thesis to which he will argue is that "The difference is
due to the accumulated influences of individuals, of their
examples, their initiatives, and their decisions."[11] The
counter-thesis is promulgated, James claims, by the "Spencerian
school" that asserts that "The changes are irrespective of
persons, and independent of individual control. They are due
to the environment, to the circumstances, the physical
geography, the ancestral conditions,"[12] and so on. What is at
stake, in other words, are the sorts of difference, if any,

that persons are able to make.

What is significant for us at this point, however, is that James construes his thesis and the Spencerian counter-thesis as developing directly from methodological differences. This is why he believes that, to settle the problem, he must state some "general remarks on the method of getting at scientific truth."[13] The Spencerians posit, according to James, that "a complete acquaintance with any one thing . . . would require a knowledge of the entire universe."[14] Based on this assumption, for example,

> we might say with perfect legitimacy that a friend of ours, who had slipped on the ice upon his door-step and cracked his skull, some months after din-ing with thirteen at the table, died because of that ominous feast. . . . The real cause of the event was not the slip, but *the conditions which engendered the slip*,--and among them his having sat at a table, six months previous, one among thirteen.[15]

James, of course, thinks that this sort of explanation is absurd, not only from a common sense standpoint, but also from a scientific point of view. He does not deny that various conditions influence or serve in causal roles (though he does imply that 'conditions' are nothing other than patterns of facts). But he does claim that the various sorts of conditions engender facts *after their own kind*, e.g., physical conditions engender physical facts and social conditions engender social facts. To illustrate his point, James remarks that

> The mold on the biscuit in the storeroom of a man of war vegetates in absolute indifference to the nationality of the flag, the direction of the voy-age, the weather and the human dramas that may go on on board; and a mycologist may study it in com-plete abstraction from all these details. Only by so studying it, in fact, is there any chance of the mental concentration by which alone he may hope to learn something of its nature.[16]

From the point of view of the investigating scientist, that is, it is necessary to regard various sets of data "as disconnected and irrelevant to one another."[17] So far as the working scientist is concerned,

> There are different cycles of operation in nature; different departments, so to speak, relatively independent of one another so that what goes on in one may be compatible with

almost any condition of things at the same time
in the next.[18]

Now James asserts that the Spencerian claims about great
men and their environments are due to a category mistake or,
as he says, the "blunder of clumping" two different cycles of
operation into one. They have, James says, conflated "the
causes of production" with "the causes of maintenance" in
their analysis of great men, i.e., geniuses who apparently
introduced some sort of material or formal difference or
change in their social environment. Mistakenly, they assert
that the social environment that *selects or neglects* the
productions of genius also *produces* the productions of genius.
But this makes no sense, in light of the fact that the
productions of genius are, by definition, social novelties:

> If anything is humanly certain it is that the
> great man's society, properly so called, does
> *not* make him before he can remake it. Physio-
> logical forces, with which the social, political,
> geographical, and to a great extent anthropo-
> logical conditions have just as much and just as
> little to do as the conditions of the crater of
> Vesuvius has to do with the flickering of this
> gas by which I write, are what make him.[19]

In committing their "blunder of clumping" the Spencerians
are merely perpetuating a category mistake that they (following Lamarck)[20] made in their analysis of the evolution of
zoological species. There, for example, they not only claimed
that "the giraffe with his peculiar neck is preserved by the
fact that there are in his environment tall trees whose leaves
he can digest." They also claimed that "the presence of the
trees . . . produced" the species or population of giraffes.

In opposition to this sort of evolutionary theory, Darwin
did two things. He demonstrated that the production of
species had more to do with "internal molecular accidents,"
i.e., contingent physiological conditions, than it had to do
with ecological conditions. Then too, he defined

> the true problem with which we have to deal when
> we study the visible effects of the environment
> on the animal. That problem is simply this: Is
> the environment more likely to preserve or destroy
> him, on account of this or that peculiarity with
> which he may be born?[21]

In other words, Darwin's greatest methodological genius lay in
specifying when and why certain sets of data are irrelevant to

the historical subject matter at hand; or conversely, when and
why data are primitive with respect to the historical matter
under study:

> In giving the name of "accidental variations" to
> those peculiarities with which an animal is born,
> Darwin does not for a moment mean to suggest that
> they are not the fixed outcome of natural law.
> If the total system of the universe be taken into
> account, the causes of these variations and the
> visible environment which preserves or destroys
> them, undoubtedly do, in some remote and round
> about way, hang together. What Darwin means is,
> that, since the environment is a perfectly known
> thing, and its relations to the organism in a way
> of destruction or preservation are tangible and
> distinct, it would utterly confuse our finite
> understanding and frustrate our hopes of science
> to mix in with it facts from such a disparate
> and incommensurable cycle as that in which the
> variations are produced.[22]

James does not doubt that the various sciences are theoreti-
cally unifiable. But such unification would depend on
establishing the logical coherence that holds among the
various sorts of primitive data with which we deal. And the
task of establishing the logical coherence of the sciences
presupposes that scientists have already discriminated both
the kinds of fact in the universe and the patterns of behavior
which those kinds of fact exhibit.

When James employs "Darwinian method," therefore, with
its two variables of variation and selection, he is led to do
three things. He is led to specify the historical subject
matter under study--a particular historical entity and the
particular problems it must resolve in order to maintain
itself. He then must identify the variant factors that bound
that entity. And finally he must identify the factors in
terms of which variants are selected or neglected as fitting
or misfitting the resolution of particular problems.

Thus, for instance, in "Great Men" James specifies the
particular sort of historical entity under study as *society*.
The problem he is trying to resolve is *how* societies develop
or change. He identifies productions of genius, i.e.,
material or formal social novelties, as the variant factors or
primitive data for that entity, society, and that problem, the
process of development or change. And he identifies sorts of

social receptivity as the factors in terms of which productions of genius are selected or neglected as fitting responses
to social problems. Thus,

> the social surroundings of the past and present
> hours exclude the possibility of accepting cer-
> tain contributions from individuals; but they
> do not positively define what contributions shall
> be accepted, for in themselves they are powerless
> to fix what the nature of the individual offer-
> ings shall be.[23]

In sum,

> social evolution is a resultant of the inter-
> action of two wholly distinct factors,--the
> individual, deriving his gifts from the play
> of physiological and infra-social forces, but
> bearing all the power of initiative and origi-
> nation in his hands; and second, the social
> environment, with its power of adopting and
> rejecting both him and his gifts. Both factors
> are essential to change. The community stag-
> nates without the impulse of the individual.
> The impulse dies away without the sympathy of
> the community.[24]

Now it is important to underscore two things. One is
that James is *not* employing Darwin's evolutionary *model* to
make any metaphysical claims. He is employing Darwin's
analytic variables, as he says, to analyze "our special
information about particular cases of change."[25] The other
point follows from the fact that he is studying "particular
cases of change." For analytic purposes, at any rate, the
problem under study is construed as peculiarly historical.
So he thinks of his task as fundamentally historiographical.
He must describe the patterns of behavior of, e.g., societies,
in light of the vicissitudes of that sort of historical thing.

The same pattern of analysis holds when James turns to
"mental evolution," i.e., the problematic of conceptual
change. There the primitive data are novel concepts, e.g.,
hypotheses, which can neither be induced nor deduced from what
is currently taken to refer to matters of fact. These
conceptual novelties which, by definition, are not among
"those abstract conceptions which were taught us with the
language into which we were born,"[26]

> are originally produced in the shape of random
> images, fancies, accidental outbirths of spon-
> taneous variation of the functional activity of
> the excessively instable brain, which the outer

> environment simply confirms or refutes, adopts
> or rejects, preserves or destroys,--selects,
> in short, just as it selects morphological or
> social variations due to molecular accidents
> of an analogous sort.[27]

Hypotheses, of course, become conceptual innovations only if
they are selected by those who have a stake in them. For
example, James remarks that

> The scientific hypothesis arouses in me a fever
> of desire for verification. I read, write,
> experiment, consult experts. Everything cor-
> roborates my notion, which being then published
> in a book spreads from review to review and
> from mouth to mouth, till at last there is no
> doubt. I am enshrined in the Pantheon of the
> great diviners of nature's ways. The environ-
> ment *preserves* the conception which it was
> unable to produce in any brain less idiosyn-
> cratic than my own.[28]

Now James's analysis of great men, great thoughts, and
their environment surely suffers from simplicity of explanation so far as the matters at hand are concerned. By this I
mean two things. (1) His specification of *both* the primitive
data and the formal data-selection mechanisms for the problems
under study are vague. For instance, with respect to the
problem of conceptual change, he does not tell us what would
serve as a scientific hypothesis; and he does not discriminate
between, e.g., *professional* selection of hypotheses (largely a
matter of selection by authority) and *epistemological*
selection of hypotheses (a matter of selection based on the
adequate fulfilment of epistemic criteria).

(2) James does not deal adequately with the fact that, in
principle, Darwin's variables of 'selection' and 'variation'
can be related in either of two quite different ways. As
Toulmin points out,

> They may take place quite independently, so that
> the factors responsible for the selective per-
> petuation of variants are entirely unrelated to
> those responsible for the original generation of
> those same variants. Or, alternatively, they
> may involve related sets of factors, so that
> the novel variants entering the relevant pool
> are already preselected for characteristics
> bearing directly on the requirements for
> selective perpetuation.[29]

There is no question but that, in fact, James focusses on the
former "decoupled" form of process in "Great Men," to the

detriment of both the latter "coupled" form and perhaps the
subject matter under study. He tends to say that the variant
factors, i.e., great men and novel conceptions, are conditioned by factors irrelevant to the factors responsible for
selection, i.e., the social and intellectual environments.
This leads to the deserved criticism that James's analysis
does not take heed of the part social conditioning plays in
the generation of genius or of the part intellectual
conditioning plays in the generation of hypotheses--at least
in "Great Men."

But James calls these shots the way he does because that
is the way he sees them, *as a matter of fact*. He may be
wrong, but if he is, he is wrong in fact. He does not rule
out the theoretical possibility of a "coupled" process in
which novel variants are preselected. Indeed, even in the
essay under study, he notes that the social environment
--though it *chiefly* selects or neglects the genius--also
"remodels him . . . to some degree by its educative influence,
and . . . this constitutes a considerable difference between
the social case and the zoological case."[30]

Indeed, we will see that at least one of James's most
important analyses, e.g., his analysis of belief, knowledge,
and the process of verification, is illustrative of a coupled
process of variation and selection, inasmuch as beliefs are
"pre-selected" by the conceptual frames in which they are bred
and which they, in turn, modify. But in "Great Men," James
focusses on the dual process of variation and selection in its
decoupled mode (1) because his paradigmatic case, genetic
mutation and ecological selection, is in fact decoupled; and
(2) because, as is often the case with James, there is a
polemical dimension to his essay. In particular, James is
arguing with thinkers who have not recognized the significance
of the distinction that Darwin made, either in respect to
zoological species or in respect to other historical entities.
Obviously, he can make his point more effectively by pointing
to cases where he thinks the distinction between factors is
absolute.

In any case, we come to realize that, for James, the
"method of getting at scientific truth" is basically

historiographical. The method of analysis that he uses across
the boards is to describe the pattern of behavior of an entity
that is constantly equilibrating or balancing itself between
the innovative factors or variations and selective factors in
its make-up. The *material*--the specific problems, data, and
selective factors--will change. But the form, both of
analysis and of the object of analysis, will remain the same.
The analysis will be descriptive of changing patterns of
behavior and the object of analysis will be something that
intrinsically is "in the making."[31] No matter whether the
subject is knowledge, ethics, religion, or psychological
behavior, James will turn to what he calls (in "The Importance
of Individuals") "the zone of formative process, the dynamic
belt of quivering uncertainty, the line where past and future
meet," or the "moving present" which is "like the soft layer
beneath the bark of the tree in which all the year's growth
is going on."[32] For this is where *both* innovative and
selective factors are still observable, the former in
competition with each other, the latter weeding out those
variants that do not fit the occasion.

We will see that in psychology, James specifies mental
states or thoughts as the primitive data for the problem of
conscious behavior; and that he describes the manner in which
the "stream of thought" selects or neglects mental states as
conscious behavior develops. In his study of knowledge, we
will find James specifying the varieties of belief as the
primitive data for the problem of epistemic behavior; and we
will analyze his description of how criteria relevant to the
process of verification select or neglect beliefs as fitting
responses to that problem. And we will see that, in his study
of religion, James is led to specify the varieties of
religious experience as primitive data, and to suggest
criteria by which to establish the kind and degree of
fittingness that each variety brings to the problem of
salvation.

The relationship between James's use of Darwinian method
and his work in metaphysics is a bit more complex. It should
be obvious that James's employment of Darwin's historiographical method is his way of turning *from* a philosophy

based on first principles *to* a philosophy of experience; from
critical work that devolves from the method of ascent employed
by, e.g., the Hegelians, to critical work that is data-
specific. It is his way of returning to experience, his way
of reforming critical philosophy. This, of course, has
consequences for metaphysics. For, instead of first specifying the conditions that make experience possible, and then
identifying only those experiences which fit those conditions,
pace Kant, James takes the contrary tack. He tries first to
specify the sorts of experience that we have. Then, instead
of extrapolating *a priori* conditions of experience, he
attempts to interpolate the conditions that hold among things,
such that they hang together the way that they do. His
metaphysics, in other words, is as *a posteriori* and as
experimental as his other sorts of study.

This means that, for James, the distinction between fact
and being is simply false. It makes no sense to consider any
sort of being that is not experienceable, and anything that is
experiencable is some sort of fact. *A priori* metaphysics
which aims to "get behind" the facts is wrongheaded inasmuch
as "fact or being is 'contingent,' or matter of 'chance' so
far as our intellect is concerned. The conditions of its
appearance are uncertain, unforeseeable, when future, and
when past, elusive."[33] Contingent facts make up the terms in
and by which we explain phenomena. And if, as James posits,
metaphysics is a specification of conditions that hold among
facts, then we commit the "blunder of clumping" when we seek,
in turn, to explain them:

> For all of us alike, Fact forms a datum, gift,
> or *Vorgefundenes*, which we cannot burrow under,
> explain, or get behind. It makes itself somehow,
> and our business is far more with its What than
> with its Whence or Why.[34]

This implies, among other things, that for James science and
metaphysics are intimately related. Insofar as metaphysics is
descriptive of conditions that hold among things, it is
dependent on the sciences that are committed to the task of
discriminating the various sorts of data that appear in the
universe. The metaphysician's task, then, is to give a
synoptic view of those sorts of data and their relations.

So James's historiographical method has two consequences
for his metaphysics, one indirect and one direct. That part
of his work that is meant to be descriptive is indirectly
dependent on the sorts of primitive data that he specifies
through historiographical analysis. More directly, when
James distinguishes between the "What" and the "Whence and
Why" of fact or being he is isolating genetic questions from
behavioral questions about fact or being, which is exactly
what he does in his analysis of great men, etc. Insofar as
facts are specified by him as primitive data, as phenomena
over which "we have no claim," they function as "spontaneous
variations." Indeed, because facts are specified by James as
primitive, their genesis is a mystery about which he can only
speculate. As far as the question of genesis is concerned,
"The question of being is the darkest in all philosophy. All
of us are beggars here, and no school can speak disdainfully
of another or give itself superior airs."[35]

This is not to say that speculative metaphysics, specula-
tion about the genesis of fact, has no place in James's work.
It is obvious that it does. It is (1) to underscore the fact
that James was self-conscious about the distinction between
descriptive and speculative metaphysics; and (2) to underscore
the fact that James's speculative metaphysics is, in principle
and in fact, couched in hypothetical terms. For James, to *do*
speculative metaphysics is to offer hypotheses about the
genesis of phenomena and/or the conditions presupposed by
phenomena that are reasonable in light of our descriptions
of matters of fact. To do this sort of work precludes the
possibility of making categorical assertions about being.

But to say that speculative metaphysics must employ
hypothetical reasoning is not to undercut its significance,
any more than the employment of hypothetical reasoning undercuts the significance of, say, speculative neurophysiology.
It is merely to underscore the contingent status of the
premises from which we reason. If there is anything fuzzy-
headed about speculative metaphysics, it is not that it is
speculative; it is that there is some difficulty with the way
in which the metaphysical problem is specified when 'metaphysics' refers to anything other than world-view.

Of one thing, James is sure. No matter what we are
speculating about, be it the nature of being, the nature of
the good, the nature of truth, or whatever, we may confirm or
disconfirm our hypotheses "in the long run of experience"--
and only in the long run of experience. *Prima facie*, this
assumption seems problematic, because it seems to imply that
there is some intrinsic mechanism that makes us "progress"
toward the resolution of our problems. Darwin's method of
analysis warrants no such implication.

In fact, one of the things that makes James's use of
Darwin remarkable is that he was able to distinguish Darwin's
use of the term 'evolution' from the pre-Darwinian (e.g.,
Lamarckian) use of the same term, at a time when most others
were confusing the two conceptions. Toulmin, among others,
has pointed out that the significance of the *Origin of Species*
was not its supposed introduction or use of the term 'evolution.' Darwin did not introduce the term, and used it
sparingly. The term had been introduced long before, first by
Herder and then by Lamarck, and was used in Darwin's day by
many, including Spencer. What was revolutionary about
Darwin's book was that it introduced the conception of organic
species as "modifiable populations, possessing not a
'specific' essence but a statistical distribution of
properties."[36] Darwin's populational approach was promulgated
to replace a doctrine of evolutionary ascent that had served
as a "naturalistic explanation of providential, progressive
change in the organic world."[37] In particular, Darwin sought
to replace a doctrine of ascent with a method by which to
analyze the descent of species.

James followed in Darwin's footsteps by developing the
analyses to which we have referred and by pitting himself
against Spencer's "philosophy of evolution" which he unmasked
as a "metaphysical creed" "disguising itself in scientific
plumes."[38]

But the problem is that both Darwin and James talk about
progress. Darwin, at the very end of the *Origins*, comforts
his reader with the message that

> we may look with more confidence to a secure future
> of great length. And as natural selection works

> solely by and for the good of each being, all
> corporeal and mental endowments will tend to
> progress toward perfection.[39]

Thayer points out that nothing in Darwin's theory warrants this inference from 'selection' to 'progress' and takes the message as a sop to possible adversaries.[40] I agree with him.

James does not specify any outcome to "progress" but he does refer to "social progress" and "mental progress" as often as he talks about social and mental "process." The question confronting us is whether James employs evolution in the same mythical way that he accuses Spencer of doing. I do not believe that he does, for the following reasons.

Toulmin points out, correctly I believe, that

> if a conception, however scientific its birth or
> ancestry, is used in practice only as a way of
> dealing with non-scientific questions--whether
> ethical, philosophical, or theological--then it
> is no longer following the trade of its fore-
> fathers, and has ceased itself to be a scientific
> term at all.[41]

It has, Toulmin says, become a "scientific myth." Instances of scientific myths are (1) the application of the second Law of Thermodynamics to the question of cosmic destination, i.e., what is going to happen after everything else has happened (whatever that might mean); and (2) the application of the notion of evolution to questions about the foundations or destiny of ethical behavior.

In both cases, the problem is that a scientific notion, with a limited and specific range of reference, and with concomitant procedures for observational confirmation or disconfirmation, is applied to a range that, by definition, is either unlimited or nonobservable or both. And as a matter of fact James was among the first critics to isolate the category mistake in drawing "pessimistic" conclusions from the law of entropy, as well as the category mistake in drawing "optimistic" conclusions from any, much less Darwin's, work in evolutionary theory.

Now the notions of "progress" and "the long run of experience" as James uses them are clearly developed from his understanding of Darwin's theory. When James says, for instance, that

> the progress of society is due to the fact that
> individuals vary from the human average in all
> sorts of directions, and that the originality is
> often so attractive or useful that they are recog-
> nized by their tribes as leaders, and become
> objects of envy or admiration, and setters of
> new ideals,[42]

he is identifying individuals as variants in a population who
serve to modify the course or pattern of behavior of that
population. And there are, indeed, a number of ways in which
an interpreter might claim that James was employing a
scientific myth to make his point.

To begin with, the relation between individuals in
society and those who envy them is categorically different
from the relation between biological mutants and their
respective species inasmuch as the behavioral pattern of the
former is, e.g., intentional, while the behavioral pattern of
the latter is not. How, so one might query, can a theory
about zoological evolution be applied to "the progress of
society" without committing a category mistake? Zoological
species, after all, are not societies, and never the twain
shall meet. But this is to miss Darwin's significance for
James--and for us, which is that he offers a method of
analysis applicable to any historical entity. If society
is an historical entity, then James has done nothing wrong.

Another way in which James might be guilty of mytho-
logizing evolutionary theory has to do with the range of its
application. It is, for instance, one thing to chart the
historical development of a given society, under observable
conditions and circumstances, with specifiable variants in its
population; and another thing to comment on the development of
society *sans phrase*. But if James is guilty of anything here,
it is merely fuzzy terminology. It would have been more
accurate for James to refer to the progresses of societies, so
as to clearly fix the range of application. But (a), it is in
fact James's working procedure to illustrate claims like the
one having to do with the "progress of society" with
particular cases; and (b) more fundamentally, James construes
generic concepts like 'society' as referring to populations of
observable entities. 'Society' is merely a "class-name" for
particular societies.

One final way in which James might be interpreted as
committing a category mistake has more specifically to do with
his use of the terms "progress" and "the long run of experience." For when we progress we do so toward some goal. And,
as we have said, there is nothing *in principle* about Darwin's
method that entails any talk about goals towards which things
could progress. But this does not preclude progress *in fact*,
i.e., progress as empirically observed. It precludes progress
as some sort of inevitable and/or necessary outcome of
historical development. Once again, the distinction between
method of analysis and object of analysis is crucial. There
is nothing about Darwinian method that entails progress. But
there is something about groups of persons or social populations, e.g., apparently purposive behavior, that allows both
for the notion of 'goal' and for a description of observable
development towards the satisfaction of goals, i.e., allows
for the notion of progress. If James misuses the notion of
progress, it is because he applies it to the wrong sort of
historical entity, or because he applies it to an entity that
is not historical. It has nothing, however, to do with mytho-
logizing Darwin's theory.

What about the notion of "the long run of experience"?
What does James mean when he talks about "the long run of
experience" possibly "weeding out" inadequate variants in
particular populations? For instance, what does he mean when
he claims that "the long run of experience may weed out the
more foolish"[43] religious faiths, i.e., those faiths which
respond inadequately to the soteric problem? Or again, what
does he mean when, in the course of his epistemology, he
refers to the possibility of "verification in the long run"?--
as if to say, there will come a time when we will know whether
or not our justified beliefs are true, because we will have
established some ultimate criterion or set of criteria by
which to measure our justifications and, *mutatis mutandis*,
our beliefs.

If read loosely, these references to the long run can
smell of the sort of progressivism that remains unwarranted by
Darwinian method. It is easy, if incorrect, to infer that
James is claiming that there is some intrinsic mechanism in

our experience which makes, for instance, ultimate verification of our justified beliefs an ineluctable event. But such
an inference finds no vindication.

The problem with interpreting James's notion of "the long
run" is in part historical. This is so because Peirce used
the same notion to refer to events or states of affairs that,
while not necessary, are inevitable.[44] He developed the
notion initially as a part of probability theory to account
for statistical inevitability. For instance, he claimed that
it is not necessary that sixes will ever turn up on the throw
of the dice, but it is inevitable in the long run. There is
no particular throw on which sixes *must* turn up, but statistical information about the frequency with which sixes have
turned up in the past can be used to generate a particular
frequency rating for the chance that they will turn up in the
future. And if we throw the dice "long enough" the ratings
will be borne out.

Now Peirce's notion is a complicated one that depends
not only on a specific understanding of 'infinity,' but also
on both formal and material rules of inference governing the
relationship between statistical laws (that are macrocosmic)
and actual states of affairs (that may be microcosmic). What
is important for us to realize is that Peirce applied this
notion of the long run to the epistemological problem. He
claimed, in particular, that the opinions of working scientists would converge in the long run, allowing us to resolve
our epistemological problems. Just what warrants the use of
"the long run" which is a limit concept in probability theory
--when applied to actual opinions of actual scientists working
on particular, discrete problems--is unclear. If anyone is
guilty of committing a 'myth of the long run,' it seems to be
Peirce.

But in any case, James does not employ "the long run" the
same way Peirce does. Two things tip us off to this fact.
Whenever James talks about the long run, he uses a modal
qualifier like 'may' or 'possibly': nothing is ever inevitable
in the long run for James. Then too, when he talks about the
long run, it is the long run *of experience*: if something is
possible in the long run for James, it is *empirically*

possible; it is possible in light of actual conditions empirically specifiable. Thus, for instance, to talk about 'verification' in the long run is not to assert that science is such that total verification of all our truth claims (whatever that would mean) is inevitable in some endless time span. It is to say that we *may* attain a set of criteria by which to verify our justified beliefs; whether we do or not depends on our experiences. It is an empirical matter. Once again, progress towards the resolution of human problems is neither necessary nor inevitable, but may in fact occur.

In summary, James deploys Darwinian method without committing any scientific myths about evolution. He uses Darwin's method, in fact, as an instrument to cut against the scientific myths prevalent in his day. And more importantly, he uses Darwin's method of historical analysis to understand the variety of problematic situations in human experience. No matter what subject he attends to, he sets the resolution of its respective problematic as a regulative ideal. And he isolates both the innovative and selective factors which comprise the terms in which the problematic is specified. Now to examine more particular ways in which he puts Darwinian analysis to work, and to see how it complements his central vision, I need to turn to his psychological and epistemological studies.

Thought and Action

James first articulates his vision of man in the universe in an early and seminal essay, "Remarks on Spencer's Definition of Mind as Correspondence."[45] There he introduces the notion of *interest* as the primitive and undefined term on which his philosophical anthropology is based. There he starts to wage his attack on the notion of mind as correspondence or man as spectator by insisting that

> the knower is not simply a mirror floating with no foothold anywhere, and passively reflecting an order that he comes upon and finds simply existing. The knower is an actor, and co-efficient of the truth on one side, whilst on the other he registers the truth which he helps to create. Mental interests, hypotheses, postulates, so far as they are bases for human

action--action which to a great extent transforms
the world--help to *make* the truth which they
declare. In other words, there belongs to mind,
from its birth upward, a spontaneity, a vote.
It is in the game, and not a mere looker-on; and
its judgments of the *should-be*, its ideals, cannot
be peeled off from the body of the *cogitandum* as
if they were excrescences, or meant, at most,
survival. We know so little about the ultimate
nature of things, or of ourselves, that it would
be sheer folly dogmatically to say that an ideal
rational order may not be real. The only objective criterion of reality is coerciveness, in the
long run, over thought. Objective facts, Spencer's
outward relations, are real only because they
coerce sensation. Any interest which should be
coercive on the same massive scale would be *eodem
jure* real. By its very essence, the reality of
a thought is proportionate to the way it grasps
us. Its intensity, its seriousness--its interest
in a word--taking these qualities, not at any
given instance, but as shown by the total upshot
of experience. If judgments of the *should-be*
are fated to grasp us in this way, they are what
"correspond."[46]

In the space of a long paragraph, James claims at least
four startling things. In revolt against a dogma as old as
Descartes and as authoritative as Kant, he claims that "the
knower is an actor," not a spectator. Contrary to classical
rationalism as well as transcendental idealism, he claims that
"mental interests," not reasons, are the bases of human
actions. In an attempt to resolve the bifurcation between
theoretical and practical reason he insists on the axiological
character of epistemic statements by claiming that "judgments
of the *should-be* . . . cannot be peeled off from the body of
the *cogitandum* as if they were excrescences." And assuming
that persons are fundamentally agents who have (to some
extent, anyway) the ability to transform their situation in
light of their interests according to "judgments of *should-be*"
or standards of appropriateness, he claims that "it would be
sheer folly dogmatically to say that an ideal rational order
may not be real." In other words, he claims that an order in
which the intentions of persons are realized and the interests
of persons are satisfied is a possibility. Or in words he
himself will come to use, there is a chance of salvation. The
rest of this section will be devoted to developing these four
claims as they relate to one another.

The knower is an actor. The difference, says James, between brute and human intellect, is that while more animals than man exhibit "intelligence," only man exhibits "intelligent intelligence."[47] By this he means that human consciousness

> seems both to supply the means and the standard
> by which they are measured. It not only *serves*
> a final purpose but *brings* a final purpose--posits,
> declares it. This purpose is not a mere hypo-
> thesis--"*if* survival is to occur, then brain must
> so perform," etc.--but an imperative decree:
> "Survival *shall* occur, and, therefore, brain *must*
> so perform![48]

It is unfortunate that James commits a category mistake here: there is at least no simple sense in which brains, as physical organisms, are the sort of thing that admit to government by imperative decree (James will become increasingly aware of the problem of "slipping into another kind,"[49] and will make efforts not to do it). But his point is well made. More living things than humans can behave satisfactorily or fulfil standards of appropriate conduct. But humans can behave satisfactorily according to standards of appropriate conduct which they posit and commit themselves to obeying. The distinction that James seems to be making is roughly equivalent to the distinction that Bennett makes between "regular" and "rule-guided" behavior[50] or the distinction that Sellars makes between "pattern-governed" and "rule-obedient" behavior:[51] trees and dogs and bees (not to mention germs and rocks and atoms) behave the way they do *because* of the pattern of things of which they are a part. But people may behave the way they do (i.e., when they are behaving reasonably) in order to satisfy "imperative decrees" or rules for conduct they hold and behave in light of under appropriate conditions.

One key neurophysiological condition that allows for the "intelligent intelligence" exhibited by people, according to James, is *"plasticity."*[52] A frog "is an extremely complex machine whose actions, so far as they go, tend to self-preservation; but still a *machine* in this sense--that it seems to contain no incalculable element."[53] Its action is simply reflex. But humans have a nervous system that allows for

response. It is "potentially adapted to respond to an
infinite variety of minute features in the situation; but its
fallibility [is] then . . . as great as its elaboration."[54]
Humans have "high brains" which perform "like dice thrown for
ever on a table"; "its hair-trigger organization makes of it
a happy-go-lucky hit-or-miss-affair."[55] But the fortunate
thing is that if human brains behave like dice, they behave
like loaded dice, and the phenomenon of "intelligent intelligence" apparently accounts for the loading:

> Loading its dice would mean bringing a more or
> less constant pressure to bear in favor of *those*
> of its performances which make for the most per-
> manent interests of the brain's owner; it would
> mean a constant inhibition of the tendencies to
> stray aside.

> Well, just such pressure and such inhibition are
> what consciousness *seems* to be exerting all the
> while. And the interests in whose favor it seems
> to exert them are its interests and its alone,
> interests which it *creates*, and which, but for
> it, would have no status in the realm of being
> whatever.[56]

James notes that we talk as if organisms have interests,
in terms of which the usefulness of organs is measured and the
correctness of reaction is plotted. But such expressions as
*"useful discharge, appropriate direction, right reaction
. . ."*

> all presuppose some Good, End, or Interest to be
> the animal's. Until this goal of his salvation
> be posited, we have no criterion by which to
> estimate the utility of any of his reactions.
> Now the important thing to notice is that the
> goal cannot be posited at all so long as we con-
> sider the purely physical order of existence.
> Matter has no ideals.[57]

In other words, it is only when "intelligent intelligence"
occurs that

> *Real* ends appear for the first time now upon
> the world's stage. The conception of conscious-
> ness as a purely cognitive form of being, which
> is the pet way of regarding it in many idealistic-
> modern as well as ancient schools is thoroughly
> anti-psychological. . . . Every actually existing
> consciousness seems to itself at any rate to be a
> *fighter for ends*, of which many, but for its
> presence, would not be ends at all. Its powers

> of cognition are mainly subservient to these ends,
> discerning which facts further them and which do
> not.58

Human thought is an instrument for the resolution of human
problems, a self-corrective instrument that enables people
to dispose themselves to behavior that accords with their
peculiar commitments.

Implicit in James's discussion is the distinction between
variant and selective factors in human consciousness. Potentially able to respond to their situation in an infinite
variety of ways, people are constantly selecting some attitudes and neglecting others, holding certain conditions to be
standard while measuring other conditions against those
standards, accepting some beliefs as true, abandoning others
as false, committing themselves to certain habits, disallowing
the establishment of other habits. The distinctive characteristic of human thought is that, at every step, *selective
factors are signified as such*. In sum, thought "is always
interested more in one part of its object than in another,
and welcomes and rejects, or chooses, all the while it
thinks."59

> The mind is at every stage a theatre of simul-
> taneous possibilities. Consciousness consists
> in the comparison of these with each other, the
> selection of some, and the suppression of the
> rest by the reinforcing and inhibiting agency
> of attention. The highest and most elaborated
> mental products are filtered from the data
> chosen by the faculty next beneath, out of the
> mass offered by the faculty below that, which
> mass in turn was sifted from a still larger
> amount of yet simpler material, and so on.60

People, in other words, are not only able to make reports
about objects of various sorts, but they are able to report
the rules according to which their observations are made. In
fact, an observation isn't distinctively human unless it is,
at least implicitly, guided by selective factors understood
as such.

Taken alone, James's description of thought as a kind of
selective industry is a bit misleading, because it sounds like
he is saying that thought is built up from a foundation of
'simples,' e.g., sensations, through a process of association

and dissociation *pace* British empiricism or mind-stuff
theorists. Such is not the case. James specifically
criticizes such architechtonic images of thought, and chooses
instead to talk of *streams of thought*. He does so to underscore the fact that the thought he is talking about is
"empirical thought"--not the *a priori* conditions of thought
but the process of thoughts in the making, the process that
occurs whenever *"thought goes on."*[61]   And the only way to
describe thought going on is the way one describes anything
that is going on: historiographically. And the best way to
do that, according to James, is to employ Darwin's variables
of populational analysis, for they allow him to take histories
without imputing or implying any providential or progressive
mechanism in history.

"A man's empirical thought," says James, "depends on the
things he has experienced, but what these shall be is to a
large extent determined by his habits of attention."[62]   People
are not first impressed with simple sensations which cause
them to perceive what they do. "No one ever had a simple
sensation by itself."[63]   Indeed, in "minds able to speak at
all there is . . . some knowledge about everything."[64]   And
the bit of knowledge about everything, or every sort of thing,
that people have is *learned*: "My experience is what I agree to
attend to."[65]   But there is nothing "simply given"[66] to me:

> Men have no eyes but for those aspects of things
> which they have already been taught to discern.
> . . .
>
> In short, *the only things which we commonly see
> are those which we preperceive*, and the only
> things which we preperceive are those which have
> been labelled for us, and the labels stamped
> into our mind. If we lost our stock of labels
> we should be intellectually lost in the midst
> of the world.[67]

In sum, people are born into languages which they must learn
to speak and to speak about in order to "think."[68]   Once their
universe of discourse has been established, it becomes the
vehicle both of world-orientation or transaction as well as
transformation.

This becomes clear, according to James, when we investigate the process of reasoning, "another form of the selective

activity of the mind."[69]

> Reasoning depends on the ability of the mind to
> break up the totality of the phenomenon reasoned
> about, into parts, and to pick out from these
> the particular one which, in our given emergency,
> may lead to the proper conclusion. Another
> predicament will need another conclusion, and
> require another element to be picked out. The
> man of genius is he who will always stick in his
> bill at the right point, and bring it out with
> the right element--'reason' if the emergency be
> theoretical, 'means' if it be practical--transfixed
> upon it.[70]

To make his point, James gives us the following illustration:
A person takes his dog to his boat only to find the boat full
of water. The fellow turns to his dog and commands, "Go get
the sponge!" The dog runs to the house, returns with the
sponge, and is stroked for good behavior. Now on James's
grounds, the dog's behavior is clearly adequate, but is it
reasonable? If not, what conditions would make it reasonable?
James claims that the dog's act was

> not yet an act of reasoning proper. It might
> fairly have been called so if, unable to find
> a sponge at the house, he had brought back a
> dipper or a mop instead. Such a substitution
> would have shown that, embedded in the very
> different appearances of these articles, he
> had been able to discriminate the identical
> partial attribute of capacity to take up water,
> and had reflected, "For the present purpose
> they are identical." This, which the dog did
> not do, any man but the very stupidest could
> not fail to do.[71]

What James is claiming positively about the dog is that his
behavior is the outcome of a "contiguous association of
ideas."[72] Despite the mistaken mentalistic idiom, James means
that the dog's behavior is a matter of simple stimulous-
response training--a kind of pattern-governed behavior. Even
more interesting are James's claims about what the dog would
have had to do in order to act reasonably. He would have to
have been aware of the sponge as a member of a class of things
having the capacity to take up water. He would need to have
been able to infer that the dipper or mop would fit the
occasion, based on his understanding of rules governing those
sorts of things. In other words, he would have to have taken

the sponge *as a sign* which could be responded to as a sign,
instead of responding the way he does.

Thus, reasoning depends on the recognition and use of
signs as signs, and can only occur "as soon as the notion of
a *sign as such*, apart from any particular import, is born."[73]
Again, to think in a distinctively human way we not only learn
to speak but to speak about our speech; we dissociate signs
from the objects to which they refer and learn to operate on
them as such in order to make more adequate transactions with
our environments.

But our focus on what goes on when we think and reason
should not obfuscate James's claim that the knower is an
actor: we think and reason in order to do things; and

> the structural unit of the nervous system is in
> fact a triad, neither of whose elements have any
> independent existence.[74]

We respond to our observations (which are preperceived) by
making certain intralinguistic moves when we reason, but "only
for the sake of calling forth the final act."

> All action is thus *re*-action upon the outer
> world; and the middle stage of consideration or
> contemplation or thinking is only a place of
> transit, the bottom of a loop, both whose ends
> have their point of application in the outer
> world. If it should ever have no roots in the
> outer world, if it should ever happen that it
> led to no active measures, it would fail of its
> essential function, and would have to be con-
> sidered either pathological or abortive. The
> current of life which runs in at our eyes or
> ears is meant to run out at our hands, feet,
> or lips. The only use of the thoughts it
> occasions while inside is to determine its
> direction to whichever of these organs shall,
> on the whole, under the circumstances actually
> present, act in the way most propitious for
> our welfare. . . . perception and thinking
> are only there for behavior's sake.[75]

But this leads to a consideration of James's *second*
claim, that *mental interests are the bases for human action*.
The knower is an actor who is born into a universe of discourse which discloses some things *as* desirous, others *as*
undesirous or even repulsive. Thought and reason may enable
us to control ourselves in ways "most propitious for our

welfare," but the interests which we acquire generate both the specifications *of* our welfare and the rules of behavior *by which to* realize it. The matter of our welfare as persons is far from simple: Contrary to Spencer's sophomoric claim that survival is the only human interest, James asserts that

> to common sense, survival is only one out of many interests--*primus inter pares*, perhaps, but still in the midst of peers. What are these interests? Most men would reply that they are all that makes survival worth securing. The social affections, all the various forms of play, the thrilling intimations of art, the delights of philosophic contemplation, the rest of religious emotion, the joy of moral self-approbation, the charm of fancy and of wit . . . and individuals who . . . satisfy these desires are protected by their fellows and enabled to survive, though their mental constitution should in other respects be lamentably ill-"adjusted" to the outward world. . . . The reason is very plain. *To the individual man, as a social being, the interests of his fellow are a part of his environment.*[76] If his powers correspond to the wants of this social environment, he may survive, even though he be ill-adapted to the natural or "outer" environment. But these wants are pure subjective ideals, with nothing outward to correspond to them.[77]

People live in worlds that are indelibly *social* and their interests are the interests of social beings, or agents and patients of communities. This is to say that, no matter how interests are specified, they will present certain shared or shareable intentions, the realization of which would consti- tute the welfare of respective communities. Thus it is that James insists that the notion of "perfect conduct"--the sort of conduct that would effect solutions for our outstanding problems as persons--is triadic in structure. "Perfect conduct" could not simply mean the adjustment of persons to their environments. It must include reference to the social "recipients" of conduct who promulgate conventional standards of adjustment. Unless the intentions of an actor suit the interests of his society, the facility with which he executes those intentions matters little: his conduct will be deemed inappropriate or misfitting.[78]

The problem is that people are usually involved with more than one society, and/or that societies are constituted around

more than one--and sometimes contradictory--set of intentions.
The beliefs and intentions that people hold are, in principle,
shareable beliefs and intentions: epistemic reality is a
social construction.[79]   But there are a variety of "worlds" or
"subuniverses" of discourse and practice that only loosely
hang together, and most people are not ascetic enough to
commit themselves to the task of abandoning beliefs and
intentions that contradict more adequate ones that they hold.

   But the philosopher is not most people. He must not only
seek "to assign to every given object of his thought its right
place in one or other of these sub-worlds, but he must also
seek to determine the relation of each sub-world to the others
in the total world which *is*."[80]   These sub-worlds include at
least

> (1) The world of sense, or of physical 'things'
> as we instinctively apprehend them. . . .
> (2) The world of science, or of physical things
> as the learned conceive them, with secondary
> qualities and 'forces' (in the popular sense)
> excluded, and nothing real but solids and fluids
> and their 'laws' (i.e., customs) of motion.
> (3) The world of ideal relations, or abstract
> truths believed or believable by all, and expres-
> sed in logical, mathematical, metaphysical,
> ethical, or aesthetic propositions.
> (4) The world of 'idols of the tribe,' illusions
> or prejudices common to the race. . . . The motion
> of the sky round the earth, for example, belongs
> to this world. . . . For certain philosophers
> 'matter' exists only as an idol of the tribe.
> For science, the 'secondary qualities' of matter
> are but 'idols of the tribe.'
> (5) The various supernatural worlds, the Christian
> heaven and hell, the world of the Hindoo mythology.
> . . . The various worlds of deliberate fable. . . .
> (6) The various worlds of individual opinion, as
> numerous as men are.
> (7) The worlds of sheer madness and vagary, also
> indefinitely numerous.[81]

So long as any object or aspect of any of these worlds appears
both "interesting and important" to us, it is practically
real for us: "*In this sense, whatever excites and stimulates
our interest is real.*"[82]   Our specification of reality is
subjective (but notice: not egocentric) because

> *as thinkers with emotional reaction, we give what
> seems to us a still higher degree of reality to
> whatever we select and emphasize and turn to* WITH

> A WILL. These are our *living* realities; and not
> only these, but all the other things which are
> intimately connected with these.[83]

This, implies James, is a simple phenomenological fact.
Whether our population of beliefs about things is dense or
sparse; whether the criteria in terms of which we accept or
reject beliefs is epistemically loose or stringent, "as
thinkers with emotional reaction, we give what seems to us a
still higher degree of reality to whatever we select and
emphasize and turn to WITH A WILL."

But if, "as a rule we believe as much as we can,"[84]

> The greatest proof that a man is *sui compos* is
> his ability to suspend belief in presence of an
> emotionally exciting idea. To give this power
> is the highest result of education. In untutored
> minds the power does not exist.[85]

Indeed, the philosopher who commits himself to the task of
understanding "how things in the broadest sense of the term
hang together in the broadest sense of the term"[86] must
suspend beliefs long enough to establish criteria by which
to warrant them.

James himself suggests several criteria for the warranting of beliefs in general. But before specifying them, it is
important to notice what *unit* of belief is in question so far
as he is concerned. Whenever James talks about the warranting
of beliefs, he focusses on beliefs as instances of complete
theories. Whenever beliefs are on trial, they are prosecuted
or defended as parts of benign or malignant conspiracies of
belief. The question always issued by James is "which system
shall carry our belief."[87] This points to the *third* major
claim that James made early on: that "judgments of the
should-be . . . cannot be peeled off from the body of the
cogitandum as if they were excrescences. . . ." *Beliefs are
theory-laden*, to borrow the more contemporary expression.
Take, to use James's own example, the belief that 'The candle
exists':

> In both existential and attributive judgments a
> synthesis is represented. The syllable *ex* in the
> word Existence, *da* in the word *Dasein*, expresses
> it. 'The candle exists' is equivalent to 'The
> candle is *over there*.' And the 'over there'

> means real space related to other reals. The
> proposition amounts to saying: 'The candle is
> in the same space with other reals.' It affirms
> of the candle a very concrete predicate--namely
> this relation to other particular concrete things.
> *Their* real existence . . . resolves itself into
> their particular relation to *ourselves*. Existence
> is thus no substantive quality when we predicate
> it of any object; it is a relation, ultimately
> terminating in ourselves, and at the moment when
> it terminates, becoming a *practical* relation.[88]

The belief that 'the candle exists' is governed by the
rules which form and transform a complete conceptual frame:
the conceptual frame of persons, events and things in our
space/time world. It is impossible to "peel off" the
categorial rules of the manifest image from the individuated
candle in the manifest image. When we believe *that* that
candle is there, we believe *in* the sub-world of sense (which
world, obviously, is subject to refinements of empirical
specification).

But given that the problem is which theory to maintain
among those presented in the variety of sub-universes of
discourse and practice, the question of criteria becomes
paramount. To answer the question, James begins by positing
that "the theoretic curiosity starts from the practical life's
demands."[89] We ask theoretic questions, in other words, in
order to get around the worlds in which we live more
adequately. Because this is the case, the world that is
manifest to us--the world pictured by ordinary language as
constituted by persons, things, and events in space and time--
is our "paramount reality"[90] at least methodologically (but
notice: not necessarily our paramount reality ontologically).
We cannot, according to James, decide which system shall carry
our beliefs without first describing our experience phenomenologically. We must first interpolate the order of the
manifest image if we are ever to extrapolate the conditions
that account for it. Thus, James posits his first criterion
of theoretic adequacy as follows:

> The conceived system, to pass for true, must at
> least include the reality of the sensible objects
> in it, by explaining them as effects on us, if
> nothing more. The system which includes the most
> of them, and definitely explains or pretends to

to explain the most of them, will, *ceteris paribus*, prevail.[91]

The reason why James insists on the methodological primacy of the manifest image is bound up with his notion of "intelligent intelligence" or distinctively human behavior. To act reasonably is to be able to resolve problematic situations according to appropriate standards of conduct that are recognized as such. James is merely pointing out that, no matter how we finally delineate the conditions of human life in the universe, we *start* delineating those conditions in response to problems and puzzles that interest, confront, and confound us here and now, in the world we observe and transact in, according to rules we commit ourselves to. No matter how we might transform our image of man in the universe, we would do so according to such rules, for the sake of satisfying various and sundry interests.

This leads to James's second criterion of theoretic adequacy:

> That theory will be most generally believed which, besides offering us objects able to account satisfactorily for our sensible experience, also offers those which are most interesting, those which appeal most urgently to our aesthetic, emotional, and active needs.[92]

If any theory depends on the phenomenon of rule-obedience as well as on the specification of interests and desires of persons as agents and patients of community, then any theory that "derealizes" persons or their interests and desires or their ability to dispose their conduct according to shared or shareable intentions is going to be found sadly lacking. It will disappoint "our dearest desires and most cherished powers."[93]   Thus, for instance,

> A pessimistic principle like Schopenhauer's incurably vicious Will-substance, or Hartmann's wicked jack-at-all-trades, the Unconscious, will perpetually call forth essays at other philosophies. Incompatibility of the future with their desires and active tendencies is, in fact, to most men a source of more fixed disquietude than uncertainty itself.[94]

Then too, any theory which undercuts the notion of problematic situations by construing persons as things simply governed by the pattern of which they are a part, is bound to be inadequate. So,

> A philosophy whose principle is so incommensurate
> with our most intimate powers as to deny them all
> relevancy in universal affairs, as to annihilate
> their motives at one blow, will be even more
> unpopular than pessimism. . . . This is why
> materialism will always fail of universal adop-
> tion, however well it may fuse things into an
> atomistic unity, however clearly it may prophesy
> the future eternity. For materialism denies
> reality to the objects of almost all the impulses
> which we most cherish. The real *meaning* of the
> impulses, it says, is something which has no
> emotional interest for us whatever. . . . Any
> philosophy which annihilates the validity of
> the reference by explaining away its objects or
> translating them into terms of no emotional
> pertinency leaves the mind with little to care
> or act for. This is the opposite condition from
> that of nightmare, but when acutely brought home
> to consciousness it produces a kindred horror.
> In nightmare we have motives to act, but no [95]
> power. Here we have powers, but no motives.

Any theory about how things in the broadest sense of the term
hang together in the broadest sense of the term is going to
account for *both* our ability to act the way we do and the
motives that make us react the way we do; or it is going to
"derealize" the conditions that lead us to theorize. For
once again:

> It is far too little recognized how entirely the
> intellect is built up of practical interests.
> The theory of Evolution is beginning to do very
> good service by its reduction of mentality to a
> type of reflex action. Cognition, in its view,
> is but a fleeting moment, a cross-section at a
> certain point of what in its totality is a motor
> phenomenon. In the lower forms of life no one
> will pretend that cognition is anything more
> than a guide to appropriate action. The germinal
> question brought for the first time before con-
> sciousness is not the theoretic 'What is that?'
> but the practical 'Who goes there?' or rather,
> as Horwicz has admirably put it, 'What is to
> be done?' . . .[96]

We make the intraconceptual moves we do in order to position
ourselves extraconceptually. We are agents; when we know we
are acting; the bases for our actions are certain, specifiable
social interests; and the rules to which we commit ourselves

in order to guide our actions toward the satisfaction of our social interests can no more be "peeled off" our objects of thought than the observable conditions which motivate our commitment to rules in the first place can be "peeled off."

Besides adequately accounting for observable conditions and for our motives and powers as persons, a theory, says James, must have intellectual and aesthetic warrant:

> The two great aesthetic principles of richness and of ease, dominate our intellectual as well as our sensuous life. And, *ceteris paribus*, no system which should not be rich, simple, and harmonious would have a chance of being chosen for belief, if rich, simple, and harmonious systems were also there.[97]

"Richness" amounts to inclusion of all observable conditions that can be accounted for. "Simplicity" amounts to an extrapolation "of the smallest possible number of permanent and independent primordial entities" from observable conditions. And 'harmony' amounts to a "definite organization" present in a system such that "relations of an inwardly rational sort obtain."[98]

Which image(s) of man in the universe, which system(s) of belief might be so warranted is another matter: "no general offhand answer can be given as to which objects mankind shall choose as its realities. The fight is still under way. Our minds are yet chaotic; and at best we make a mixture and a compromise, as we yield to the claim of this interest or that, and follow first one and then another principle in turn."[99] And this state of affairs leads to James's *fourth* claim, that *it would be sheer folly to say that an ideal rational order may not be real*.

Now the specification of such an "ideal rational order" is, on James's grounds, a metaphysical task--it is part of making a picture of the whole world; any detailed consideration of it must be put off until we consider James's metaphysics in the next chapter. But in his more strictly psychological work, he does *indicate* such an order, and it is construed soterically.

Remember: people are agents and patients of communities who commit themselves to a variety of rules, including

epistemic rules, in order to make adequate transactions with
their environments, which adequacy is specified according to
a variety of interests. The "ideal rational order" in this
light would be an order in which the behavior of persons, as
persons, is simply *fitting*. Such behavior would result in
"the Sentiment of Rationality,"[100] the feelings of "ease,
peace, rest," which come in transition "from a state of puzzle
and perplexity" to a state of solution, a state in which
(specified) problems are resolved.[101] If the universe(s) in
which people find themselves were *transformable* to such a
state of solution, it might be *made* rational. Early on, James
simply calls such a condition of the universe(s) "God or 'Soul
of the World.'"[102] He claims that this "God," this condition
of the universe which allows for the solution of our puzzles
and perplexities, is "the normal object of the mind's
belief."[103] His point is psychological, not either epistemological or ontological: whether "God" is "really the living
truth is another matter."[104] But "God" is the normal object
of the mind's belief, because, "so far as we can see, the
given world is there only for the sake of the operation."[105]
In other words, conditions of things in general seem to
support our ability as persons to transform our situations
sufficiently and adequately enough to overcome outstanding
problems. To believe that there is god or a god or some gods,
on these grounds, is to believe that conditions, or a condition, or some conditions somehow support our transactions as
persons, and is to expect that such conditions will continue
to prevail. This sort of belief is "rational" because it
provides an adequate stimulus for our "practical nature."[106]
Were god the case,

> All Science and History would thus be accounted
> for in the deepest and simplest fashion. The
> very room in which I sit, its sensible walls and
> floor, and the feeling of air and fire within it
> give me, no less than the 'scientific' concep-
> tions which I am urged to frame concerning the
> mode of existence of all these phenomena when my
> back is turned, would then all be corroborated,
> not derealized, by the ultimate principle of my
> belief. The World-soul sends me just those
> phenomena in order that I may react upon them;
> and among the reactions is the intellectual
> one of spinning these conceptions. What is

> beyond the crude experience is not an *alterna-*
> *tive* to them, but something that *means* them
> for me here and now. It is safe to say that,
> if ever such a system is satisfactorily
> excogitated, mankind will drop all other
> systems and cling to that one alone as real.[107]

The problem is that such a system has not, in James's
view, been satisfactorily excogitated. Were conditions such
as to support our activity as persons, then things would seem
utterly rational, and no one would question whether life is
worth living. But numerous conditions specified in numerous
ways seem to obstruct the satisfaction of our socially
construed interests; and some are led to wonder indeed whether
life is worth living, for some become convinced that our world
is a place "in which we can never volitionally feel at
home."[108]

Just how James understands the process by which we might
come to know the truth about our situation is the subject of
the next section; and just how he understands the problem of
the self, the problem whether life is worth living, is the
subject of the section after that.

Belief, Knowledge, and the Search for Truth

James develops his epistemological position primarily in
two books, *Pragmatism* and *The Meaning of Truth*.[109] Insofar as
his work in these books is epistemological (and it is much
else besides), he argues toward the claim that

> Truth may well consist of certain opinions, and
> does indeed consist of nothing but opinions, tho
> not every opinion need be true.[110]

According to James, we believe many things, i.e., we assert
many things with conviction and conduct ourselves accordingly.
And some of the things we believe, we possibly know. To
reformulate James's claim: "If we know anything, our knowledge
consists of some of our beliefs, some of the things we assert
with conviction, though not all of our beliefs, not all of the
things we assert with conviction, are true." In other words,
if we know that p, we believe that p; but our belief that p
does not entail our knowledge that p. This is only common
sense: some of our beliefs have turned out to be false.

Indeed, James will make the stronger claim, inferred from
instances of conceptual change, that any one of our beliefs
might turn out to be false. So, as he sees it, knowledge must
entail other conditions than belief. To be sure, knowledge
is indelibly subjective, soaked as it is in conviction. But
there must be safeguards that will preclude our claiming to
know something that turns out to be false. So James is led,
like most epistemologists, to address two separate questions:

What do we know?

and

What are the criteria of knowledge?

Now in one sense the answer to the first question is
simple. If we know anything, we know facts; we know that some
things are the case. But if we construe the first question to
mean, 'what are candidates in competition for the office of
knowledge?' then the answer is 'beliefs.' If we didn't
believe anything, it would be silly to ask either question.
In other words, beliefs are the *data* for epistemology, or the
science of knowledge. If James can answer the second
question, then he will have established criteria for the
selection or neglection of beliefs as adequate responses to
the epistemic problem, 'what do we know?'

But *prima facie* the two questions taken together generate
a vicious circle. Chisholm, in a grand tradition, points this
out in his lecture, *The Problem of the Criterion*.[111] Para-
phrasing Montaigne, he formulates the problem this way:

> To know whether things really are as they seem
> to be, we must have a procedure for distinguish-
> ing appearances that are true from appearances
> that are false. But to know whether our pro-
> cedure is a good procedure, we have to know
> whether it really succeeds in distinguishing
> appearances that are true from appearances that
> are false. And we cannot know whether it really
> does succeed unless we know which appearances
> are true and which ones false. And so we are
> caught in a circle.[112]

Chisholm, of course, uses appearance language, but the problem
remains when we use belief language: To know whether our
beliefs are true, we must have a procedure for distinguishing

true beliefs from false ones. But to know whether our
procedure is adequate, we have to know whether it actually
succeeds in distinguishing true beliefs from false ones. And
we cannot know whether it does unless we know which beliefs
are true.

Now Chisholm claims that there are three responses to
this problem, but none of those responses covers James's
pragmatic position. Chisholm says that an epistemologist can
accept the circularity entailed by the two questions. If he
does, Chisholm says he has only one option: he must espouse
the *sceptical* position and say, "you cannot know what, if
anything, you know, and there is no possible way for you to
decide in any particular case."[113] Or, Chisholm goes on, an
epistemologist can beg the question, and take either of two
positions. He can assume that he has an answer to the first
one and, based on that answer, generate an answer to the
second one. In this case he takes the "particularist"
position. Or he can assume that he has an answer to the
second one and, based on that answer, generate an answer to
the first one. In this case, he takes the "methodist" position. Now before we show why James does not take any of
these positions, we must examine each one.

The *sceptic's* position boils down to the following:

The two questions generate a vicious circle;
therefore,

If S believes that p, there is some chance that
S is incorrect in his belief; and

If there is some chance that S is incorrect in
his belief that p, then S does not know that p;
therefore,

S is ignorant.

Based on the chance of error, in other words, the sceptic is
led to develop what amounts to a theory of ignorance, not a
theory of knowledge.

What about the other two positions? According to
Chisholm, he himself, Reid, and Moore, among others, hold the
particularist position. In spite of their differences, each
one of these epistemologists asserts that we can answer the

question 'What do we know?' They claim that some of our
beliefs are incorrigible, self-justifying, self-evident, and
therefore guaranteed of being true. In other words, they all
claim that there is a kind of belief that p such that to
believe that p is to know that p. For instance,

> G. E. Moore would raise his hand and say: "I
> know very well this is a hand, and so do you.
> If you come across some philosophical theory
> that implies that you and I cannot know that
> this is a hand, then so much the worse for the
> theory."114

And Chisholm, on his own behalf, says that

> If I report to you the things I now see and
> hear and feel--or, if you prefer, the things I
> now think I see and hear and feel--the chances
> are that my report will be correct; I will be
> telling you something I know. . . . To be sure,
> there are hallucinations and illusions. . . .
> But from this fact--that our senses do sometimes
> deceive us--it hardly follows that your senses
> and mine are deceiving you and me right now.
> . . . In short, the senses should be regarded
> as innocent until there is some positive reason,
> on some particular occasion, for thinking that
> they are guilty on that particular occasion.115

Particularists, therefore, start with assertions of fact.
They say that there are *basic* beliefs that are basic because
they refer without inference to matters of fact, i.e., they
refer to facts that we do not infer from anything else because
they are self-presenting or noncomparative in nature.
Particularists may claim, for instance, that perceptions are
basic beliefs, or that memories are basic beliefs, or that
revelations from God are basic beliefs. In general, the
particularist position is that

> There are basic beliefs that refer without
> inference to matters of fact.
>
> These beliefs are self-evident or self-justified.
>
> Any belief that is self-evident is guaranteed of
> being true.
>
> If S basically believes that p, S knows that p.

Methodists, on the other hand, start with assertions of
principle, and go on to instantiate those principles with

reference to particular occasions. Both Locke and Hume, for instance, claim that the only way a person can know that p is to derive that information from sense experience. If it is derived from sense-experience, they would say, then we know it. This empirical principle, they claim, is incorrigible: it is categorical in form and universal in application. In sum:

Certain principles are categorically true.

If S believes that p, and p meets the conditions of a principle that is categorically
true, S knows that p.

All in all, therefore, sceptics claim that any belief may be false, and develop a theory of ignorance. Particularists claim that certain beliefs are basic because they refer without inference to matters of fact, and develop an epistemology from this foundation. Methodists claim that certain principles are categorically true, because they condition, invariantly, what is the case, and develop an epistemology from this foundation. In light of these three positions, Chisholm closes his lectures on the problem of the criterion with the following admission:

What few philosophers have had the courage to
recognize is this: We can deal with the problem
only by begging the question. . . . One may
object: "Doesn't this mean, then, that the
sceptic is right after all?" I would answer:
"Not at all. His view is only one of the three
possibilities and in itself has no more to
recommend it than the others do. And in favor
of our approach [which is particularist] there
is the fact that we do know many things after
all."116

James apparently agrees with Chisholm's parting words when he says that "the most hardened epistemologist never really doubts that knowledge somehow does come off."117 If he did, he would stop being an epistemologist and develop a theory of ignorance like the sceptic does.

But we have not taken the trouble to specify Chisholm's three responses to the problem of the criterion because we think that James would agree with his analysis. To the contrary, James's epistemology engineers an attack on the

whole assumption that either epistemology is developed on the
basis of some foundation or epistemology is abandoned. In
fact, his epistemology generates the claim that we may know,
but we have no guarantee that we know. And he argues generally from the phenomenon of conceptual change. In his own
words:

> Since it is impossible to deny secular alterations
> in our sentiments and needs, it would be absurd to
> affirm that one's own age of the world can be
> beyond correction by the next age. Scepticism
> cannot, therefore, be ruled out by any set of
> thinkers as a possibility against which their
> conclusions are secure; and no empiricist ought
> to claim exemption from this universal liability.
> But to admit one's liability to correction is one
> thing, and to embark upon a wanton sea of doubt
> is another. Of willfully playing into the hands
> of scepticism we cannot be accused. He who
> acknowledges the imperfectness of his instrument,
> and makes allowances for it in discerning his
> observations, is in a much better position for
> gaining truth than if he claimed his instrument
> to be infallible.[118]

In other words, he grants the sceptic that

> If S believes that p, there is some chance that
> S is incorrect in his belief;

but he attempts to develop an epistemology in light of the
corrigible status of beliefs. As he sees it, to admit the
risk of error can be construed legitimately as admitting the
chance of truth.

James believes that he can construct such an epistemology
by describing the "observable process which Schiller and Dewey
particularly singled out for generalization," i.e., "the
process by which an individual settles into new opinions."[119]
Take notice: an historical process is under observation, and
the population under study is the population of beliefs held
by a person:

> The process here is always the same. The indi-
> vidual has a stock of old opinions already, but
> he meets a new experience that puts them to a
> strain. Somebody contradicts them; or in a
> reflective moment he discovers that they con-
> tradict each other; or he hears of facts with
> which they are incompatible; or desires arise
> in him which they cease to satisfy. The result
> is an inward trouble to which his mind till

> then has been a stranger, and from which he seeks
> to escape by modifying his previous mass of
> opinions. He saves as much of it as he can, for
> in this manner of belief we are all extreme
> conservatives. So he tries to change first this
> opinion, and then that (for they resist change
> very variously) until at last some new idea
> comes up which he can graft upon the ancient
> stock with a minimum of disturbance of the
> latter, some idea that mediates between the
> stock and the new experience and runs them
> into one another most felicitously and
> expediently.[120]

In other words, James attempts to describe how an individual
goes about *deciding* whether or not, and if so how, to amend
his stock of beliefs when faced with optional or alternative
ones. Some of those decisions generate less drastic changes
than others, but *wholesale* change is possible:

> With science, *naif* realism ceases: 'Secondary'
> qualities become unreal; primary ones alone
> remain. With critical philosophy . . . the
> common sense categories one and all cease to
> represent anything in the way of *being*; they
> are but sublime tricks of human thought, our
> ways of escaping bewilderment in the midst of
> sensation's irremediable flow.[121]

Thus, James prefigures philosophers like Neurath who conceive
of knowledge, not as resting on some firm foundation of
incorrigible beliefs or categorical principles, but as a
vehicle which, in principle, can be constantly rebuilt, 'one
plank at a time':[122]

> We patch and tinker more than we renew. The
> novelty soaks in; it stains the ancient mass;
> but it is also tinged by what absorbs it. Our
> past apperceives and co-operates; and in the
> new equilibrium in which each step forward in
> the process of learning terminates, it happens
> relatively seldom that the new fact is added
> *raw*. More usually, it is embedded cooked, as
> one might say, or stewed down in the sauce of
> the old.[123]

Here we cash in on our promissory note that James does
describe historical processes, the innovative and selective
factors of which are *coupled*. When James describes the
process of "learning," he describes novel beliefs *"along with
the whole environment of social communication of which they
are a part and out of which they take their rise."* [124] Like

law and language, the development of knowledge is a *social* process:

> These things *make themselves* as we go. Our
> rights, wrongs, prohibitions, penalties, words,
> forms, idioms, beliefs, are so many new crea-
> tions that add themselves as fast as history
> proceeds. Far from being antecedent principles
> that animate the process, law, language, truth
> are but abstract names for its results.[125]

But if knowledge does not rely on any antecedent foundation, then it becomes difficult to claim that any belief is
basic, in the strong sense that particularists must specify
beliefs as basic, or to claim that any principle is categorically true. So James can neither be a particularist nor be
a methodist.

There may have been a time when James was a particularist. In any case, he has been praised and blamed for being
one. When critics do praise him (e.g., Perry, Ayer) or blame
him (e.g., Royce) for being a particularist, they turn
primarily to the first two essays in *The Meaning of Truth* for
supporting evidence, i.e., they turn to "The Function of
Cognition" and "The Tigers in India." There James distinguishes between "knowledge by acquaintance" or intuitive
knowledge or direct knowledge of "sensible termini" and
"knowledge about" or conceptual knowledge or information.
When we specify what we know about "the white paper before
our eyes," James says, we place "the white paper" in context.
"The knowledge *about* it is *it* with a context added. Undo *it*,
and what is added cannot be *con*text."[126]

In other words, in these two essays, James argues that
percepts like "the whiteness, smoothness, or squareness of
this paper" are "ultimate data."[127]

> These percepts, these termini, these sensible
> things, these mere matters-of-acquaintance,
> are the only realities that we ever directly
> know, and the whole history of our thought is
> the history of our substitution of one of them
> for another, and the reduction of the substitute
> to the status of conceptual sign.[128]

Percepts, so this argument goes, are "the mother earth, the
anchorage, the stable rock, the first and last limits, the
terminus a quo and the *terminus ad quem* of the mind."[129]

Given the direct knowledge that we have of certain experiences, James apparently answers the question 'What do we
know?' and generates the following generalization in answer
to the question concerning epistemic criteria:

> A percept knows whatever reality it directly or
> indirectly operates on and resembles; a conceptual
> feeling, or thought knows a reality whenever it
> actually or potentially terminates in a percept
> that operates on, or resembles that reality, or
> is otherwise connected with it or with its con-
> text.130

Thus, to verify the 'conceptual claim' that 'there are tigers
in India' we must 'cash' it empirically: We must, in principle, be able to observe some tiger in India:

> The pointing of our thought to the tigers is
> known simply and solely as a procession of
> mental associates and motor consequences that
> follow on the thought, and that would lead har-
> moniously, if followed out, into some ideal or
> real context, or even into the immediate presence
> of the tigers.131

Can there be any question that James argues along the lines
espoused by particularists here? No. But the problem with
construing James as a particularist is that these two essays
were written early-on in his philosophical career--and that
by the time he edited them for *The Meaning of Truth*, he
actually professed that what was particularistic about them
is a "defect." "The treatment . . . of percepts as the only
realm of reality" is a defect. "The undue prominence given
to resembling," that stems from the naively realistic assumption that percepts and facts mirror one another, is a defect.
He admits that he avoids "raising the idealistic controversy,"
i.e., the controversy concerning the manner in which signs
might relate to objects, or be rooted in them.132 What is
more, the lectures on pragmatism, while maintaining an
allegiance to facts and to the principle of verification,
abandon the claim that any belief--of fact or principle--can
be asserted to be categorically true, or refer without
inference to matters of fact. The same is the case with the
essays in *The Meaning of Truth* that were written after those
lectures, in development and defense of them. Thus, in the
lectures he asserts that

> Purely objective truth, truth in whose establish-
> ment the function of giving human satisfaction in
> marrying previous parts of experience with newer
> parts played no role whatsoever, is nowhere to be
> found. The reasons why we call things true is the
> reason why they *are* true, for "to be true" means
> only to perform this marriage function.133

Now whatever James means by "this marriage function" and
however he is using the term 'true' here, and no matter what
he means by "experience," he is saying that our knowledge is
conditional. He is saying that we cannot know that p without
placing our belief that p in the context of "experience" and
inferring its truth from the part that it plays in that
context. If, to be a particularist, one must found an
epistemology on the ability to refer without inference to
matters of fact, then James is no particularist. Notice:
this does not preclude James from generating an epistemology
that is fact-oriented, and it does not preclude him from
generating a realistic epistemology. It merely precludes him
from founding his epistemology on any myth of the given--a
myth that he abandons the moment he claims that

> Our whole notion of a standing reality grows up
> in the form of an ideal limit to the series of
> successive termini to which our thoughts have led
> us and are still leading us. Each terminus proves
> provisional by leaving us unsatisfied. The true
> idea is the one that pushes farther; so we are
> ever beckoned on by the ideal notion of an ulti-
> mate completely satisfactory terminus.134

Reality stands at the end of inquiry, not at its beginning.
Obviously, we need to clarify just how James is using terms
like "true" and "experience" and "satisfaction" and so on,
but before we do, we must show why James is not an epistemological methodist either.

It is true that James promulgates a pragmatic method or
process of verification; i.e., he does establish criteria by
which to completely justify our beliefs. But no matter how
he specifies that pragmatic principle, he does not make any
categorical claims about it. Generally speaking, "theories
. . . become instruments, not answers to enigmas on which we
rest."135 They are as conditional, in principle, as the facts
that instantiate them. Indeed,

> no theory is absolutely a transcript of reality,
> but any one of them may from some point of view
> be useful. Their great use is to summarize old
> facts and to lead to new ones. They are only a
> man-made language, a conceptual shorthand . . .
> in which we write our reports of nature. . . .136

The pragmatic method, says James, is "the attitude of looking
away from first things, principles, 'categories,' supposed
necessities; and of looking towards last things, fruits,
consequences, facts."[137] The pragmatist "clings to facts and
concreteness, observes truth at its work in particular cases,
and generalizes."[138] If, to be a methodist, one must found an
epistemology on principles that are categorically true, then
James is no methodist. But notice again: this does not
preclude James from generating an epistemology that includes
criteria for the justification of beliefs; it does not
preclude him from generating an epistemology that is theoret-
ically sound. Once again, it merely precludes him from
founding his epistemology on epistemic conditions that, in
principle, are invariant.

But if James's pragmatism precludes both unconditional
principles and direct knowledge of matters of fact, then he
apparently is left without answers to either epistemic
question. Indeed, as we have seen, he admits the sceptic's
premise that if S believes that p, there is some chance that
S is incorrect in his belief. But he does not generate a
theory of ignorance: He generates an epistemology in which,
not foundations, but consequences, i.e., *expected epistemic
utility*, play the crucial role. In other words, beliefs are
selected or neglected in James's scheme of things in terms of
their epistemic value. This must be underscored. James says
that "the true is the name of whatever proves itself good in
the way of belief . . . for definite, assignable reasons";
that "the true . . . is only the expedient in the way of our
thinking."[139] In doing so, it is obvious that he claims that
knowledge is fundamentally axiological. When a person decides
to believe that x, he may do so for definite reasons, none of
which needs be epistemic. But when a person *who is searching
for the truth* decides to believe that x, he does so for
definite *epistemic* reasons. James is searching for the truth;

he is addressing his epistemology to people who are searching
for the truth, and if he finds certain beliefs more satisfactory than others, it is not because he values them *sans
phrase*, not because they further his welfare generally
speaking, but because he values them epistemically and
because they further his epistemic welfare in particular.
For anyone to claim that he knows that x, according to James,
he must justify his belief that it is better to believe that
x than any other belief that might compete with his belief
that x. "Beliefs 'pass' so long as nothing challenges them,
just as banknotes pass so long as nobody refuses them."[140]
Justification is called into play, however, when there is an
"actual competition of opinions."[141] It is in the "actual
competition of opinions," i.e., in the development of our set
of beliefs, that we need to compute the relative value of
variant and vying convictions.

But to say that knowledge is axiological is not to
confuse epistemology and ethics. James says that the true is
the expedient in the way of our thinking, and he makes a point
of drawing an analogy between the true and "the right" which
he specifies as "the expedient in the way of our behaving."[142]
But to make an analogy is precisely not to claim an equiva-
lence. Thus when James argues that "True ideas are those we
can assimilate, validate, corroborate, and verify. False
ideas are those that we cannot,"[143] he is suggesting that
there is a procedure by which to evaluate beliefs epistemically. He is arguing that if I am to make the claim that I
know that p, I need certain warrants to support my claim--but
the warrants I need are amoral.

Some critics have claimed that James's epistemology is,
in some sense, *immoral*. Royce, for instance, called it
"capricious."[144] He claimed that, because James's epistemology rests neither on invariant principles nor on any
direct knowledge, it allows for all sorts of wishful thinking. James's answer to this sort of claim is forthright:

> That men do exist who are 'opinionated,' in the
> sense that their opinions are self-willed, is
> unfortunately a fact that must be admitted, no
> matter what one's notion of truth in general may
> be. But that this fact should make it impossible

> for truth to form itself authentically out of the
> life of opinion is what no critic has yet proved.[145]

It makes no more sense to call James's epistemology "capricious" than it does to call his ethical position "subjective."
Beliefs *may* have little or no epistemic value, just like
intentions *may* be materially egocentric. But to admit this is
hardly to preclude the claim that

> Truth may well consist of certain opinions, and
> does indeed consist of nothing but opinion, tho
> not every opinion need be true

any more than it is to preclude James's ethical claim that
obligations consist of certain intentions, and consist of
nothing but intentions, though not every intention is
obligatory. To claim that the stuff of knowledge, i.e.,
belief, is inherently corrigible hardly proves the sceptic's
claim that we are not able to know anything.

Why not? Because we can justify certain beliefs
adequately enough to say that we may, i.e., probably, know,
without *guaranteeing* that we know. James is neither a
sceptic, nor a particularist, nor a methodist, because those
sorts of thinkers assume that if we know that p, then our
belief that p must be incorrigible. James does not agree with
this assumption. Instead, he promulgates a pragmatic analysis
of knowledge.

Now before we finally turn to James's own analysis of
knowledge, it will be worthwhile to backtrack historically,
briefly and sketchily, to indicate the pragmatic heritage that
he self-consciously espouses. If there is one key epistemological stance which characterizes pragmatism, it is the
claim that there are no epistemological givens: if we have
warrants for our beliefs, they are not antecedent or
foundational; they are consequential and behavioral. This
'pragmatic stance' is grounded in certain distinctions that
Kant made concerning (i) different sorts of practical law
(i.e., laws governing the behavior of persons) and (ii)
different sorts of belief (i.e., convictions which either have
not or cannot be verified empirically).[146]

Kant claimed that there are two sorts of practical law.
There are moral laws which are generated *a priori* from the

conditions of personhood. But there are also pragmatic laws
of free action, which are generated from empirical (i.e.,
psychological and biological) principles. Pragmatic laws
regulate the behavior of persons "for the attainment of those
ends which are commended to us by the senses,"[147] i.e.,
pragmatic laws are empirically conditioned. For instance,
Kant's 'rules of prudence,' derived from the notion of
happiness or satisfaction, are pragmatic laws.

Now within this context Kant defines pragmatic belief as
the sort of conviction which is "concerned with optional and
contingent ends," "yet forms the ground for the actual employment of means to certain actions."[148] For Kant, a pragmatic
belief is a rational bet: a hypothetical assertion, held with
lesser or greater conviction, that something will be taken
empirically to be the case, given certain empirical conditions. For instance,

> The physician must do something for a patient in
> danger, but does not know the nature of his
> illness. He observes the symptoms and if he
> can find no other likely alternative, judges
> it to be a case of phthisis. Now even in his
> own estimation his belief is contingent only;
> another observer might perhaps come to a sounder
> conclusion.[149]

The physician's belief is (i) hypothetical, (ii) regulative of
his behavior *as* a physician attempting to heal this particular
patient, and (iii) cashed as valid or justified by a process
of empirical verification (i.e., by the success or failure of
the medical treatment which, *ceteris paribus*, would heal his
patient were the latter actually suffering from phthisis).

Peirce's revolution, it seems to me, lies in his appropriation of Kant's notion of pragmatic belief to analyze all
assertions. In other words, he develops a theory of meaning
in which all assertions are held to be hypothetical, empirically conditioned, regulative ideas, or rules for action. For
Peirce, the significance of assertions is judged according to
the consequent, dispositional conditions which they possibly
imply: Hence Peirce's claim that

> If one can define accurately all the conceivable
> experimental phenomena which the affirmation or
> denial of a concept could imply, one will have

> therein a complete definition of the concept, *and*
> *there is absolutely nothing more in it.*150

Peirce's appropriation represents a departure from Kant inasmuch as he applies his pragmatic maxim to specify the significance of *all* assertions, both 'practical' and 'theoretical.'
Kant, to the contrary, had claimed that 'pragmatic belief'
concerned only 'practical' matters.

For Peirce, then, there are no concepts that are foundational, i.e., that refer without inference to matters of fact.
All concepts are defined contextually and indirectly through
the trial and error processes of empirical procedure. The
significance of a concept lies in its observable effect on our
behavior as persons. Charles Morris ably reformulates
Peirce's maxim as follows:

> The meaning of an intellectual concept involves
> an intrinsic connection between action and
> experience such that if such and such kinds of
> action were to be performed, then such and such
> kinds of experiential results would necessarily
> be obtained.151

Now if Peirce appropriated Kant's notion of 'pragmatic
belief' to generate a theory of meaning, James in turn
appropriated the latter to analyze 'belief,' 'knowledge,' and
'truth.' James applied what *he* took to be Peirce's maxim
(others, including Peirce, construed it differently) to the
epistemic problematic, and generated a *dispositional* theory of
belief, an *instrumental* theory of justification, an
eliminative theory of truth, and a *probabilistic* theory of
knowledge. Now these adjectives--as they are used here--are
mine, not James's, but I believe that the following description of James's analysis of the epistemic problem will give
them warrant.

The most lucid articulation of James's understanding of
the pragmatic principle is found neither in *Pragmatism* nor in
The Meaning of Truth, but in his Gifford Lectures on the
varieties of religious experience.152 There James says,

> Thought in movement has for its only conceivable
> motive the attainment of belief, or thought at
> rest. Only when our thought about a subject has
> found its rest in belief can our action on the
> subject firmly and safely begin. Beliefs, in

short, are rules for action; and the whole function of thinking is but one step in the production
of active habits. If there were any part of a
thought that made no difference in the thought's
practical consequences, then that part would be
no proper element in the thought's significance.
To develop a thought's meaning we need therefore
only determine what conduct it is fitted to produce: that conduct is for us its sole significance;
and the tangible fact at the root of all our
thought-distinctions is that there is no one of
them so fine as to consist in anything but a possible difference of practice. To attain perfect
clearness in our thoughts of an object, we need
then only consider what sensations, immediate
or remote, we are conceivably to expect from
it, and what conduct we must prepare in case
the object should be true. Our conception of
these practical consequences is for us the whole
of our conception of the object, so far as that
conception has positive significance at all.153

Equipped with this understanding of how we think and its
epistemic implications, James is led to claim, along with
the sceptic, that

If S believes that p, there is some chance that
S is incorrect in his belief.

But he does not go on then to claim that

If there is some chance that S is incorrect in
his belief that p, then S does not know that p.

Instead, he is led to claim that

If there is some chance that S is incorrect in
his belief that p, then he may know that p,
and he may not.

Philosophically convinced that epistemic certainty is a sham,
in other words, he develops a probabilistic epistemology. As
usual, his method is to establish an objective, to isolate the
relevant data, and to determine the criteria by which the
relevant data are selected or neglected as fitting responses
to the problem under study.

In the science of knowledge, the objective is a statement
of the truth. No pragmatist, says James, "who ever actually
walked the earth has denied the regulative character in his
own thinking of the notion of absolute truth."154 To know
that p, it must be true 'that p.' The data under study are
beliefs, the "rules for action" that, whether correct or

incorrect, are generated by our thinking. To know that p, we must believe that p. But some beliefs serve as fitting responses to the epistemic problem and others do not. Hence, to know that p, we must be justified in our belief that p. Finally, we realize from the phenomenon of radical conceptual change that it is possible to justify beliefs based on false premises. Ptolemy was justified in holding his cosmological beliefs, because his arguments were based on valid rules of inference and conventional beliefs. They were bad arguments, however, because they were based on false statements. Hence, to know that p, the justification that warrants our belief that p must not, in turn, depend on any false beliefs. All in all, as James sees it,

> S knows that p if and only if (i) it is true that p; (ii) S believes that p; (iii) S is justified in believing that p; and (iv) the justification that S proposes on behalf of his belief that p does not, in turn, depend upon any false belief.

Let us turn to the first condition of knowledge, which is truth. James devoted a good deal of effort to supporting the claim that, if S knows that p, it is true that p. Indeed, in the preface to *The Meaning of Truth*, James says that

> The pivotal part of my book named *Pragmatism* is its account of the relation called 'truth,' which may obtain between an idea (opinion, belief, statement or whatnot) and its object.[155]

The problem with interpreting James's "theory of truth" is that it is really two theories. Following the idiom of his day, he meant, in part, what we today mean by 'theory of epistemic justification.' When he asks, for example, "What is the truth's cash-value in experiential terms?"[156] and answers generally that its cash-value is *verifiability* and then goes on to specify the conditions of verification, he is generating an instrumental theory of justification. He is saying that we call a statement of belief 'true' *because* it is a verified, or verifiable, statement. This is hardly an analysis of the term 'truth.' But if it is a sin to call this sort of work "theory of truth," then it is likewise a sin to call 'coherence' and 'correspondence' theories of truth, 'theories of truth,' because they also answer the question of

justification. They too ask why our belief that p is true,
and answer (respectively), *because* p coheres with a system of
accepted propositions; or, *because* p corresponds to matters of
fact. Theories of justification address the 'because' questions, not theories of truth.

James, however, does more than posit a theory of justification. He analyzes the term 'truth.' "Empiricists," he
says, "think that truth in general is distilled from single
men's beliefs; and the so-called pragmatists 'go them one
better' by trying to define what it consists in when it
comes."[157]

The first claim that James makes about the term 'truth'
is now old hat:

> Realities are not *true*, they *are*; and beliefs are
> true *of* them. But I suspect that in the anti-
> pragmatist mind the two notions sometimes swap
> their attributes. The reality itself, I fear,
> is treated as if 'true,' and conversely.[158]

Truth, in other words, is something that we claim on behalf of
statements, not on behalf of matters of fact. James does not
commit the sin of confusing signs and objects. For him, truth
represents "a property of the idea"; it is not "something
mysteriously connected with the object known."[159] To make
this claim in James's day was to draw blood from philosophers
in the Hegelian mold, like Royce, who construed truth as a
property inseparably epistemological *and* ontological.

But once this first move is made, it becomes possible to
construe truth as a condition of knowledge without any
explicit *reference* to it. In other words, it becomes evident
that our claiming that Q is true, where Q is a statement of
belief which *means* that p, is equivalent to our claiming that,
if we know that p, then p. For instance:

> S knows that 'snow is white' is true and that
> 'snow is white' means that snow is white if and
> only if S knows that snow is white and that
> 'snow is white' means that snow is white.

When we say that 'snow is white' is true, we say no more nor
less than that, if we know that snow is white, then snow is
white. And James means nothing more nor less than this when
he claims that "truth and knowledge are terms correlative and

interdependent":[160]

> If there is to be truth . . . both realities
> and beliefs about them must conspire to make it;
> but whether there ever is such a thing, or how
> anyone can be sure that his own beliefs possess
> it, [pragmatism] never pretends to determine.[161]

But isn't James begging the question? And isn't he saying
that in order for us to claim that Q is true we must already
know that p (where Q *means* p)? The answer to the first
question is, 'No, James is not begging the question.' The
answer to the second question is, 'Yes, James is saying that
in order for us to claim that Q is true, we must already know
that p.' Keith Lehrer explains why more succinctly than I
could. He suggests that some people are inclined to object
to the truth condition of knowledge

> on the grounds that we have no way of deciding
> whether the truth condition is satisfied until
> we know that it is, and therefore making truth
> a condition of knowledge renders it impossible
> to decide whether we know anything. The answer
> is that such a condition of knowledge is not
> one that we must find to be satisfied *before* we
> find out that we know; it is rather part of an
> analysis of knowledge and hence a condition that
> must be satisfied *when* we know.[162]

James brings this point home in the final pages of *The Meaning
of Truth*. There he posits that "wherever knowledge is
conceivable truth is conceivable, wherever knowledge is
possible, truth is possible, wherever knowledge is actual,
truth is actual": there, and nowhere else; then, and not
before. This is why James says to the "Anti-Pragmatist" in
"A Dialogue" that

> Where you see three distinct entities in the
> field, the reality, the knowing, and the truth,
> I see only two. Moreover, I can see what each
> of my two entities is *known-as*, but when I ask
> myself what your third entity, the truth, is
> known-as, I can find nothing distinct from the
> reality on the one hand, and the ways in which
> it may be known on the other.[163]

The reference to truth may therefore be *eliminated* in the
formulation of the truth condition of knowledge. To insist
on the truth condition is only to insist that, if we know
that something is the case, then it is the case.

Belief is the next condition of knowledge. We have already seen that James specifies belief as a "rule for action." Alternatively, he specifies it as an "instrument of action," i.e., as a rule, held with greater or lesser conviction, that disposes its holder to behave in a particular sort of way in particular sorts of circumstance.[164] On this reading, to know that something is the case is to hold a belief, a rule for behavior, that correctly fits an empirically specifiable occasion. In James's words, we not only believe, but we know, if our belief "*fits*, in fact, and adapts our life to the reality's whole setting. . . ."[165]

Now there are a number of arguments against claiming that if S knows that p, S believes that p, though James considers only one of them. First, one could argue that it makes perfectly good sense to say: "I do not believe that p. I know that p."[166] Here, of course, the speaker construes belief as contrary to knowledge. The argument, however, goes on to imply that if belief is contrary to knowledge, then belief is contradictory to knowledge; and, therefore, that belief cannot be a condition of knowledge. But this is simply not the case. It is the case that belief is *contrary* to knowledge, and James would have no trouble accepting the claim that it is. But contraries can either be contradictory or they can be complementary.[167] In the case of belief and knowledge, they are complementary. We recognize this when we realize that, "I do not believe that p. I know that p.," is *elliptical* for the statement that, "I not only believe that p. I (even) know that p."

Second, it may be contended that counter-examples are available that undercut the claim that belief is a condition of knowledge. For instance, it has been posited that a person can offer the correct answer to a question without believing that his answer is correct. In these cases, so the argument goes, the person in question knows the answer. He just does not believe either the answer or that he knows the answer.[168] But there is a gross error in this argument: To give a correct answer is hardly the same as knowing that the answer is correct. A well-trained mynah bird can give correct answers to some questions if trained appropriately. But the

best-trained mynah bird does not know anything. If a person
does not believe that p is the correct answer, but states
'that p' in answer to it, and 'that p' is the correct answer,
then that person is a lucky guesser--no more and no less.

Third, some claim that 'if S knows that p, then S
believes that p' is false because 'belief' and 'knowledge'
belong to two different orders of fact. 'Belief' is a
psychological state; 'knowledge' is an epistemological state:
To know that p is to have all the correct information about
p; to believe that p is to have some degree of conviction that
p is the case.[169] James's answer to this argument is clear
and provocative:

> I defy anyone to show any difference between
> logic and psychology here. The logical relation
> stands to the psychological relation between
> idea and object only as saltatory abstractness
> stands to ambulatory concreteness. Both rela-
> tions need a psychological vehicle. . . .[170]

In a sense, this claim of James's drives us to the heart of
his entire epistemological project. For James, to do
epistemology is to describe how persons who are searching
for the truth--persons that Lehrer aptly titles "veracious"[171]--decide among competing beliefs which ones to hold.
As far as he is concerned, 'conviction' is the name of the
game. For, along with the various myths of the given that he
gave up on becoming a pragmatist, he also gave up the sort of
epistemology that goes with them--the sort of epistemology in
which the epistemologist plays spectator attempting to copy
correctly a static scene. For James, the heart of epistemology is the logic of *inquiry*, not the logic of *revelation*. And
if James is correct in construing epistemology this way, then
it is difficult to accept this last sort of criticism of the
belief condition of knowledge.

It might be different were James to claim that conviction
was the *cause* of belief and/or knowledge; but he does not. He
claims that it is a condition of belief and of knowledge. His
epistemology is explicitly *not* "an inquiry into the 'how it
comes,' but into the 'what it is' of cognition."[172] It is
descriptive, not *genetic* in any causal sense. For James to
say that his epistemological account is "ambulatory" is not to

say that it is genetic in any *causal* sense. It is to say that
it is historiographical, or descriptive of the conditions
under which knowledge is developed.

In any case, James does not claim that either belief or
truth or both serve as sufficient conditions of knowledge. If
S knows that p, then S is justified in believing that p.
Prior to pragmatism, the two basic positions that a philosopher could take on the matter of justification were "correspondence theory" and "coherence theory," to which we have
referred already. Correspondence theorists justify beliefs in
terms of *evidence*. They claim that it is reasonable to hold a
belief if and only if that belief is self-evident or if that
belief is directly or indirectly related to a belief that is
self-evident. Coherence theorists, to the contrary, deny that
there are any self-evident beliefs. They justify particular
beliefs in terms of relations that hold among those particular
beliefs and others in a given conceptual framework.

What about James? Well, at first glance, he looks like a
correspondence theorist, inasmuch as he claims that "Truth
. . . is a property of certain of our ideas. It means their
'agreement,' as falsity means their disagreement with
'reality.'"[173] Now, like correspondence theorists, he seems
to be saying that some of our ideas are basic, i.e., they
refer without inference to matters of fact; and these ideas,
as well as others that are based on them, are true.

But at second glance, he looks like a coherence theorist,
because it turns out that he construes 'agreement' as "workability" and 'reality,' at least in part, as the beliefs that
we value epistemically. Along these lines, he says that, if
a belief is to "work," it must

> derange common sense and previous belief as
> little as possible, and it must lead to some
> sensible terminus or other that can be verified
> exactly. To 'work' means both these things;
> and the squeeze is so tight that there is
> little loose play for any hypothesis.[174]

When we remember that James construes sensible termini as
"provisional," i.e., as observation-reports that are, in
principle, intersubjectively held beliefs about what is
particularly the case, it becomes rather easy for us to

reformulate his specification of "workability" to read
simply, "a belief works if and only if it coheres with the
other beliefs we value epistemically."

But to read James either as a correspondence theorist or
as a coherence theorist is to miss the point of his being a
pragmatist, which is to shift the burden of justification
from the antecedent conditions of belief *to* their consequences. For him, the success of an idea is judged not only
in light of the system of propositions with which it coheres,
but also according to its applicability to future events. It
must "lead *towards*, or *up to*, or *against*, a reality. . . ."[175]
"Leading" is the key term. Should a belief ever lose its
referential value, should it ever fail to carry us to the
edges of language, it would lose its justification, no matter
how ensconced it is in our system of beliefs.

Thayer suggests that "agreement" means essentially social
or intersubjective acceptability for James.[176] He says that
"'agreement' has to do with a social, or interpersonal way of
adaptation to the common situation as a consequence of the
statement made and the character of the conditions it
asserts."[177] This interpretation is tempting. If we look
again at James's specification of 'reality,' we find three
sorts of belief that are each logically intersubjective:
(a) common sense, (b) previous belief, i.e., the belief we
inherit, and (c) sensible termini, i.e., the things *anyone* can
observe. But the fact of the matter is that, while sensible
termini are *in principle* intersubjective, they may not be in
fact. James is too dyed-in-the-wool a realist to buy the
claim that, if S is justified in believing that p, then the
belief that p is socially acceptable. Once again:

> Each terminus proves provisional by leaving us
> unsatisfied. The truer idea is the one that
> pushes farther; so we are ever beckoned on by
> the ideal notion of an ultimate completely
> satisfactory terminus. . . . Can we imagine a
> man absolutely satisfied with an idea and with
> all its other relations to his other ideas and
> to his sensible experiences, who should yet *not*
> take its content as a true account of reality?[178]

Would it matter if his veracious colleagues thought him crazy,
or epistemically off-balance? Surely the man would argue on

behalf of his belief that it was an "opinion in which all men
might agree, and which no man should ever wish to change,"
i.e., he would argue for its truth and, therefore, for its
intersubjective *accessibility*. But to say that something is
accessible is hardly to say it is acceptable. James's theory
of justification is not finally social but instrumental. A
veracious person decides to maintain this belief and not that
one, is convinced more of these than of those in terms of
expected epistemic utility, to which both correspondence and
coherence are subordinated. We value the beliefs that we do,
he says,

> That we may better foresee the course of our
> experience, communicate with one another, and
> steer our lives by rule. Also that we may have
> a cleaner, clearer, more inclusive mental view.[179]

Just *how* we choose one belief over another is something that
James never makes clear, and this is an inadequacy of his
theory of justification. *That* our belief system(s) stand in
need of constant correction is clear for James. But, frankly,
his theory lacks sophistication insofar as he does not give us
the decision-theoretic moves by which we might decide to
revalue the probability rating of one belief, while devaluing
another, while refurbishing another, while abandoning another,
and so on. I find James's theory of justification warranted
as far as it goes--but he left it in need of development.[180]

Even so, he was ingenious enough to realize that if a
person knows that p, it is not merely because 'that p' is one
belief in a corrected system of beliefs. He never states, but
implies that if S knows that p, then the justification that S
proposes on behalf of his belief that p does not, in turn,
depend upon any false belief: "I myself," James says,

> as a pragmatist, believe in my own account of
> truth as firmly as any rationalist can possibly
> believe in his. And I believe in it for the
> very reason that I *have* the idea of truth which
> my learned adversaries contend that no pragmatist
> can frame. I expect, namely, that the more fully
> men discuss and test my account, the more they
> will agree that it fits, and the less will they
> desire a change. I may of course be premature
> in this confidence, and the glory of being truth
> final and absolute may fall upon some later
> revision and correction of my scheme, *which*

> *later will then be judged untrue in just the*
> *measure in which it departs from that finally*
> *satisfactory formulation.* To admit, as we
> pragmatists do, that we are liable to correc-
> tion (even tho we may not expect it) *involves*
> the use on our part of an ideal standard.[181]

Again, the truth, and the reality to which it refers, comes at
the end of inquiry, and only at the end. This is the essence
of self-criticism and the brilliance of pragmatism. James
--as a man searching for the truth, i.e., a man committed to
our epistemic welfare--claims that he not only needs to
correct his set of beliefs so as to maintain only those that
are of maximum epistemic utility. (He has done *this* in the
formulation of his epistemology.) He claims that he must also
be prepared to exchange all of the beliefs in his corrected
system that *turn out to be false*, for their verific alternatives.

What do we know? According to James, we may not know
anything, but we probably do. What are the criteria of
knowledge? Well, in James's view, if we know anything, what
we know is true, believed, justified; indeed, is justified in
such a way as to depend on no false belief. Notice: A
veracious person is one who commits himself to the search for
truth. A veracious person would exchange any false belief in
his "corrected doxastic system" for its verific alternatives.
And this implies that he would commit himself to rules of
conduct *intended* to be simply fitting. But whether or not his
rules actually lead to such conduct is a matter of chance, a
risk he binds himself to as a result of his commitment.

Persons

Where James's epistemology revolves around the problem of
establishing and satisfying our epistemic welfare, his
philosophy of persons revolves around the problem of establishing and satisfying our welfare in general. To establish
our "welfare," for James, is to consider and try to specify
life's worth. And to satisfy our welfare in general is to
dispose ourselves successfully to conduct we take to be
fitting. James addresses these problems and the issues that
fall out from them in his multifaceted analysis of "the self."

At first glance, James's analysis of the self appears to be full of disparate and sometimes contradictory statements. Some of the claims that James makes have to do with *what we are conscious of when we say we are self-conscious*. For example, he claims:

> In the widest possible sense . . . a man's self is the sum total of all he *can* call his, not only his body and his psychic powers, but his clothes and his house, his wife and his children, his ancestors and his friends, his reputation and his works, his lands and horse, and yacht and bank account.[182]

> What we conceptually identify ourselves with and say we are thinking of at any given time is the center; but our full self is the whole field, with all those infinitely radiating subconscious possibilities of increase that we can only feel without conceiving, and can hardly begin to analyze.[183]

James makes other claims about the self that have to do with *the way we identify ourselves*. For example:

> The sense of our personal identity . . . is exactly like any one of our other perceptions of sameness among phenomena. It is a conclusion grounded either on the resemblance in a fundamental respect, or on the continuity before the mind, of the phenomena compared.[184]

> There is nothing more remarkable in making a judgment of sameness in the first person than in the second or the third.[185]

Still other claims that he makes about the self have to do with *specifying criteria for reidentifying individual people*. Thus:

> The word 'I' is primarily a noun of position, like 'this' and 'here.'[186]

> The identity found by the *I* in its *me* is a loosely constructed thing.[187]

> The body, and the central adjustments, which accompany the act of thinking, in the head . . . are the real nucleus of our personal identity.[188]

> The commonest element of all . . . is the possession of the same memories.[189]

> The 'I think' which Kant said must be able to
> accompany all my objects is the 'I breathe'
> which actually does accompany them.[190]

Still other claims have to do with *the specification of an
epistemological subject*. For example:

> The Ego is simply *nothing*.[191]

> Our 'Thought'--a cognitive phenomenal event in
> time--is, if it exist at all, itself the only
> thinker which the facts require.[192]

Finally, James makes claims about what he calls "self-regard."
That is, he makes some claims about *how we go about evaluating
our individual lives*. And he makes other claims about *the
conditions that allow for self-evaluation*. As regards the
former sort, he says:

> Men have arranged the various selves which they
> seek in a hierarchical scale according to their
> worth.[193]

> We make a combination of two things in judging
> the total significance of a human being. We feel
> it to be some sort of product . . . of his inner
> virtue *and* his outer place.[194]

As regards the latter sort, he says:

> Our self-feeling in this world depends entirely
> on what we *back* ourselves to be and do.[195]

> The innermost of the empirical selves of a man
> is a Self of the *social* sort.[196]

> The question whether life is worth living . . .
> does, indeed, depend on you *the liver*.[197]

> This life *is* worth living, we can say, *since it
> is what we make it* from the moral point of view.[198]

The problem with interpreting this variety of claims
about the self is that James never came flat-out with his own
understanding of how they relate to one another. He does not
even sort them, as I have attempted to do. But if we grant
two things about James's work, I believe we can make sense of
all these claims. First, we must grant that James is employing a particular sort of historiographical method to describe
persons, whom he construes as agents and patients of communities with intentional abilities to devise ways to feel at home

in the universe; or less metaphorically, to adapt selectively
to a variety of environments. Second, we must grant that his
center of vision is soteric. He is concerned with specifying
the conditions that would have to hold if the interests and
intentions of persons, as persons, are to be fulfilled. And
one of the ways in which he clarifies the conditions that
would allow for salvation is to ask the question whether life
is worth living. I believe that if we take James's claims
about self-regard as the key to his analysis of the self, his
other claims about self-consciousness, personal identity, and
epistemological subjectivity fall into place.

So let us assume that the problem confronting James in
his analysis of the self amounts to the question whether life
is worth living. What, then, are the conditions that allow an
individual to ask this question about his own life, as well as
the conditions that allow individuals to estimate the lives of
others?

As always, the first task to which James attends is the
identification of the relevant data in terms of which his
problem might be resolved. In particular, he tries to
describe all the sorts of things that we are apt to call our
selves or our own. In his terms, he describes the "empirical
me." Now, according to James (*pace* Hume), there is no one
thing that we identify as our self or our own. There is a
whole population of things. Generally, James says, we
identify ourselves with the things we value most of all:

> The Empirical Self of each of us is all that he
> is tempted to call by the name of *me*. But it is
> clear that between what a man calls *me* and what he
> simply calls *mine* the line is difficult to draw.
> We feel and act about certain things that are ours
> very much as we feel and act about ourselves. Our
> fame, our children, the work of our hands may be
> as dear to us as our bodies are, and arouse the
> same feelings and the same acts of reprisal if
> attacked.199

In other words, there is a whole variety of things that are
similar inasmuch as we seek to maintain and preserve them
despite great cost. These things are the standards in terms
of which one measures his "actual success or failure, and
the good or bad actual position one holds in the world."200

James says that the constituents of the empirical or "historical" self are a) the material self, b) the social self, and c) the spiritual self. By this he means that the variety of things we call me or mine can be *sorted* three different ways. We construe our selves as "material" when we depict them as "the objects of instinctive preferences coupled with the most important practical interests of life."[201] For instance, if we construe our selves as organisms that must breathe, eat, and so on, in order to maintain life, then we construe our selves as material. We describe our selves as "social" when we specify them in terms of how we think other people notice them. A person has "as many different social selves as there are distinct *groups* of persons about whose opinion he cares":

> He generally shows a different side of himself to each of these different groups. Many a youth who is demure enough before his parents and teachers, swears and swaggers like a pirate among his 'tough' young friends.[202]

If we construe our selves as "spiritual," we depict them as agents; we describe them as being "the home of interests . . . the source of effort and attention, and the place from which appear to emanate the fiats of the will."[203]

In many ways, James treats these three *sorts* as if they were actually discrete phenomena; as if, on introspection, we could actually see some selves that are utterly spiritual, others that are only material, and still others that are just social. For instance, he talks about valuing spiritual selves more than social selves and social selves more than material selves. This has led some interpreters, e.g., Wild, to search for some "essential self," some "pure subjective center of our lived experience"[204] in James's work. I think this sort of search is mistaken. The material, social, and spiritual selves do not describe actual people. They serve as the analytic variables in terms of which each and any empirical me must be unpacked. One variety of personal experience may be construed as more material than another, another less socially than the first, but no self, in James's view, is devoid of material, social, or spiritual significance. There is no more striking evidence for this fact than James's

attempt to locate *the* spiritual self or what he calls the
"self of all the other selves," and "the innermost of the
empirical selves."[205]   After abandoning, in principle, all
nonobservable agents like the soul, he identifies the
spiritual self *as* material at one point and *as* social at
another.   Whenever James attempts to describe himself as
agent, whenever his

> introspective glance succeeds in turning round
> quickly enough to catch one of these manifesta-
> tions of spontaneity in the act, all it can ever
> feel distinctly is some bodily process, for the
> most part taking place within the head.[206]

So the self of all the other selves, the agent that "welcomes
or rejects," must be specified materially.   But because there
simply is no observable agent who could live out of community,
outside the walls of some ethical republic (see below, p. 92
f.), "the innermost of the empirical selves of a man is a Self
of the *social* sort."[207]

Now to specify the spiritual self as material and social
just does not make any sense unless we construe James to be
saying that, no matter *which* self we claim to value more than
any other, we must not only specify it psychologically as this
or that set of intentions, but also materially as this or that
body, and socially as this or that community member.   This is
only to reiterate what James has already indicated in his
specification of the various sub-universes: persons are
psychophysical agents and patients in and of communities or
groups whose members are able to share intentions.   Each self
must be specified in terms of all three variables.

So the varieties of personal experience, the things we
describe as me and mine, provide the data in terms of which
individuals can resolve the question whether life is worth
living.   Each such experience can be construed as a mutation
of self, and can be selected or neglected as valuable for
resolving the problem at hand, the resolution of which would
generate "a self I can *care for*," "some *object* interesting
enough to make me instinctively wish to appropriate it for
its *own* sake."[208]

To this end, James suggests, people *order* the varieties
of personal experience: they devise hierarchies of selves.

"I am often confronted," he says,

> by the necessity of standing by one of my empir-
> ical selves, and relinquishing the rest. Not that
> I would not, if I could, be both handsome and fat
> and well-dressed, and a great athlete, and make a
> million a year, be a wit, *bon-vivant*, and a lady-
> killer as well as a philosopher. . . . But the
> thing is simply impossible. . . . Such different
> characters may conceivably at the outset of life
> be alike *possible* to a man. But to make one of
> them actual, the rest must more or less be sup-
> pressed. So the seeker of his truest, strongest,
> deepest self must review the list carefully, and
> pick out the one on which to stake his salvation.
> . . . This is as strong an example as there is
> of that selective industry of the mind on which I
> insisted some pages back [see p. 37 f.]. Our
> thought, incessantly deciding, among many things
> of a kind, which one for it shall be realities,
> here chooses one of many possible selves or
> characters, and forthwith reckons it no shame
> to fail in any of those not adopted expressly
> as its own.[209]

Out of the data pool of actual and potential me's, people are
able to select which to identify with or dispose themselves to
or become. In general, "The problem with . . . man is less
what act he shall now choose to do, than what being he shall
now resolve to become."[210]

But this picture of the process of self-evaluation needs
a good deal of supporting argument. First, *prima facie*, it is
unclear how we *can* identify ourselves at all if, in principle,
the data in terms of which we might do so is subject to
constant change. Hume saw this problem, and was led to take
a sceptical position towards identity in general. Second,
suppose we could specify who we conceive ourselves to be, and
think we dispose ourselves more or less characteristically.
Isn't it possible that we lack sufficient information and/or
criteria to judge or evaluate our own behavior? (Suppose we
decide we have no self we can care for--but only because we
lack information about ourselves that others might have which
could lead us to make a different, life-saving, evaluation?)

As far as the first problem is concerned, James has a
good deal to say. As I have mentioned, he claims that

> The sense of our personal identity is exactly like
> any one of our other perceptions of sameness among
> phenomena. It is a conclusion grounded either on

the resemblance in a fundamental respect, or on
the continuity before the mind, of the phenomena
compared.[211]

Now there are two sorts of identity, and James is aware of
both. As regards the notion of *numerical identity*, sameness
and change are incompatible. If something is numerically
identical,

'. . . it can't run on from next to next. Continuity can't mean mere absence of gap; for if
you say two things are in immediate contact, *at*
the contact how can they be two? If, on the
other hand, you put a relation of transition
between them, that itself is a third thing, and
needs to be related or hitched to its terms.
An infinite series is involved,' and so on.[212]

Comparative identity, to the contrary, allows for compatible
sameness and change. For something to be comparatively
identical, it need only be subject to reidentification despite
its vicissitudes. James, of course, is claiming that people
remain comparatively identical: somehow they are able to
remain the same despite mutation.

This is the case for James because he assumes that the
things we can look at in the world, the things we can attempt
to describe, are all mutable or subject to change. Selves are
no different from other phenomena in this respect. Your
character develops over a period of years. But I can describe
the development of your character, because your behavior is
continuous enough for me to reidentify you (or it) over and
over again. I can describe not only the development of your
character (roughly, the development of your attitudes and
dispositions), but also his and my own in the same sort of
way (though maybe not with the same accuracy). This is so
inasmuch as "there is nothing more remarkable in making a
judgment of sameness in the first person than in the second
or the third."[213] No matter whose changing character I am
describing--mine, yours, or his--the data are, in principle
if not in fact, there for anyone to see.

All this amounts to saying that, for James, personal
identity is not really a puzzlement, at least like it was for
some other philosophers, e.g., Locke and Hume, who did not
distinguish adequately between numerical and comparative sorts

of identity. Locke was led to espouse a form of substantial-
ism, and Hume a kind of scepticism, but they both shared the
same premise: the same cannot change. If the same cannot
change, and people change, then people cannot remain the same,
so people cannot maintain identity.

James turns the problem of personal identity on its head.
He argues that, as a matter of fact, we all count it as simple
truth that (the same) people change (even if some people are
not actually able to reidentify themselves or others). The
question is not whether, but how we are able to reidentify
ourselves and others. Here James introduces the herd-metaphor
to which both Linschoten and Dooley refer in their interpretations of James's analysis of self.[214] James says that our
ability to recognize ourselves is like the ability a cattle
owner has when he "picks out and sorts together when the time
for the round-up comes in the spring, all the beasts on which
he finds his particular brand":

> As we think we see an identical bodily thing
> when, in spite of changes in structure, it exists
> continuously before our eyes, or when, however
> interrupted its presence, its quality returns
> unchanged, so here we think we experience an
> identical *self* when it appears to us in an anal-
> ogous way. Continuity makes us unite what dis-
> similarity might otherwise separate; similarity
> makes us unite what discontinuity might hold
> apart.[215]

There is no absolute unity of self and there is no metaphysical substance of self. "The past and the present selves
compared are the same just so far as they *are* the same, and
no farther."[216] Their (comparative) unity is *generic*, not
ontological. "But this generic unity coexists with generic
differences just as real as the unity. And if from one point
of view they are one self, from others they are as truly not
one but many selves. . . . Where the resemblance and the
continuity are no longer felt, the sense of personal identity
goes too."[217]

James asserts, therefore, that self-identity "can only
be a relative identity, that of a slow shifting in which there
is always some common ingredient retained."[218] The case,
James says, is like Pope's story about Sir John Cutler's

socks.   Sir John "had a pair of black worsted stockings, which
his maid darned so often with silk that they became at last a
pair of silk stockings."[219]   From Sir John's point of view,
the socks retained their identity throughout: they continued
to conform to his feet from first to last.   For him, they
remained "intimate" and "warm."

Traditionally, either memory or bodily continuity or both
have served as the "herd-mark," the criteria for identity of
persons.   Thus, some have claimed that it is either a necessary or sufficient condition of saying correctly that this
person is Michalson, that the body which this person before us
has is the body that Michalson had.   And others have claimed
that it is either a necessary or sufficient condition of
saying correctly that this person is Michalson, that he should
have memories of doing Michalson's actions or of having
Michalson's experiences.[220]   If one stance is maintained
without the other, as can happen when a philosopher is a
metaphysical dualist, puzzle cases arise (e.g., cases in
which memories are continuous while bodies are transferred).

James can be read as equivocating on the issue of
criteria for reidentification of persons.   Consider the fact
that in the very same paragraph he says both that "the central
part of the *me* is the feeling of the body. . . ." and that
"the commonest element of all, the most uniform, is the
possession of the same memories."[221]   But I believe that to
read him as equivocating is to presume that he rests his
analysis of the self on a metaphysical dualism--which is not
in fact the case.   James can and should, therefore, be read
as claiming simply that, in practice, we use both criteria,
sometimes together, sometimes apart, and that our use of
either depends on our particular point of view.   (Obviously,
memory plays more of a part in autobiographical statements
than in biographical statements or historical statements about
persons.)   The crucial point is that, because both memories
and behavior are subject to alteration or mutation,

> the identity found by the I in its me is only a
> loosely constructed thing, an identity 'on the
> whole' just like that which any outside observer
> might find in the same assemblage of facts.   We
> often say of a man 'he is so changed one would

> not know him'; and so does a man, less often,
> speak of himself. These changes in the *me*,
> recognized by the *I*, or by outside observers,
> may be grave or slight.[222]

But so long as some "common ingredient" is retained from a
particular point of view, identity is maintained *from that
point of view.*[223]

The notion of 'view-point' that comes to the fore in
James's work has epistemological implications of some import.
This is the case because it allows him to find a *via media*
between Hume's radical disjunction of empirical selves and
Kant's postulation of a transcendental ego, i.e., a nonobservable epistemological subject. James agrees with Hume's
claim that

> when I enter most intimately into what I call
> *myself*, I always stumble on some particular or
> other of heat or cold, light or shade, love or
> hatred, pain or pleasure. I never can catch
> *myself* at any one time without a perception, and
> never can observe anything but a perception.[224]

He chides Moore and Natorp for claiming that we have an
immediate consciousness of consciousness and asserts that

> To say that I am self-conscious, or conscious of
> putting forth volition, means only that certain
> contents, for which "self" and "effort of will"
> are the names, are not without witness as they
> occur.[225]

But unlike Hume, he does not "pour out the child with the
bath"; he does not deny that "a thread of resemblance" can be
maintained. He does not accept Hume's claim that a succession
of ideas "connected by a close relation affords to an accurate
view as perfect a notion of diversity as if there was no
matter of relation"[226] at all. Instead, he asserts that there
are empirically identifiable "points of view" or 'witnesses,'
for which the word 'I' serves as index: As he says, "The word
'I' is primarily a noun of position, like 'this' and
'here.'"[227]

By merely asserting empirically identifiable points of
view, James avoids the Kantian response to Hume. Faced with
Hume's bundle of perceptions, Kant introduced what he called
the transcendental Ego of apperception, which he specified as

"the simple and utterly empty idea: I; of which we cannot even
say we have a notion, but only a consciousness which accompanies all notions."[228]   Kant was correct, from James's point
of view, in protesting against Hume's scepticism concerning
personal identity. But according to James, Kant's

> service has been ill-performed, for the Egoists
> themselves, let them say what they will, believe
> in the bundle, and in their own system merely *tie
> it up*, with their special transcendental string,
> invented for that use alone. Besides, they talk
> as if, with this miraculous tying or 'relating,'
> the Ego's duties were done. Of its far more
> important duty of choosing some of the things
> it ties and appropriating them, to the exclusion
> of the rest, they tell us never a word.[229]

James's point is that Kant introduces an 'I' that does not do
the kind of work that needs to be done by any epistemological
subject that can make any difference. On Kant's view, the 'I'
reports discrete thoughts and sense-impressions that go
whirling by. But what needs to be done by any empirically
discriminable epistemological subject is to make judgments
about what to say and how to behave from a particular point of
view. People need not postulate any nonobservable condition
of apperception to maintain a sense of identity. All they
need do is point to their own thought, "a cognitive phenomenal
event in time."[230]   All they need do is observe that they are
able to reinfer what they have already inferred about things,
or as James says, repossess what they have already possessed.
"Who owns the last self owns the self before the last, for
what possesses the possessor possesses the possessed."[231]
Following up on the herd metaphor, James says that

> the herdsman is there, in the shape of something
> not among the things collected, but superior to
> them all, namely the real, present, on-looking,
> remembering 'judging thought.' . . . This is what
> collects,--'owns' some of the past facts which it
> surveys, and disowns the rest,--and so makes a
> unity that is actualized and anchored and does not
> merely float in the blue air of possibility.[232]

The "superiority" which James accords the "judging thought" is
temporal and *epistemic* inasmuch as it reiterates (at the very
least) what is taken to be the case from that personal point
of view. The "judging thought" amounts to a person's current

evaluation of things, not least of which are his selves.

By identifying the current "judging thought" of a person with the ability to select and neglect information available to him, James allows both for personal identity (unlike Hume) and the dissolution of personal identity (unlike Kant). An individual can repossess enough information about himself to maintain a sense of identity. But he may not. There is nothing in principle supporting the implication of Kant's position, that there is some invariant condition that we cannot observe but which is necessary for cognition to occur. Selves dissolve. People forget, undergo amnesia, become insane and exhibit split personalities, have accidents that turn them into neural vegetables. They undergo all these sorts of mutation that James catalogues in *The Principles* and elsewhere.[233] And when they do, we no longer can maintain a comparatively identical point of view, we slip into talk about their 'selves' instead of their 'self' (as do they) or begin to talk about them as if they were not selves at all, but things (which have no point of view).

'View-point' not only allows James to find a *via media* between Hume and Kant on the questions of personal identity and epistemological subjectivity. It also allows him to draw certain distinctions between first-person ascriptions and third-person descriptions. True, according to James, there is nothing in principle that I can observe about myself that cannot be shared with others. To be sure, you cannot feel my pain or witness my stream of consciousness, but I can tell you as much about them as I know myself. I can, however, and probably do evaluate what I observe about myself in ways that you do not. Moreover, that is my privilege: I represent a particular point of view. My "total empirical selfhood . . . my historic Me" is "a collection of objective facts."[234] But I select and neglect, i.e., evaluate the facts about my self in a way that you may not. (You might evaluate them the same way. Then, were it not for the fact that we have discriminable bodies, it would be difficult to tell us apart: We would share the same intentions, dispose ourselves to behave the same way, and so on.)

Now James does *not* say that I may know more about myself

than you or he ever could. If anything, I know less. Who
knows more depends on the perspective, the time and place
from which the facts about myself are described and evaluated.
But he does say that, no matter whether I know more or less
about myself than either you or he, my point of view is
particular, and is the only point of view from which I can
ultimately evaluate my life (though, obviously, I can and do
take into consideration your view of me as well as his).

But this brings us to our second question which I will
now repeat: Isn't it possible that we lack sufficient information to evaluate our selves adequately? *Prima facie*, this is
a silly question. Certainly there is bound to be information
about my self that I am not aware of. Part and parcel of
thought and action is the *neglection* of data. But that does
not bother anybody in practice. In fact, it facilitates
practice. If we didn't neglect data about ourselves (which
is in fact available *ad infinitum*), we could never decide to
do anything. But as things stand, we decide to do things all
the time.

One might, however, argue that there may be relevant
information about myself that prevents me from making an
adequate evaluation about myself. Consider the fact that a
psychiatrist may be able to tell me more about myself than I
could ever have guessed. Or (to avoid the question of myth-
acquisition) consider the fact that, all things being equal,
a biographer can tell more about a person's life than the
sincerest of autobiographers can tell about himself. An
autobiographer can observe only what he selects. But a
biographer can observe both what his subject selects and what
he neglects, but other relevant witnesses select. The data-
base is the same, but the 'take' is different. The ability to
evaluate the significance of one's self is enhanced with time
and the perspectives which it brings. And everybody knows
this. Indeed, James says, many people are haunted by these
considerations.

Certainly, according to James, "our self-feeling in this
world depends on what we *back* ourselves to be and do."[235] We
identify with this occupation or that cause, or these dispositions or those attitudes. Our self-esteem is "determined by

the ratio of our actualities to our supposed potentiali-
ties."[236]   Indeed, James points out that "such a fraction may
be increased as well by diminishing the denominator as by
increasing the numerator."[237]   To this extent "Our self-
feeling is in our power."[238]   But things are complicated by
the fact that our pretensions are inevitably social pretensions:

> the emotion that beckons me on is indubitably
> the pursuit of an ideal social self, is a self
> that is at least *worthy* of approving recogni-
> tion by the highest *possible* judging companion,
> if such companion there be. This self is the
> true, the intimate, the ultimate, the permanent
> Me which I seek. This judge is God. . . .[239]

When we make claims about ourselves, we do so in the hope that
those claims will be funded by our fellows, the people with
whom we are able to share intentions. This becomes clear,
James believes, when we take a look at the behavior of a
person who is in the process of deliberately changing himself:

> When, as a protestant, I turn catholic; as a
> catholic, freethinker; as a 'regular practi-
> tioner,' homeopath, or what not, I am always
> inwardly strengthened in my own course and
> steeled against the loss of my actual social
> self by the thought of other and better *possible*
> social judges than those whose verdict goes
> against me now. The ideal social self which I
> thus seek in appealing to their decision may be
> very remote: it may be represented as barely
> possible. I may not hope for its realization
> during my lifetime; I may even expect the future
> generations, which would approve me if they knew
> me, to know nothing about me when I am dead and
> gone.[240]

James's point is that there is no self for which I could
be able to care that could not conceivably be valued as worthy
or unworthy from other points of view. This is so, because
there is no conceivable way to construe the behavior of
persons asocially. A person promotes his resolutions for
social funding: he is able to care solely for socially
valuable selves. So when a person resolves to do and be
things that his communities in fact reject, he appears to
behave egocentrically. He appears to be what James calls a
"social suicide."[241]   He appears to have ventured beyond the

realm of acceptable, much less accepted, behavior. He appears
to behave in ways for which nobody else cares.

But "social suicides" are able to maintain a sense of
personal identity so long as they are able to presume that, in
the long run of experience, the self they care about may come
to be judged worthy of care. In fact, according to James, it
is this sort of presumption that generates prayer. The reason
why we pray, if we do, says James,

> is simply that we cannot *help* praying. . . . The
> impulse to pray is a necessary consequence of the
> fact that whilst the innermost of the empirical
> selves of a man is a Self of the *social* sort, it
> yet can find its only adequate *Socius* in an ideal
> world.242

The problem of the self, for James, is ultimately a religious
problem.

Because of James's position that persons are historical,
psychophysical organisms with empirically describable points
of view, there is no lasting problem concerning personal
identity. Because James does not consider a person's self-
knowledge to be privileged in any telling sense, there is no
lasting problem about epistemological subjectivity. In fact,
people are at a disadvantage when it comes to evaluating their
own lives because of their inevitable lack of perspective.
People depend on the judgment of others to sanction their own
resolutions. But when there are no others who do in fact
sanction their resolutions, they may either stop caring ("That
life is *not* worth living the whole army of suicides
declare");243 or they may assume that there *must* be an
"adequate *Socius*" for them; or they may suppose that there
might possibly be such a *Socius*. But in any case each is able
to vote with his feet despite the fact that no actual society
accepts and funds his resolutions:

> For most of us a world with no such inner refuge
> when the outer social self failed and dropped
> from us would be the abyss of horror. I say 'for
> most of us' because it is probable that individuals
> differ a good deal in the degree in which they are
> haunted by this sense of an ideal spectator. It
> is a much more essential part of the consciousness
> of some men than of others. Those who have the
> most of it are possibly the most *religious* men.
> But I am sure that even those who say they are

altogether without it deceive themselves, and
really have it in some degree. Only a non-
gregarious animal could be completely without
it.[244]

Once one realizes the religious context in which James's
analysis of the self is placed, the classic debate among
James-interpreters (typified by Dewey and Capek) as to James's
analysis is somewhat trivialized. Dewey argues in "The
Vanishing Subject in the Psychology of James,"[245] that there
are two strains in the *Principles*. One accepts "epistemological dualism." The other construes the subject as an
"organism . . . having no existence save in interaction with
environing conditions."[246] Dewey argues, as I do, that the
latter strain predominates and is developed in James's later
work. He points out, as I do, that James construes persons
as psychophysical beings; that the criteria of mentality is
"the pursuance of future ends and choice of means for their
attainment";[247] and that James abandons any reference to a
transcendental ego or any nonobservable self or condition of
self. But notice: of the three variables which constitute the
empirical self, Dewey's analysis only considers two. He shows
that James specified the self both materially and intentionally
(or spiritually). But he failed to attend to the social
aspect of self, which is the crucial aspect insofar as the
question whether life is worth living is concerned.

Capek provided a kind of counter-argument to Dewey in
"The Reappearance of the Self in the Last Philosophy of
William James."[248] In this article, he accepted Dewey's claim
that James abandoned an epistemological subject transcendental
to observation. But he agreed with Jean Wahl that we should
"distinguish between the Ego denied by James and the Self
affirmed by him."[249] He argued that James ultimately affirms
"the theory that personal activity is a genuine and irreducible fact and not a simple epiphenomenon or a verbal
entity."[250]

To begin with, however, it is not clear that Dewey denied
James's acceptance of the sort of personal activity that Capek
affirms. For instance, he recognized that the organisms James
called selves are "personal beings,"[251] who have the ability
to "choose means" to attain future ends. So he affirmed that

James's 'persons' behave intentionally. He merely insisted
that James specified intentional behavior as observable.

But be that as it may, neither Dewey nor Capek gave any
reference to the social variable or to the problem of self-
evaluation. This led Dewey to lose sight of the fact that the
"environing conditions" most significant for the problem of
the self are the conditions of *social* environment. While
Dewey underscored the physiological specification of the "Self
of selves," he overlooked the social specification that
occurred in the very same paragraph in *The Principles*.[252]
While he emphasized James's claim that "our body" is "the
origin of co-ordinates, the constant place of stress in all
that experience-train,"[253] he did not attend to James's claim
that persons are not persons outside of "ethical republics,"[254] that any 'I' is necessarily one of us, necessarily
a member of some *"Socius,"* necessarily the index to a point of
view which is, in principle if not in fact, intersubjective.

Capek fared no better by selecting those of James's
assertions that apparently underscore the irreducibility of
personal activity, because he paid no attention to the social
variable. He promulgated his discussion without ever
approaching the problem of self-evaluation or the religious
question whether life is worth living. By failing to come to
grips with these aspects of James's work, he misconstrued the
significance of some key claims that James made. For
instance, Capek asserted that the following claim shows that
James affirmed some nonobservable self:

> What we conceptually identify ourselves with and
> say we are thinking of at any time is the center,
> but our *full self* is the whole field, with all
> those indefinitely radiating subconscious possi-
> bilities of increase that we can only feel without
> conceiving, and can hardly begin to analyze.[255]

Capek inferred that James was claiming that there is some nonobservable potential self. But the quote above does not
contradict James's earlier claim that "my total empirical
selfhood . . . my historic Me [is] a collection of objective
facts."[256] It merely confirms our suspicions about the asym-
metry that holds between first-person ascription and third-
person description. James is merely claiming that I know less

about myself (even though I may have hunches about where I am
tending) than I could know were I able to view my entire life
in biographical and/or historical perspective. The facts
about my "total self" are "historical" and therefore "objective" but I need to assume some "ideal spectator" whose point
of view is adequate enough to bring my life into total view--
in order to specify the facts about it and evaluate them.

It seems plausible that Dewey and Capek never attended to
the social aspect of self in James's work, because they
construed James's problem about the self respectively as
epistemological and ontological. But to do so is to mis-
construe James's center of vision and so to fail to connect
his massive analysis of the self with the question whether
life is worth living. Dewey was right in claiming, on James's
behalf, that persons have "no existence save for environing
conditions" (though misleading in failing to specify those
conditions socially). But he failed to see that James was
led to the claim as a resolution to the problem of self-
evaluation. He failed to note James's claim that

> We make a combination of two things in judging
> the total *significance* of a human being. We
> feel it to be some product . . . of his inner
> virtue and his outer place,257

and that the outer place for virtues is obviously society:
People are not virtuous as bodies or centers of intentional
behavior so much as agents and patients in groups that are
able to share intentions.

Capek was right in claiming a kind of irreducibility of
personal activity on James's behalf (though simply wrong in
implying the nonobservability of James's 'self'). But he
failed to see that James was led to make the claim by way of
coming to grips with the "chance of salvation," or the
question about the possibility of an eventually adequate
socius for my resolutions. He failed to notice that James
finally claimed that the "question whether life is worth
living does, indeed, depend on you *the liver*,"258 *not* because
persons are ontologically irreducible or epistemologically
privileged, but because the question never seriously occurs to
anyone save "social suicides" who may or may not imagine it

possible for an adequate *socius* to eventuate; and who, therefore, may or may not maintain any interest in living.
Personal activity, for James, is "irreducible" insofar as
persons are able to care for themselves when no one else in
fact thinks them worthy--though even then, persons depend on
some unseen "Companion" to vindicate their worth in the long
run of experience.

If James's only specification of self as social had come
in his chapter on self-consciousness in *The Principles*, the
confusions typified by Dewey and Capek would be somewhat
excusable. But we have seen that James specifies interests
as social and construes the various sub-universes of discourse
and practice (save the world of madness) as based upon shareable beliefs and intentions. What is more, James's essay,
"The Moral Philosopher and the Moral Life,"[259] claims, among
other things, that persons are agents and patients of more or
less inclusive "republics," the shared intentions of which
are prescriptive for members.

Now "The Moral Philosopher" has been criticized for
developing two contradictory ethical views.[260] It has been
said that James generates a utilitarian view, in which the
intentions and desires of individuals are subordinated to the
shared intentions of the common society (or societies) to
which they belong, for the sake of the general welfare of each
and every member. It has also been said that James generates
an intuitive view, in which the intentions and desires of
individuals play first fiddle. How, it is asked, can one
reconcile statements like

> 'those ideals must be written highest which pre-
> vail at the least cost. . . . the laws and usages
> of the land are what yield the maximum of satis-
> faction to the thinkers taken all together. The
> presumption in cases of conflict must always be[261]
> in favor of the conventionally recognized good.

on the one hand, and statements like

> 'the *highest* ethical life--however few may be
> called to bear its burdens--consists at all
> times in the breaking of rules which have
> grown too narrow for the actual case'[262]

on the other? The former statement seems to assert the

normative status of shared intentions or obligations, whereas
the latter statement seems to assert the normative status of
(some) individual claims or resolutions. Given these two
contrary norms, how is it possible to answer the criteriological question in ethics?

James's answer is clear and cogent. He claims that

> There is but one unconditional commandment, which
> is that we should seek incessantly, with fear and
> trembling, so to vote and to act as to bring about
> the very largest total universe of good which we
> can see.[263]

In other words, he claims that if and when a person is living
an ethical life, he is attempting to maximize what he
construes to be good (no matter how he construes good to be).
If behaving according to socially constructed standards
subserves that goal, then he should do his duty, *in so far
forth*. If breaking social law and custom subserves that goal,
he should follow his own inclinations, *in so far forth*. The
parallel with *epistemic* welfare is instructive: Just as the
veracious person is committed to exchanging false beliefs for
more adequate ones, no matter whether the ones he considers
more adequate are accepted as such by other veracious people,
so the strenuous ethical person is committed to behaving in
ways he construes as more fitting, no matter whether the
conduct he considers more fitting is accepted as such by
other people in his "ethical republic." Indeed,

> ethical science is just like physical science,
> and instead of being deducible all at once from
> abstract principles, must simply bide its time,
> and be ready to revise its conclusions from day
> to day. The presumption, of course, in both
> sciences, is that the vulgarly accepted opinions
> are true, and the right casuistic order that
> which public opinion believes in; and surely it
> would be folly quite as great, in most of us, to
> strike out independently and to aim at original-
> ity in ethics as in physics. Every now and then,
> however, someone is born with the right to be
> original, and his revolutionary thought or action
> may bear prosperous fruit. He may replace old
> 'laws of nature' by better ones; he may, by
> breaking old moral rules in a certain place, bring
> in a total condition of things more ideal than
> would have followed had the rules been kept.[264]

Hence, James squares individual claims or resolutions with

obligations or shared intentions by asserting *"not only that without a claim made by some concrete person, there can be no obligation, but that there is some obligation wherever there is a claim."*[265] A "claim" or individual resolution is nothing other than a *presumptive* obligation, and an obligation is nothing other than a *funded* claim. For one person to be able to discuss with another what ought to be done, according to James, *presupposes* that both are members of the same society or "republic." Persons *forge* communities, and intentions which come to be shared actually may have to be claimed by individuals somewhere and sometime.

What distinguishes the individual from his group is not the form of his intentions or claims or resolutions, but may be the material or content of those claims. His claims, insofar as they are ethical, are intersubjective in principle. But the community or "socius" in which those claims are normative *may* not actually exist. Again: the individual may not live in an adequate socius. The recipients of his executed intentions may construe them incorrectly.

In any case, just as the veracious person has to be serious enough to constantly prune his population of beliefs, the person committed to realizing our welfare in general must learn to "live with energy, though energy bring pain";[266] he must learn to lead what James calls "the strenuous life."[267] The strenuous life or "mood" is the sort of life that can be led by an individual who has no adequate socius for his resolutions, but who predicates his conduct on the assumption that there may be some (unseen) associate who could fund his resolutions, even here and now:

> The capacity of the strenuous mood lies so deep down among our natural human possibilities that even if there were no metaphysical or traditional grounds for believing in a God, men would postulate one simply as a pretext for living hard, and getting out of the game of existence its keenest possibilities of zest. . . . Every sort of energy and endurance, of courage and capacity for handling life's evils, is set free in those who have religious faith. For this reason the strenuous type of character will . . . always outwear the easy-going type, and religion will drive irreligion to the wall.[268]

But whether the religious problem of the self can ever be solved, whether god is simply postulated for living hard or is some possible condition or agency or force that can effect the "strong relief,"[269] the salvation, which strenuous livers demand, is another question: It is a question that might be answered only if we picture how things in the broadest sense of the term hang together in the broadest sense of the term. In other words, it is a question that depends on metaphysical inquiry. James realizes this, and turns to the task.

[1] *TC*, I:463 ff.; and Philip Wiener, *Evolution and the Founders of Pragmatism* (Philadelphia: University of Pennsylvania Press, 1972), pp. 97-133. On page 105, Wiener makes the claim that the idea of "Darwinian evolution functioned as a huge ganglion or nerve center" for James.

[2] *TC*, I:469.

[3] Wiener, *op. cit.*, p. 99.

[4] Max Fisch, "The Classic Period in American Philosophy," in *Classic American Philosophers*, p. 10, quoted in Israel Scheffler, *Four Pragmatists* (New York: Humanities Press, 1974), p. 4.

[5] *Ibid.*

[6] For a useful exposition of Darwinian historiographic analysis, see Stephen Toulmin, *Human Understanding*, vol. 1 (Princeton: Princeton University Press, 1972), pp. 319-363.

[7] *Ibid.*, pp. 353 f.

[8] Hereafter cited as "Great Men" and found in *Will*, pp. 216-254.

[9] In *Will*, pp. 255-262.

[10] "Great Men," p. 218.

[11] *Ibid.*

[12] *Ibid.*

[13] *Ibid.*, p. 216.

[14] *Ibid.*

[15] *Ibid.*, p. 217.

[16] *Ibid.*, pp. 220-221.

[17] *Ibid.*, p. 220.

[18]*Ibid.*

[19]*Ibid.*, pp. 234-235.

[20]Toulmin, *op. cit.*, p. 334, remarks that "Herbert Spencer was a Social Lamarckist, not a Social Darwinist." He bases this claim, correctly I believe, on the fact that Spencer endorsed the Lamarckian doctrine that the development of biological evolution was unidirectional and irreversible. This doctrine does *not* follow from the Darwinian schema which accounts for local changes in populations by relating them to their adaptive advantages.

[21]"Great Men," p. 222.

[22]*Ibid.*, p. 223.

[23]*Ibid.*, p. 231.

[24]*Ibid.*, p. 232.

[25]*Ibid.*, p. 253.

[26]*Ibid.*, p. 246.

[27]*Ibid.*, p. 247.

[28]*Ibid.*, p. 250.

[29]Toulmin, *op. cit.*, p. 337.

[30]"Great Men," p. 246.

[31]"The Importance of Individuals," p. 260.

[32]*Ibid.*, pp. 258-259.

[33]*Problems*, p. 45.

[34]*Ibid.*, p. 46.

[35]*Ibid.*

[36]Toulmin, *op. cit.*, p. 324.

[37]*Ibid.*

[38]"Great Men," p. 254.

[39]As quoted in H. S. Thayer, *Meaning and Action: A Critical History of Pragmatism* (Indianapolis: The Bobbs-Merrill Co., 1968), p. 62.

[40]*Ibid.*

[41]Stephen Toulmin *et al.*, *Metaphysical Beliefs* (London: SCM Press, 1957), p. 27.

[42]*Problems*, p. 3.

[43]*Ibid.*, p. 231. Cf. also, William James, *Pragmatism: A New Name for some Old Ways of Thinking* (New York: Longmans, Green, and Co., 1907), p. 222. Hereafter cited as *Pragmatism*.

[44]See C. S. Peirce, *Collected Papers*, ed. Hartshorne and Weiss (Cambridge: Belknap Press, Harvard, 1931-35), 6 vols., 5:22, for his definition of "the long run." See Thayer, *op. cit.*, pp. 112 ff., for an excellent discussion of the notion as employed by Peirce.

[45]In *Collected Essays and Reviews*, pp. 43-68; hereafter cited as "Spencer."

[46]*Ibid.*, pp. 67-68.

[47]*Ibid.*, p. 64.

[48]*Ibid.*

[49]See William James, *The Principles of Psychology* (New York: Dover Publications, Inc., 1950), 2 vols., vol. 1, p. 134. Hereafter cited as *PP* followed by a Roman numeral indicating volume followed by a colon followed by a page number (e.g., *PP*I:134).

[50]See Jonathan Bennett, *Rationality: An Essay Towards Analysis* (London: Routledge & Kegan Paul, 1964), pp. 8-21.

[51]See Wilfrid Sellars, "Some Reflections on Language Games," in *Science, Perception, and Reality* (London: Routledge & Kegan Paul, 1963), pp. 321-358, especially pp. 324-327.

[52]*PP*I:105. My italics.

[53]*Ibid.*, p. 17.

[54]William James, "Are We Automata?" in *Mind*, Vol. 4, No. 13 (January, 1879), p. 5. Hereafter cited as "Automata."

[55] *Ibid.*

[56] *PP*I:140.

[57] "Automata," p. 6.

[58] *PP*I:141.

[59] *Ibid.*, p. 284.

[60] *Ibid.*, p. 288.

[61] *Ibid.*, p. 225.

[62] *Ibid.*, p. 286.

[63] *Ibid.*, p. 224.

[64] *Ibid.*, p. 221.

[65] *Ibid.*, p. 402.

[66] *Ibid.*

[67] *Ibid.*, pp. 443-444.

[68] *PP*II:356-358.

[69] *PP*I:287.

[70] *Ibid.*

[71] *PP*II:349-350.

[72] *Ibid.*, p. 349.

[73] *Ibid.*, p. 357.

[74] William James, "Reflex Action and Theism," in *Will*, p. 113. Hereafter cited as "Reflex."

[75] *Ibid.*, p. 114.

[76] My italics.

[77] "Spencer," pp. 52-53.

[78]*Varieties*, p. 347.

[79]The notion of "the social construction of reality" has been recently developed and popularized by Peter L. Berger and Thomas Luckmann in *The Social Construction of Reality* (Garden City: Doubleday & Co., 1966). Their work is based on the work of Alfred Schutz. See, for instance, *Collected Papers*, vol. 1: *The Problem of Social Reality* (The Hague: Martinus Nijhoff, 1962), which, in great part, is based on Schutz's reading of James. See, in particular, pp. 340-346, for a discussion of "multiple realities" based on James's chapter XXI of *PP*.

[80]*PP*II:291.

[81]*PP*II:292.

[82]*PP*II:295.

[83]*Ibid.*, p. 297.

[84]*Ibid.*, p. 299.

[85]*Ibid.*, p. 308.

[86]The phrase belongs to Sellars, *op. cit.*, p. 1; but it fits James like a glove and is derived from James's pragmatic vocabulary.

[87]*PP*II:312.

[88]*Ibid.*, p. 290.

[89]*Ibid.*, p. 309.

[90]*Ibid.*, p. 299. Perhaps more than anyone else, Wild, *op. cit.*, has underscored the paramount reality of the manifest image of (as he puts it in current phenomenological jargon) "the life-world" in James's work. But where I interpret James as holding the manifest image as primitive for *methodological* reasons, Wild interprets James as taking the life-world as "really real," i.e., holding it as primitive for ontological reasons. See, in particular, pp. 152-159. We will see, however, that James insists that no "general offhand answer can be given as to which objects mankind shall choose as its realities."

[91]*PP*II:312.

[92]*Ibid.*

[93]William James, "The Sentiment of Rationality," in *Will*, p. 82.   Hereafter cited as "Sentiment."

[94]*Ibid.*

[95]*Ibid.*, pp. 82-83.

[96]*Ibid.*, p. 84.

[97]*PP*II:315.

[98]*Ibid.*, p. 316.

[99]*Ibid.*, pp. 316-317.

[100]See "Sentiment," pp. 63-110 in *Will*.

[101]*Ibid.*, p. 63.

[102]*PP*II:317.

[103]"Reflex," p. 116.   See also *PP*II:317.

[104]"Reflex," p. 116.

[105]*Ibid.*, p. 130.

[106]*Ibid.*, p. 134.

[107]*PP*II:317.

[108]"Reflex," p. 126.

[109]William James, *The Meaning of Truth* (Ann Arbor: The University of Michigan Press, 1970), intro. by Ralph Ross. Hereafter cited as *Meaning*.

[110]*Ibid.*, p. 271.

[111]Roderick Chisholm, *The Problem of the Criterion* (Milwaukee: Marquette University Press, 1973).

[112]*Ibid.*, p. 3.

[113]*Ibid.*, p. 14.

[114]*Ibid.*, p. 21.

[115]*Ibid.*, pp. 22-24.

[116]*Ibid.*, pp. 37-38.

[117]*Problems*, p. 87.

[118]*Varieties*, pp. 324-325.

[119]*Pragmatism*, p. 59.

[120]*Ibid.*, pp. 59-60.

[121]*Ibid.*, p. 186.

[122]Otto Neurath developed this metaphor in "Protokoll-satze," *Erkenntnis*, Vol. 3 (1932), pp. 204-214.

[123]*Pragmatism*, p. 169. See also James's 'Stocking' example in *PPI*:372.

[124]*Meaning*, p. 269. My italics.

[125]*Pragmatism*, p. 242.

[126]*Meaning*, p. 15. Cf. also *PPI*:221-223 and 258-259.

[127]*Meaning*, p. 47.

[128]*Ibid.*, p. 39.

[129]*Ibid.*

[130]*Ibid.*, p. 32.

[131]*Ibid.*, pp. 44-45.

[132]See *ibid.*, pp. 41-42 and p. 50.

[133]*Pragmatism*, p. 198.

[134]*Meaning*, p. 159.

[135]*Pragmatism*, p. 53.

[136]*Ibid.*, p. 57.

[137]*Ibid.*, pp. 54-55.

138 *Ibid.*, p. 68.

139 *Ibid.*, p. 76.

140 *Ibid.*, p. 207.

141 *Meaning*, p. 205.

142 *Pragmatism*, p. 222.

143 *Ibid.*, p. 201.

144 See Josiah Royce, "The Problem of Truth in the Light of Recent Discussion," in *Royce's Logical Essays*, ed. Daniel S. Robinson (Dubuque: William C. Brown Co., 1951), pp. 63-97. Royce does not refer to James by name, but it is obvious from the context that he is criticizing James's epistemology.

145 *Meaning*, p. 271.

146 Cf. Murray G. Murphy's lucid article, "Kant's Children: The Cambridge Pragmatists," in *C. S. Peirce Society Transactions*, 1968:4, for an incisive discussion of Kant's influence on Peirce, James, and the other members of the 'Cambridge Metaphysical Club.'

147 Kant, *op. cit.*, p. 632.

148 *Ibid.*, p. 647.

149 *Ibid.*, pp. 647-648.

150 Peirce, *op. cit.*, 5:412.

151 Charles Morris, *The Pragmatic Movement in American Philosophy* (New York: George Braziller, 1970), p. 22.

152 Cf. also *Problems*, pp. 59-60; "Philosophical Conceptions," pp. 410-412; *Pragmatism*, pp. 45-49; and *Meaning*, pp. xxix-xliv.

153 *Varieties*, p. 435.

154 *Meaning*, pp. 265-266.

155 *Ibid.*, p. xxix.

156 *Ibid.*

[157]*Ibid.*, p. 262.   Cf. also p. 183.

[158]*Ibid.*, p. 196.

[159]*Ibid.*, p. xi.

[160]*Ibid.*, p. 296.

[161]*Ibid.*, pp. 296-297.

[162]Keith Lehrer, *Knowledge* (Oxford: Clarendon Press, 1974), p. 48.

[163]*Meaning*, p. 296 and p. 295.

[164]*Pragmatism*, p. 202.

[165]*Ibid.*

[166]Cf., e.g., Austin Duncan-Jones, "Further Questions about 'Know' and 'Think,'" in *Philosophy and Analysis*, ed. Margaret Macdonald (Oxford: Basil Blackwell, 1966), p. 97.

[167]I am following the logic of contraries as construed by Wilfrid Sellars, *Science and Metaphysics* (London: Routledge & Kegan Paul, 1968), pp. 121 f.

[168]Cf., e.g., A. D. Woozley, "Knowing and Not Knowing," in *Knowledge and Belief*, ed. A. Phillips Griffiths (Oxford: Oxford University Press, 1967), pp. 82-99.

[169]Both Russell and Moore criticized James on these grounds. See Bertrand Russell, *Philosophical Essays* (New York: Simon and Schuster, 1966), pp. 79-130; and also G. E. Moore, *Philosophical Studies* (London: K. Paul, Trench, Trubner & Co., 1922), pp. 123-146.

[170]*Meaning*, pp. 152-153.

[171]Lehrer, *op. cit.*, pp. 190 ff.

[172]*Meaning*, p. 1.

[173]*Pragmatism*, p. 198.

[174]*Ibid.*, pp. 216-217.

[175]*Meaning*, p. 157.

[176]Thayer, *op. cit.*, p. 151.

[177]*Ibid.*

[178]*Meaning*, p. 159; cf. also pp. 70-73.

[179]*Ibid.*, pp. 62-63.

[180]The decision-theoretic moves that Lehrer suggests in *op. cit.* might prove to be a correction to James's theory of justification. Cf. particularly pages 187-235 where Lehrer suggests the moves a veracious man would have to make in order to maintain a corrected "doxastic" or self-correcting belief system.

[181]*Meaning*, p. 264. My italics.

[182]PPI:291.

[183]*Universe*, p. 289.

[184]PPI:334.

[185]*Ibid.*, p. 331.

[186]William James, *Essays in Radical Empiricism* (New York: Longmans, Green, and Co., 1943), ed. Ralph Barton Perry, p. 170. Hereafter cited as *Radical Empiricism*.

[187]PPI:372.

[188]*Ibid.*, p. 341.

[189]*Ibid.*, p. 372.

[190]*Radical Empiricism*, p. 37.

[191]PPI:365.

[192]*Ibid.*, p. 369.

[193]*Ibid.*, p. 314.

[194]William James, *Talks to Teachers on Psychology; and to Students on Some of Life's Ideals* (New York: W. W. Norton & Co., Inc., 1958), p. 181. Hereafter cited as *Talks*.

[195]PPI:310.

[196]*Ibid.*, p. 316.

[197]*Will*, pp. 59-60.

[198]*Ibid.*, p. 61.

[199]*PP*I:291.

[200]*Ibid.*, p. 306.

[201]*Ibid.*, p. 292.

[202]*Ibid.*, p. 294.

[203]*Ibid.*, p. 296.

[204]Wild, *op. cit.*, pp. 87-92.

[205]See particularly *PP*I:296-305.

[206]*Ibid.*, p. 300.

[207]*Ibid.*, p. 316. Of all of James's major interpreters, only Wild, *op. cit.*, discusses the social self at any length. See pages 83-86. But he fails to notice James's claim that the innermost self is a self of the social sort and goes on to specify the "inner citadel of selfhood" in terms of "body," *pace* Merleau-Ponty.

[208]*PP*I:319.

[209]*Ibid.*, pp. 309-310.

[210]*PP*I:288.

[211]*Ibid.*, p. 334.

[212]*Radical Empiricism*, pp. 50-51.

[213]*PP*I:331.

[214]See Hans Linschoten, *On the Way Toward A Phenomenological Psychology: The Psychology of William James*, trans. and ed. Amedeo Giorgi (Pittsburgh: Duquesne University Press, 1968), pp. 285-290; and Patrick K. Dooley, *Pragmatism as Humanism: The Philosophy of William James* (Chicago: Nelson Hall, 1974), pp. 27-36.

[215]*PP*I:334.

[216]*Ibid.*, p. 335.

[217]*Ibid.*

[218]*Ibid.*, p. 372.

[219]See *ibid.*, f.n., p. 372.

[220]For a lucid discussion of the problem of criteria for reidentification of persons, see Terence Penelhum's article on "Personal Identity," in the *Encyclopedia of Philosophy*, Vol. 6, pp. 95-106.

[221]*PPI*:372.

[222]*Ibid.*

[223]Cf. *TC*II:757 where James says that "all consciousness is *positional*, is a 'point of view,' measures things from a *here*, etc. . . ."

[224]Quoted in *PPI*:351.

[225]*Radical Empiricism*, p. 6.

[226]Quoted in *PPI*:352.

[227]*Radical Empiricism*, p. 170.

[228]Quoted in *PPI*:362.

[229]*Ibid.*, p. 370.

[230]*Ibid.*, p. 369.

[231]*Ibid.*, p. 340.

[232]*Ibid.*, pp. 337-338.

[233]Cf. James's section on "The Mutations of the Self," in *PPI*:373-400, as well as his article on "The Hidden Self," in *Scribner's Magazine*, Vol. VII (1890), pp. 361-373.

[234]*PPI*:322.

[235]*Ibid.*, p. 310.

[236]*Ibid.*

[237] *Ibid.*, p. 311.

[238] *Ibid.*

[239] *Ibid.*, p. 315.

[240] *Ibid.*

[241] *Ibid.*, p. 317.

[242] *Ibid.*, p. 316.

[243] *Will*, p. 37.

[244] *PPI*:316.

[245] Reprinted in John Dewey, *The Problems of Men* (New York: Philosophical Library, 1946), pp. 396-409.

[246] *Ibid.*, p. 396.

[247] Quoted in *ibid.*, p. 400.

[248] Milec Capek, in *Philosophical Review*, 62 (1953), pp. 526-544.

[249] *Ibid.*, p. 526. Cf. also Jean Wahl, *Les Philosophies pluralistes d'Angleterre et d'Amérique* (Paris: Librairie Félix Alcan, 1920), pp. 118-136.

[250] Capek, *op. cit.*, p. 526.

[251] Dewey, *op. cit.*, p. 400.

[252] *PPI*:316-317.

[253] Quoted in Dewey, *op. cit.*, p. 409.

[254] See my discussion of James's "ethical republics" below, pp. 92-95.

[255] Quoted from *Universe* in Capek, *op. cit.*, p. 543.

[256] *PPI*:322.

[257] *Talks*, p. 181.

[258]*Will*, pp. 59-60.

[259]In *Will*, pp. 184-215.

[260]See Perry's discussion of James's "inclusive" ethical principle (which I have associated with utilitarianism) and his "exclusive" ethical principle (which I have associated with intuitionism), in *Spirit*, pp. 129 ff.; in particular, pp. 130-131, where he says, "For James was a heroic and fighting partisan, who gave his final allegiance to the cause of kindness and peace. This paradox is so central not only to James, but to the cult of liberalism, that I should like to translate into my own terms, and formulate it as the conflict between the *exclusive* and *inclusive* principles of life." Roth, in *Freedom and the Moral Life: The Ethics of William James* (Philadelphia: Westminster Press, 1969), claims that James's apparent contradiction leads to "basic inadequacies in the particular principles that James develops in this essay." But this claim makes sense only if we take the essay as an attempt at normative ethics, which it is not. The essay is fundamentally criteriological. Wild, in his persistent attempt to turn James into an existentialist, downplays the aspect of James's ethical statement which depends on the notion of shared intention or obligation, by equating the latter with what James calls "the easy-going mood." This is unfair to the complexity of James's statement and to the part obligation plays in it. See Wild, *op. cit.*, pp. 218 ff. Ayer on the other hand claims that while "James is not exactly a Utilitarian . . . the position at which he arrives . . . is not very different from theirs." See *op. cit.*, p. 200. But Ayer's claim is rather empty, until one isolates the relation between claims and obligations in James's work.

[261]*Will*, pp. 205-206.

[262]*Ibid.*, p. 209.

[263]*Ibid.*

[264]*Ibid.*, p. 208.

[265]*Ibid.*, p. 194. My italics.

[266]*Ibid.*, p. 85.

[267]*Ibid.*, p. 211.

[268]*Ibid.*

[269]*Ibid.*

*The Religious Demand, the Esthetic Response,
and the Pragmatic Argument*

It has been some time now since W. H. Walsh suggested to
the contemporary philosophical community that many metaphysi-
cians have construed their task as rather more esthetic than
ontological, and that relevant metaphysical claims ought to
be assessed accordingly.[1] Metaphysical assertions, Walsh
said,

> can be seen, that is to say, as a series of
> attempts to tell us how to get the different
> aspects of our experience into perspective.
> And though it is characteristic of such attempts
> to announce that all sorts of unfamiliar entities
> exist (even materialism tells us that nothing is
> ultimately there except matter), it is perhaps a
> mistake to treat such announcements as intended
> to convey information.[2]

On this reading, metaphysics does not claim to add any new set
of facts to those which science and common sense supply. It
merely supplies an "overall interpretive scheme,"[3] a point of
view from which to organize the facts that are at hand. In
this sense, it *complements* the sorts of analysis generated in
the sciences, but the criteria for acceptability or unaccept-
ability of its claims are *different* from those on which
scientific assertions are based. As Walsh says,

> decisions about whether to accept or reject a
> scientific proposition are possible because
> science is an activity which proceeds under
> agreed rules, rules which, among other things,
> specify what is to count as evidence for or
> against. In metaphysics, by contrast, we are
> not so much working under rules as advocating
> them, with the result that objective proof,
> proof that is to say which any right-thinking
> person would acknowledge, is not to be had.[4]

James's metaphysical work is sound evidence for Walsh's
position. If *ontological statements* amount to statements that
make categorical claims about what there is, then James simply
does not make any. Doing metaphysics, for him, amounts to

"making a picture of the whole world,"[5] and results in a kind
of esthetic stance, or roughly, a place from which to view
'things' in the broadest sense of the term. It is, he says,
a "personal vision" expressing our own temperament.[6] Stated
a little differently, "it is our individual way of just
seeing and feeling the total push and pressure of the
cosmos."[7]

James's statements about what he is doing when he does
metaphysics are not meant to be loose or vague. They are
meant to force metaphysical claims into the right sort of
forum. To argue as if people could generate categorical
assertions about what there is, on his reading, is absurd.
His psychological and epistemological studies have persuaded
him that a) no experiences are simply given, and b) "necessary
truths" are simply those we intend to hold invariant. Contra
myths of the given he says: "We have no organ or faculty to
appreciate the simply given order."[8] There are no epistemic
simples to found our knowledge on. Then too, "The word 'I'
is primarily a noun of position, like 'this' and 'here.'"[9]
There is no substantial self on which to found our knowledge
of things in general. *Contra* necessary truths, he says that
in opposition to "Kantism" which imposes human laws "a priori
on all experience as 'legislative,'" his brand of pragmatism
is attempting to specify "human ways of thinking that grow up
piecemeal among the details of experience because on the whole
they work best."[10] We take some statements for granted, but
in no strong sense are they *a priori* truths. What is more,
the distinction that Kant makes between analytic and synthetic
truths is one of his "most unhappy legacies, for the reason
that it is impossible to make sharp."[11] So as far as James
is concerned, people are just not in a position to make
categorical assertions about anything at all. What they can
do, if they are so compelled, is present a vision of things
in general. And if they do so, the sort of vision that they
present will likely express the sort of compulsion that led
them to do it.

In James's own case, a certain religious question that
science left unanswered demanded the sort of esthetic response
that metaphysical inquiry alone might provide. For, in

James's view, science left unresolved the problem of the self, or the question whether a "socius" could eventuate that would satisfy the resolutions of its individual members. So the question that governs his metaphysics is whether things in general are structured in a way that allows for the *chance* or possibility of salvation. In fact, James was pretty sure that the problem of salvation generally speaking probably governed the metaphysical inquiries of most philosophers. "Whether we be empiricists or rationalists," he says along these lines, "we are, ourselves, parts of the universe, and share the same one deep concern in its destinies. We crave alike to feel more truly at home with it, and to contribute our mite to its amelioration."[12]

Besides the religious demand and the esthetic response, there is a third, and equally significant, constituent of Jamesian metaphysics: it must be justified. For James, this means that the *vision* which he presents must be defended as providing the most adequate framework for our experiences or observations. His metaphysics, therefore, is both

> the final outlook, belief, or attitude to which
> it brings us, and the reasonings by which that
> attitude is reached and mediated. A philosophy
> . . . must indeed be true, but that is the least
> of its requirements. One may be true without
> being a philosopher, true by guesswork or by
> revelation. What distinguishes a philosopher's
> truth is that it is *reasoned*. Argument, not
> supposition, must have put it in his possession.[13]

Quite simply, what is philosophical about metaphysics is neither the demand that generates the task, nor the vision articulated by the task but the justification for that particular vision. The business of metaphysics is forecast, not fiction. It deals in "grounded possibilities," not wishful thoughts. It attempts to specify what the universe "promises" in the sense of delineating the best of all *possible* worlds and not in the sense of delineating the best of all *conceivable* worlds. For these reasons, James tells us that

> the first thing to notice is this, that the only
> material we have at our disposal for making a
> picture of the whole world is supplied by the
> various portions of that world of which we have
> already had experience. We can invent no new

forms of conception, applicable to the whole
exclusively, and not suggested originally by
the parts.[14]

Indeed, the metaphysical vision itself must be conceived
"after the analogy of some particular feature" of the universe.[15] And the argument for that vision must employ the
same *methods* that any reasonable person making claims about
particular observations should employ: "He observes, discrim-
inates, classifies, looks for causes, traces analogies, and
makes hypotheses."[16]

James's vision, responding as it does to the question of
salvation, is a picture of a *salvable* world. The temperament
or esthetic stance that it expresses is "neither optimistic
nor pessimistic, but melioristic, rather. The world, it
thinks, may be saved, on condition that its parts shall do
their best. But shipwreck in detail, or even on the whole,
are among the open possibilities."[17] Pretending to be a
creative god, James says that

> I am going to make a world not certain to be
> saved, a world the perfection of which shall be
> conditional merely, the condition being that
> each several agent does its own 'level best.'
> I offer you the chance of taking part in such a
> world. Its safety, you see, is unwarranted. It
> is a real adventure, with real danger, yet it
> may win through.[18]

This is the vision that James maintains throughout his metaphysical project; this is the vision that James tries to
justify.

Even as a vision, however, James's salvable world is
problematic. For what does it mean to say that things in
general are structured in a way that makes salvation possible?
If it means that the best of all possible worlds is a world in
which salvation is possible, then it also means that the best
of all possible worlds is a world in which salvation is not
actual. And if that is the case, then salvation, no matter
how it is specified, is as elusive as the end of the rainbow.
If it means that the best of all possible worlds is a world
that is saved, then it means that the best of all possible
worlds is so disanalogous to the one we live in--with its
crimes, diseases, and absurdities--that it may be criticized

as fantasy.

But pragmatically speaking, the dilemma is besides the point. The point is that what James's metaphysics is "known-as" is a stance from which to view things generally--the advocacy of some rules in terms of which to organize our experiences. It is not "known-as" a set of categorical assertions about what there is that may be confirmed someday. (This does *not* imply that James's vision is neither confirm-able nor disconfirmable; it simply implies that, on James's view, to live in light of the chance of salvation is the most rational way to live.) To use Walsh's suggestive phrase, James's vision of a *salvable world* should be taken "as a series of recommendations about the here and now instead of as news from nowhere."[19] From our vantage point, says James, "some conditions of the world's salvation are actually extant . . . and should the residual conditions come, salvation would become an accomplished reality."[20] So from our point of view not as "the readers but the very personages of the world drama,"[21] there may be nothing that precludes our behaving as if the world could be saved.

Another problem concerns the specification of 'salva-tion.' But here James is deliberately vague: "You may," he says, "interpret the word 'salvation' in any way you like, and make it as diffuse and distributive, or as climacteric and integral a phenomenon as you please."

> Take, for example, any one of us in this room
> with the ideals he cherishes and is willing to
> live and work for. Every such ideal realized
> will be one moment in the world's salvation.
> But these particular ideals are not bare abstract
> possibilities. They are grounded, they are *live*
> possibilities, for we are their live champions
> and pledges, and if the complimentary conditions
> come and add themselves, our ideals will become
> actual things.[22]

James *cannot* specify salvation on his own grounds because, as he sees it, the demand for salvation is generated precisely in those situations where the resolutions of individuals find no satisfaction--are not recognized as worthy--in any actual "socius" or like-membered population.

It is no coincidence, therefore, that James's vision of a

salvable world is "conceived after a social analogy." In
fact, he conceives of it after the analogy of his own "federal
republic."[23]   Like a federal republic, it is constituted "as a
pluralism of independent powers" that will

> succeed just in proportion as more of these work
> for its success. If none work, it will fail. If
> each does his best, it will not fail. Its destiny
> thus hangs on an *if*, or on a lot of *ifs*--which
> amounts to saying (in the technical language of
> logic) that, the world being as yet unfinished,
> its total character can be expressed only by
> *hypothetical* and not by *categorical* propositions.[24]

It is, in other words, "a social scheme of work genuinely to
be done," in which the task at hand is accomplishable only if
"you trust yourself and trust the other agents enough to face
the risk."[25]

James is saying that if you behave toward things in
general the way you behave toward other members of your own
"ethical republic"--in which you posit your own resolutions as
presumptive obligations and trust the intentions of others so
far as you are able--you will probably behave in the most
adequate way. The world, like such a republic, should be
viewed as a government of, by, and for its constituents, or
at least those of its constituents who are able to share
intentions. Like a republic, the world or universe should be
construed as regulated by a variety of institutions. It
should be construed as modifiable both under law and in law
by (some of) its constituents. And it should be construed as
both regulated and innovative *relative to* the purposes held
in common by its constituents, or at least those of its
constituents who are able to share intentions.

James's pluralistic universe argues for the *variety*,
novelty, and *activity* in our universe(s) of discourse and
practice, in order to make reasonable his vision of a salvable
world. So we must turn to each of these three conditions in
order to see how his vision of things fares.

Variety

The first analogy that James advocates as holding between
the world and a federal republic is the analogy of variety.
Each thing in the world, according to James, must adapt its

behavior to the variety of environments to which it belongs,
just as each member (person and/or institution) of a federal
republic must adapt itself to a variety of institutions to
which it belongs. Federal republics are governments of the
people. The behavior of each thing in the universe is, to
some extent at least, forced by external conditions. Thus it
is that James says rather metaphorically that

> everything is in an environment, a surrounding
> world of other things, and . . . if you leave it
> to work there it will inevitably meet with fric-
> tion and opposition from its neighbors. Its
> rivals and enemies will destroy it unless it can
> buy them off by compromising some part of its
> original pretensions.[26]

The first rule of interpretation that James advocates is
simply that *everything is in an environment external to it*.

This is significant for a number of reasons as far as
James is concerned. First of all, if things did not have to
adapt themselves to conditions external or foreign to them, it
would be difficult to imagine why salvation might be a
problem. Certainly people make the religious demands they do
in response to conditions that apparently repel or undercut
their intentions. So, as regards James's own compulsion to
present a metaphysical vision, this first condition must hold.

Secondly, the condition of variety dictates the way in
which James's vision can be articulated. For if things behave
as they do in response to external conditions, then there is
simply no way to picture the world or universe 'as a whole.'
No matter how complex the thing is that we are observing, it
is part of some larger or more complex pattern or variety of
patterns. So James must articulate his vision of the world
distributively. In fact, this is, on his view, what makes
him a "pluralist":

> Does reality exist distributively? or collect-
> ively?--in the shape of *eaches*, *everys*, *anys*,
> *eithers*, or only in the shape of an *all* or *whole*?
> An identical content is compatible with either
> form obtaining. . . . Pluralism stands for the
> distributive, monism for the collective form of
> being.[27]

Thirdly, the condition of variety dictates the sort of
argument that James can bring to bear in support of his

vision. If James's metaphysical project is to carry any
weight at all, we must assure ourselves that he is not engaged
in generating some kind of scientific myth or grandiose
category mistake. That is precisely what he would be doing if
he applied scientific and/or common sensical notions, that
have limited and specific ranges of reference, to a 'world'
conceived of as some collective "whole" and therefore
categorically different from everything in it. But in
advocating the condition of variety, James simply denies
that it is possible to conceive the world collectively. He
denies the acceptability of claims that take the form, 'The
whole world is x,' or 'The whole world behaves x-ly.' His
statements about the world take a distributive and conditional form; e.g., 'each thing in the world, under so and so
conditions, behaves x-ly.' By making claims about the world
in this form, he allows for ranges of reference that are
limited and specific enough for confirmation and disconfirmation. In other words, the metaphysical rule that everything
is in an environment external to it makes scientific analysis
possible.

It does not take much on our part to accept James's first
condition, because it is now taken to be almost common sense--
and therefore nothing that needs extensive advocacy. Such was
not the case in his own time. In fact, if you accept James's
claim that the only *reasonable* form in which to say things
about the world is the distributive form, then you let him
quickly count coup on enemies that historically were difficult
to best. James's battle was fought against the two prevailing
sorts of monism at the turn of the century: Victorian
scientific naturalism and post-Hegelian absolute idealism.
Both sorts of monism were essentialist or necessitarian. Both
claimed the right to make categorical or unconditional statements about the world in its entirety. What distinguished
them (or at least the advocates of absolute idealism from some
of the advocates of scientific naturalism)[28] were the sorts of
foundation they advocated as governing the behavior of all
things unconditionally. The scientific naturalists claimed
that all things are essentially comprised of atomic material,
and that everything behaves necessarily the way it does as a

result. The absolute idealists claimed that all things are
generated intentionally by some absolute mind or agent, and
behave necessarily the way he intends them to behave. Thus
for each sort of monism, the one nonintentional, the other
intentional, conditionality and its presupposed logical
category of possibility are simply nonexistent. Things and/
or events are either necessary or impossible. All things are
internally and systematically related to everything else, in
much the same way that circuits are related in a solid state
electronic system: to observe how each part behaves, you must
have a map or plan of the whole thing.

Now both scientific naturalism and absolute idealism were
generated within a particular metaphysical context. This is
to say that both shared certain rules of interpretation for
the organization of experience, even though one pictured the
world essentially as mind and the other as matter. In
particular, both let the Parmenidean question about the one
and the many dictate the shape of their visions. They both
responded to the question, 'How do the permanent, eternal
objects of the world preserve their underlying identity,
through all the surface appearances of change?'[29] Hence,
they *assumed* that the world of appearance must rest on some
unconditional foundation, and developed their visions in terms
of the assumption.

James did not. He challenged the Parmenidean question
explicitly. True enough, he called the problem of the one and
the many "the most central of all philosophic problems."[30]
In fact, he said that "if you know whether a man is a decided
monist or a decided pluralist, you perhaps know more about the
rest of his opinions than if you gave him any other name
ending in *ist*."[31] But when we see how James *construes* the
problem of the one and the many, we find that he has turned
Parmenides' question on its head. Instead of asking how
permanent things maintain their identity despite the appearance of change, James asks how things maintain their coherence
and continuity, despite all the real changes they undergo. In
other words, James draws up the problem of the one and the
many in a way that will articulate at the most general level
what he has already articulated in each specific study in

which he has been engaged. Surely his populational analyses
of social intentions, mental events, and persons have been
based on the ruling that these sorts of things are *historical*.
His problem in each case has been, at the very least, to
figure out how these changing things maintain coherence and
continuity. What James does as metaphysician is to turn the
claim that things are historical into a rule of thumb. For
him, things *look* historical, so people should *see* them that
way. Things appear to maintain coherence and continuity
through a process of balance between variant and selective
factors in a population of constituent elements, so people
should view the identity of things that way. For James, the
point is that

> in every series of real terms, not only do the
> terms themselves and their associates and envi-
> ronments change, but we change, and their
> *meaning* for us changes, so that new kinds of
> sameness and types of causation continually come
> into view and appeal to our interest. Our earlier
> lines, having grown irrelevant, are then dropped.
> The old terms can no longer be substituted or the
> relations "transferred," because of so many new
> dimensions into which experience has opened.[32]

On this view,

> the world is "one" in some respects, and "many"
> in others. But the respects must be distinctly
> specified if either statement is to be more than
> the emptiest abstraction. Once we are committed
> to this soberer view, the question of the One and
> the Many may well cease to appear important. The
> amount either of unity or of plurality is, in
> short, only a matter for observation to ascertain
> and write down in statements that will have to be
> complicated in spite of every effort to be
> concise.[33]

By establishing the problem on these lines, James effectively
switches the focus of the problem of the one and the many from
the behavior of presumably permanent things to "the finite
world *as such*, and with things that have a history."[34] He
dissolves the Parmenidean question by claiming that historiographically, "oneness and manyness are absolutely coordinate.
. . . Neither is primordial or more essential or more
excellent than the other."[35] In other words, neither oneness
nor manyness has any ontological status, neither serves as the

foundation for the other. They are simply tools we use to
make sense of things generally inasmuch as any thing we can
observe is conjoined with similar things in populations that
must adapt to distinguishably external environments.

So if we turn away from construing monism as "a vague
conviction of the world's unity"[36] and likewise turn away from
construing pluralism as a no-less-vague conviction of the
world's variety, we can still observe the sorts of unity and
variety that people actually experience in the world. When
we *look* at things, says James, we see a variety of unities.
We see causal unities, generic unities, teleological unities,
esthetic unities, and noetic or epistemic unities. In other
words, even if the world were "one" we would have to decide
among these sorts of oneness. If there were complete causal
unity (as the scientific naturalists actually claimed), then
the behavior of each thing in the world would be systematically effected and affected by everything else. If there were
generic unity (as James himself will claim in his advocacy of
'pure experience'), then everything in the world would be of
the same sort, e.g., material, mental, historical, observable.
If there were teleological unity, then everything in the world
would serve the same purpose (as the absolute idealists
actually claimed). If there were esthetic unity, then each
thing in the world would be part of the same story or history
(as many absolute idealists and scientific naturalists
actually claimed). And finally, if there were noetic unity,
it would be because an "all knower" became "acquainted at one
stroke with every part of what exists."[37]

But when we look at things--in fact the *more* critically
we look at things--we see various causal orders or systems,
not one. For instance,

> not all the parts of our world are united *mechani-*
> *cally*, for some can move without the others moving.
> They all seem united by *gravitation*, however, so
> far as they are material things. Some of these
> are united *chemically*, while others are not; and
> the like is true of thermal, optical, electrical,
> and other *physical* connections. These connections
> are specifications of what we mean by the word
> oneness when we apply it to our world. We should
> not call it one unless its parts were connected in
> these and other ways. But then it is clear that

> by the same logic we ought to call it "many" so
> far as its parts are disconnected in these same
> ways, chemically inert towards one another or non-
> conductors to electricity, light, and heat. . . .
> There is thus neither absolute oneness nor abso-
> lute manyness from the physical point of view, but
> a mixture of well definable modes of both.[38]

James's point is that the scientific naturalists engage in
scientific mythology inasmuch as they claim causal unity for
the world without specifying or limiting the range of their
claim. If we are to refrain from this "blunder of clumping,"
we must distinguish the sorts of causal connection that we are
inspecting. When we do limit and specify the range of our
reference,

> the result is innumerable little hangings-
> together of the world's parts within the larger
> hangings-together, little worlds, not only of
> discourse but of operation, within the wider
> universe. Each system exemplifies one type or
> grade of union, its parts being strung on that
> particular kind of relation, and the same part
> may figure in many different systems, as a man
> may hold various offices and belong to several
> clubs. From this "systematic" point of view,
> therefore, the pragmatic value of the world's
> unity is that all these definite networks actu-
> ally and practically exist.[39]

James does not preclude the *possibility* of the causal unity
of phenomena. He states, for instance, that "if the minor
causal influences among things should converge towards one
common causal origin of them,"[40] then we could construe the
world as causally unified. But we would do so upon the
specification of causal connections that we do not as yet
observe.

The same is the case with the other sorts of unity. When
we specify them, they all turn out to be "little hangings-
together of the world's parts within the larger hangings-
together, little worlds, not only of discourse but of operation, within the wider universe."[41] With respect to
teleological unity, we cannot specify with any adequacy a
general purpose governing all things. In fact, the actual
specification of any particular purpose is liable to change:

> Any resultant . . . *may* have been purposed in
> advance, but none of the results we actually know

in this world have in point of fact been purposed
in advance in all their details. Men and nations
start with a vague notion of being rich, or great,
or good. Each step they make brings unforeseen
chances into sight, and shuts out older vistas,
and the specifications of the general purpose have
to be changed daily. What is reached in the end
may be better or worse than what was proposed, but
it is always more complex and different.[42]

So "everything makes strongly for the view that our world is
incompletely unified teleologically, and is still trying to
get its unification better organized."[43]

When we specify certain things as exemplifying esthetic
unity, we end up construing that unity as limited, disconnected with some other aspects of its environment, and
oftentimes unfinished:

Retrospectively, we can see that altho no definite purpose presided over a chain of events, yet
the events fell into a dramatic form, with a
start, a middle, and a finish. In point of fact
all stories end; and here again, the point of
view of a many is the natural one to take. The
world is full of partial stories that run parallel to one another, beginning and ending at odd
times. They mutually interlace and interfere at
points, but we cannot unify them completely in
our minds. In following your life-history, I
must temporarily turn my attention away from my
own. Even a biographer of twins would have to
press them alternatively upon his reader's
attention.[44]

And finally, the same holds for noetic or epistemic
unity. As we have quoted James saying: Not only do epistemic
"terms themselves and their associates and environments
change, but we change, and their *meaning* for us changes."[45]
The absolute idealists, on James's view, were correct in
criticizing the traditional correspondence theories of truth
(or actually, of justification) promulgated by both empiricism
and rationalism. They were correct in claiming that words
have meaning solely within conceptual context. Their mistake
was to claim that all words belong to one conceptual frame
which is closed and self-sufficient inasmuch as it rests on,
or is generated from, unconditional truths or principles.

Now there is no need to retrace James's arguments against
the sort of strong coherence theory of justification and

methodist epistemology that absolute idealism represents.[46]
The point is that once the Parmenidean eternal one is replaced
by the Heraclitean historical many as an organizing principle
for our observations, we no longer need assume that either
there are invariant and standard theoretical and practical
truths, or there is epistemic and moral chaos. So long as
the concepts and theories allow us to deal adequately with
the problems we confront in our environment, what better
justification do we need? And to argue that they may in fact
turn out to be inadequate is to admit their external relation
to environments of discourse and of operation.

In other words, once we turn the problem of the one and
the many on its head, as James has done, there is no need to
make the claim that things are true *ex vi terminorum*, because
we can make functional or pragmatic sense of things without
having to refer to linguistically independent meanings. In
fact, to claim that any statement is true *ex vi terminorum* is
to make a mistake inasmuch as whole populations of concepts or
words can undergo semantic change. We believe, in other
words, since the coming of Quine, that analyticity holds no
water. There may have been a time, for instance, when the
statement that 'bachelors are unmarried' was taken to be true
by virtue of the meaning of the terms. But, as Harman points
out,

> This shows how philosophy becomes tied to an
> outmoded morality. As non-philosophers know,
> in this era of unstable marriages there are
> many bachelors who are still technically married.[47]

The point is not that we live in epistemic chaos. It is that,
in principle, thoughts are specified in terms of how they
function in conceptual environments that are subject to change
at every level. To cite Harman again:

> It *is* true that cats are animals, another commonly
> cited analytic truth. But Putnam points out that
> inability to imagine this false is a matter of
> lack of imagination. Imagine the discovery that
> all furry things we've been calling cats are
> really made of plastic and are radio-controlled
> spy devices from Mars. What we have imagined is
> that cats are not animals.[48]

There are, surely, statements about things that we firmly

accept and even claim to know, "but there is no real distinction between meaning postulates and others or between change in view and in meaning."[49]

So even if there were an absolute mind or agent, it wouldn't make any difference so far as James is concerned. In fact, it would just generate problems becuase "it does not account for our finite consciousness";[50] and because it "contradicts the character of reality as perceptually experienced,"[51] or roughly, as observed. For we persons "know things without other things,"[52] inasmuch as we live in environments, aspects of which are epistemically foreign to us. If there is some absolute mind or agent who exists as "a being without environment, upon which nothing alien can be forced,"[53] then we cannot simply exist as its object or as the result of its intention because we "know differently from its knowing."[54] We see things in eaches, everys, anys, eithers. It would see things as alls or wholes.

So no matter how complex or inclusive the 'worlds of discourse and of operation' that we can observe seem to be, they are liable to change in response to specifiable selective factors in their external environments. If we stick to James's assumption that "we can invent no new forms of conception, applicable to the whole exclusively, and not suggested originally by the parts,"[55] then we must preclude metaphysical visions of the absolute.

But if James's first rule of interpretation, that 'everything is in an environment external to it,' precludes visions of the absolute, it nonetheless allows for the vision of a *universe*. James turns the Parmenidean question on its head, and claims that "what really exists is not things made but things in the making."[56] In so doing, he does not *abandon* the concept of identity. He redefines it to meet the needs of historical entities. He says that "without losing its identity a thing can either take up or drop another thing."[57] To use Toulmin's suggestive term again, things are able to maintain a transient identity.[58] This, of course, undercuts the notion of numerical identity as universally applicable. But James says that

> real life laughs at logic's veto. Imagine a heavy
> log which takes two men to carry it. First A and
> B take it. Then C takes hold and A drops off;
> then D takes hold and B drops off, so that C and
> D now bear it; and so on. The log meanwhile never
> drops, and keeps its sameness throughout the
> journey. Even so it is with all our experiences.
> Their changes are not complete annihilations fol-
> lowed by complete creations of something absolutely
> novel. There is partial decay and partial growth,
> and all the while a nucleus of relative constancy
> from which what decays drops off, and which takes
> into itself whatever is grafted on, *until at
> length something wholly different has taken its
> place.*[59]

James's illustration may not be the best example, because it
is so commonsensical (it might have been better to illustrate
his point by saying, e.g., that every cell in a person's body
is supposed to change over a five-year period and yet we claim
it to be the same body). But his point should be clear
enough: Specifications of the universe can be completely
refurbished, yet still allow for what James calls a
"concatenated" and "continuous" universe. Thus,

> enormous as is the amount of disconnection among
> things . . . everything that exists is influ-
> enced in *some* way by something else, if you can
> only pick the way out rightly. Loosely speaking,
> and in general, it may be said that all things
> cohere and adhere to each-other *somehow*, and
> that the universe exists practically in reticu-
> lated or concatenated forms which make it a
> continuous or integrated affair.[60]

From the point of view of its many sorts of environment, "the
world hangs together from next to next in a variety of ways,
so that when you are off of one thing, you can always be on to
something else, without ever dropping out of your world."[61]
Like a federal republic with its variety of institutions with
their written and/or unwritten rules, the world is constituted
of a variety of environments that regulate patterns of
behavior. And just as the institutions in a republic can
undergo various sorts and degrees of transformation without
ever dissolving the rule of law, so can the world be construed
in process without dissolving its integration. If the structure of things is loose enough to allow for the religious
demand of salvation, it is concatenated or integrated enough

to allow for historical development. It provides, therefore,
one of the conditions that would make eventual salvation
possible.

Novelty

The second analogy that James advocates as holding
between 'things' in the broadest sense of the term and a
'federal republic' is the analogy of novelty. Federal republics are structured, in principle anyhow, not only in a way
that generates social accommodation on the part of its
constituents. They are also structured in a way that allows
for the assimilation of novel proposals generated by specifiable constituents at a variety of social levels. Federal
republics are not only governments of citizens, but also
government by citizens. In other words, if we look at what
is going on in a federal republic, we see a process that
depends formally on two major variables: regulation and
innovation. There are rules, laws, and regulations that
govern the behavior of citizens, but they are amendable in
principle by citizens. In principle, there are procedures
that enable each constituent to propose changes; and these
procedures complement the rules and laws that the republic
has funded, and that each citizen has the responsibility to
adhere to.

So too with James's universe. If his first principle of
interpretation demanded that each thing in the universe
accommodate its behavior to the environmental pattern(s) of
which it is a part, his second rule advocates that everything
hangs together in a way that allows for the assimilation of
novel factors that can make a difference. According to this
rule, if we look at what is going on in the universe, once
again we see a process that is dependent on two variables:
regulation and innovation. We see that its make-up depends
as much on the novel factors that emerge in it as it does on
the regulative factors that result from cumulative environmental selection. Simply put, "reality grows";[62] it develops
"piecemeal by the contribution of its several parts,"[63] and
not as generated by "the integral world itself."[64]

The analogy of novelty is crucial so far as James's

vision of a salvable world is concerned. Without novelty,
there could be no possibility for the development of a
universe hospitable enough to satisfy the resolutions that,
left unrealized, motivate people to pray. By emphasizing that
each thing is constituted in relation to external environments, he drives home the point that everything adapts its
behavior to conditions that are "foreign" to it and that
"resist" it. If environmental government *alone* accounted for
the behavior of things, people would be left in the position
of having to submit to the brutalization of some of their most
deeply held intentions. This is, in fact, what James took
both absolute idealism and scientific naturalism to imply.
He took them both to be claiming that "whatever occurs,
necessarily occurs.' He took that to mean "your way is
blocked in all directions save one."[65] He took that to imply
that 'things could not have been different.' In other words,
he construed both absolute idealism and scientific naturalism
as sorts of determinism, and claimed that

> Determinism, in denying that anything else can
> be in its stead, virtually defines the universe
> as a place in which what ought to be is impos-
> sible,--in other words, as an organism whose
> constitution is afflicted with an incurable
> taint, an irremediable flaw.[66]

The "indeterminism" that James wants to advocate instead
is meant to support the parts contingency, deliberation, and
decision play in the lives of people and the world they live
in. He wants to say that, as a rule, "from the point of view
of what is already given, what comes may have to be treated as
a matter of chance";[67] and that at any given time "the next
turn in events can . . . genuinely be ambiguous, i.e.,
possibly this, but also possibly that."[68] In other words,
he wants to advocate real possibility.

Now Thayer has pointed out that James's notions of a
world 'in the making' or of a 'plastic' universe

> hint of something more than the metaphors convey.
> These augur vaguely of a principle of certain
> equi-possible, but mutually exclusive classes
> of events, some of whose actualization at one
> time is a causal condition of the actualization
> of only some of a class of possible events at

> a future time. Far from making an appeal to
> objective chance, this stated principle holds
> that the actualization of some (as against
> other present possible) events "determines"
> the future actualization of some (as against
> other) events. But, obviously, the entire
> thesis of a "world in the making" needs an
> explicit and detailed formulation.[69]

Thayer goes on to point out that no classical pragmatist gave the explicit and detailed formulation required.[70] And as a matter of historical note, just the *problems* that such a formulation would entail were not articulated carefully until Goodman published his essays on real possibility and counterfactuals now collected in *Fact, Fiction, and Forecast*.[71] But Thayer's point does throw light on how James construed his indeterminism and the part novelty plays in the scheme of things. For James *never* advocates a vision of things which, because they are subject to contingency, implies that the way things hang together is irrational or makes no sense. And he *never* advocates the sort of indeterminism which precludes the determination of things in retrospect. He claims that his indeterminism better accounts for what is going on in the world. And the *sort* of indeterminism that he advocates is one that says, roughly, we are able to determine what has happened (with some high degree of approximation) but less able to *predict* what will happen.

The classic presentation of James's indeterminism comes in his essay, "The Dilemma of Determinism."[72] There James ties the problem of novelty directly to the problem of salvation. For it is there that James tries to show that the religious optimism of the absolute idealists and the religious pessimism of the scientific naturalists result from their supposition of sorts of determinism that cannot account for our ordinary view of human life. In "The Dilemma" James makes it clear that *if we find ourselves in need of salvation, it is because we are faced with problems of evil which seem, prima facie, to be insurmountable*. He uses the term 'evil' to account for the variety of phenomena that thwart our shareable intentions--natural phenomena like illness, pain, and disaster, social phenomena like murder, and "noetic" phenomena like despair and the sense of meaninglessness or absurdity.[73]

And he claims that optimism, pessimism, and meliorism are the
three options available to people who take problems of evil
seriously by attempting to respond to them.

He actually limits the debate in "The Dilemma" to one
kind of determinism. He distinguishes between "hard" and
"soft" determinists and claims that "hard" determinists really
deny that evil is a problem, inasmuch as they construe
purposive behavior as epiphenomenal and believe that all
statements about such behavior can be reduced to some sort of
nonintentional language. So, really, he is focussing on the
post-Hegelian absolute idealists alone. These latter do not
deny that evil is a problem but claim that evil is either
destined or sanctioned to be part of our experience. They do
not deny that our behavior is purposive, but claim that we are
the instruments of some absolute being whose will generates
all events ineluctably.

Now the first thing that James does in his debate against
these "soft" determinists who admit teleology but preclude
possibility is to establish the fact that the advocacy of
"determinism" or "indeterminism" is a matter of metaphysics.
Science, James points out, insofar as it is a self-correcting
procedure for determining the behavior of observable things,
can do no more than offer evidence for determinism or
indeterminism, which remain rules by which to organize our
observations. Indeed, he claims that "all our scientific and
philosophic ideals are altars to unknown gods. Uniformity as
much as free-will."[74] And

> what divides us into possibility men and anti-
> possibility men is different faiths or postulates
> --postulates of rationality. To this man the
> world seems more rational with possibilities in
> it,--to that man more rational with possibilities
> excluded.[75]

As we have said, therefore, James goes out of his way to claim
that his inclusion of "chance" in the universe gives no
support to the hypothesis that the way things hang together
is irrational. It is, to the contrary, an assertion that
indeterminism more adequately accounts for the way things,
and in particular, people, behave.

The second thing James does is to point out that, once a

person has done something, and we talk about what has
occurred, as spectators of an event that is now passed, the
debate between the determinist and the indeterminist is
interminable. For if I claim to have done x on purpose, the
soft determinist will claim that my doing of x "will have been
fated," whereas the indeterminist will claim that my doing of
x was the actualization of one (of several) equi-possible
pattern(s) of behavior, and that I could have behaved
differently.[76] If the determinist is correct, then my
decision to behave this way instead of that way cannot
possibly play an effective role in the universe. If the
indeterminist is correct, then decisions may "make nature
continuous." They may serve

> in their strange and intense function of granting
> consent to one possibility and withholding it
> from another, to transform an equivocal and double
> future into an unalterable and simple past.[77]

Far from meaning 'irrationality' or chaos, James's "chance"
therefore means

> exactly the same thing as the idea of gift . . .
> anything on which we have no effective *claim*.
> And whether the world be the better or the worse
> for having either chance or gifts in it will
> depend altogether on *what* these uncertain and
> unclaimable things turn out to be.[78]

But if James admits from the outset that, as spectators,
we cannot know whether the universe is finally deterministic
or indeterministic, because our evidence is ambiguous, he is
sure that on ethical grounds, and from our standpoint as
agents, the soft determinists are in a quandary. And their
quandary concerns the problem of evil.

The quandary has to do with what James calls judgments
of regret. All sorts of events occur such that, *ex post
facto*, we wish that we had done something to preclude their
happening. And most of the time we take our wish not to be
wishful, i.e., we think we *really could have* done something
to develop things differently. Soft determinists cannot
account for such judgments. Consider the response of the soft
determinist to the case of the "Brockton murderer" who, to rid
himself of his boring wife,

> inveigled her into a desert spot, shot her four
> times, and then, as she lay on the ground and
> said to him, "You didn't do it on purpose, did
> you dear?" replied, "No, I didn't do it on pur-
> pose," as he raised a rock and smashed her skull.[79]

Now we might ordinarily express regret that such an event
occurred. Indeed, we are likely to say that things would
have been better off had the murder not occurred. But if
we are soft determinists, either we have to assert that
"though it *couldn't* be, yet it would have been a better
universe with something different from the Brockton murder
in it,"[80] i.e., respond pessimistically, or we have to say
something like, 'Because it happened, it must have had the
moral sanction of Geist, or independent, intentional subjectivity recognizing itself or actualizing its will.' The
problem with either response is that, from the agent's point
of view, *there is nothing to do*. Both necessitarian pessimism
and optimism generate a response to evil that James tren-
chantly calls "indifference." The pessimist is convinced that
the murder is fated by "the whole" while the optimist is
convinced that the murder is actually sanctioned by the
Absolute, for reasons of self-recognition and/or self-
realization. The former resigns himself to the conviction
that intentional behavior, while a fact, is absurd, and the
latter celebrates evil as a condition of deepening our understanding of the essence of good. Both lead to one brand of
fatalism or another.

In the face of the dilemma presented by soft determinism,
James claims that "the only escape is by the practical way."
He offers a stance in which "conduct, and not sensibility,"
the point of view of the agent and not the point of view of
the spectator, "is the ultimate fact for our recognition.
With the vision of certain works to be done, of certain
outward changes to be wrought or resisted, it says our
intellectual horizon terminates."[81] In brief, his *moral*
justification for the metaphysical rule of novelty is this:

> I cannot understand the willingness to act, no
> matter how we feel, without the belief that acts
> are really good and bad. I cannot understand the
> belief that an act is bad, without regret at its
> happening. I cannot understand regret without

the admission of real genuine possibilities in the
world. Only *then* is it other than mockery to feel,
after we have failed to do our best, that an irrep-
arable opportunity is gone from the universe, the
loss of which it must forever after mourn.[82]

It is important to keep in mind, however, that the point
James wants to make is *not* a moral one, but a metaphysical
one: one about how to construe things generally. And even in
"The Dilemma," James is explicit about this:

The quarrel which determinism has with chance
fortunately has nothing to do with this or that
psychological detail. It is a quarrel altogether
metaphysical. Determinism denies the ambiguity
of future volitions, *because it affirms that
nothing future can be ambiguous.*[83]

James's indeterminism, to the contrary,

says that the parts have a certain amount of
loose play on one another, so that the laying
down of one of them does not necessarily determine what the others shall be. It admits that
possibilities may be in excess of actualities,
and that things not yet revealed to our knowledge
may really in themselves be ambiguous. Of two
alternative futures which we conceive, both may
now be really possible; and the one become impossible only at the very moment when the other
excludes it by becoming real itself. Indeterminism thus denies the world to be one unbending
unit of fact. It says there is a certain
ultimate pluralism in it; and so saying, it
corroborates our ordinary unsophisticated view
of things.[84]

Indeterminism, that is, provides the metaphysical rule in
terms of which we account for contingent behavior of all
sorts. Purposive behavior is merely a *sort* of contingent
behavior.

Now it is important to realize that James's "indeterminism" is, in no sense, antiscientific. It is not antiscientific, at least, if by 'science' we mean a kind of self-
corrective process of investigation based on observation
reports about phenomena. In fact, it allows for the determination of conditions *once* those conditions are *there* to
observe. It merely says that, from the point of view of what
we already know, certain conditions appear fortuitously,
i.e., in ways that do not seem to be generated by prior
conditions.

If the word 'chance' is bothersome, it surely is not because 'chance' is an unscientific variable:

> The sting of the word 'chance' seems to lie in the assumption that it means something positive, and that if anything happens by chance, it must needs be something of an intrinsically irrational and preposterous sort. Now chance means nothing of the kind. It is a purely negative and relative term, giving us no information about that of which it is predicated, except that it happens to be disconnected with something else,--not controlled, secured, or necessitated by other things. As this point is the most subtile one of the whole lecture, and at the same time the point on which all the rest hinges, I beg you to pay particular attention to it.[85]

It is 'subtile' and important because it means that James's "indeterminism" is a *temporal* indeterminism: it is an indeterminism relative to *prediction*, not to conditions per se. James never says that things are indetermin*able*. He says, "What comes is determined only when it comes. *Ab extra,* it appears only as a possible gift or graft."[86]

Consider the example of a chance-event that James gives:

> What is meant by saying that my choice of which way to walk home after the lecture is ambiguous and matter of chance as far as the present moment is concerned? It means that both Divinity Avenue and Oxford Street are called; but that only one, and that only *either* one, shall be chosen. Now, I ask you seriously to suppose that this ambiguity of my choice is real; and then to make the impossible hypothesis that the choice is made twice over, and each time falls on a different street. . . . You as passive spectators, look on and see the two alternative universes, one of them with me walking through Divinity Avenue in it, the other with the same me walking through Oxford Street. Now, if you are determinists, you believe one of these universes to have been from eternity impossible: you believe it to have been impossible because of the intrinsic irrationality or accidentality somewhere involved in it. But looking outwardly at these universes, can you say which is the impossible and accidental one, and which the rational and necessary one? I doubt if the most ironclad determinist among you could have the slightest glimmer of light on this point. In other words, either universe *after the fact* and once there would, to our means of observation and understanding, appear just as rational as the other. There would be absolutely no

criterion by which we might judge one necessary
and the other matter of chance.[87]

There is nothing mysterious about this sort of chance-event,
but it *may* make a difference, because what *happens* with James
on Oxford instead of Divinity or vice versa may be different.
Notice, however, that, in James's example, the *alternatives*
that make up the ambiguity are *"kinds* of things already here
and based in the existing frame of nature."[88] And if this is
all that James's indeterminism amounts to, it is pretty weak;
for it amounts to saying that, given the lawlike patterns of
behavior that we know to hold in the universe, we can specify
the following sorts of happenings in which leeway may occur as
to details. It is, surely, along these lines that James asks
rhetorically: "Is anyone ever tempted to produce an *absolute*
accident, something utterly irrelevant to the rest of the
world?"[89]

Indeed, when we consider James's *first* rule of interpretation, which demanded that each thing in the universe
accommodate its behavior to the environmental pattern(s) of
which it is a part, a picture begins to emerge at the metaphysical level that will support his Darwinian kind of
historiographic analysis at the scientific level. For he
seems to be saying that, whatever it is we are describing,
it will break down upon analysis into two factors that
equilibrate one another: regulative (or:selective) ones and
innovative (or:chance) ones. Hence the distinction that he
implicitly makes between "chance-events" and "absolute
accidents" (within, note well, the same seminal essay).[90]
Chance-events are events that we could not have predicted,
but events that are supportable in terms of the lawlike
behavior of things. For an "absolute accident" to occur, on
the other hand, environmental regulation would have to go
completely lax--which on James's own grounds would amount to
chaos.

In other words, chance-events play the same role in
James's universe that they did in Darwin's zoological populations: they account, in interaction with regulative factors,
for change. The claim is that, wherever we look, we see some
things tending to adhere to established patterns, other things

tending to force mutation in patterns, and never one sort of
thing without the other.

Now the Divinity Avenue/Oxford Street example is so tame,
because the alternative patterns of behavior that make up the
ambiguity can be accounted for so easily in terms of relevant
sorts of rules (e.g., moral, practical, physiological, and
psychological rules). But if James's analogy of novelty is
to hold, then the rules of behavior themselves must be liable
to mutation. In other words, if his social analogy is to
hold, then like the amendable constitution of a federal
republic, the constitution of the universe--the rules of its
government--must be subject to changes *in law* as well as
changes and variations *under law*, without being subject to
lawlessness.

And, indeed, James does so construe things in the
broadest sense of the term. Thayer points out that "in the
latter part of his life," James "moved from an earlier
espoused tychism to a view of the emerging of novelties that,
unlike tychism, did not leave novel events irrelevant to and
unnaturally discontinuous with the rest of nature."[91]   Now I
think that Thayer is wrong to drive a wedge between James's
tychism (i.e., the position taken on chance-events in "The
Dilemma") and his doctrine of emergence. I believe that had
Thayer recognized the distinction that James makes between
'absolute accident' and 'chance-event' he would have seen that
the difference between the earlier and later work is not a
difference in doctrine or analysis but a difference in
reference: the earlier work refers to changes under rule while
the later work refers to changes in rule: both analyze change
the same way; it is just that the changes analyzed are of two
different sorts. In any case, the thrust of Thayer's point is
correct: In *Pragmatism, A Pluralistic Universe* and *Some
Problems in Philosophy*, James focusses on a doctrine of
emergence, i.e., on noting and attempting to account for the
fact that the same (in a transient sense of same) elements in
the universe interact differently at different 'levels of
behavior.'

The first thing that James does in this respect is to
give a pragmatic analysis of the term 'possibility': Asking,

"What may the word 'possible' definitely mean?" he says that

> to unreflecting men it means a sort of third
> estate of *being*, less real than existence, more
> real than non-existence, a twilight realm, a
> hybrid status, a limbo into which and out of
> which realities ever and anon are made to pass.[92]

But this *de re* construal of 'possibility' depends on the sort
of ontological claim that James prohibits himself from making.
And, in any case, it is "too vague and nondescript to satisfy
us."[93]   So he is led to ask:

> When you say that a thing is possible, what dif-
> ference does it make? It makes at least this
> difference that if anyone calls it impossible you
> can contradict *him*, and if anyone calls it neces-
> sary you can contradict him too.[94]

This *de dicto* construal of 'possibility' is less off the mark
than the naive *de re* construal. Yet, "these privileges of
contradiction don't amount to much,"[95] unless they refer to
actual patterns of behavior. On James's reading, then,
'possibility' characterizes neither *being* nor simply *statements*, but historical conditions. 'Possibility'

> makes at least this negative difference that if
> the statement be true, it follows that there is
> nothing extant capable of preventing the possible
> thing. The absence of real grounds of interfer-
> ence may thus be said to make things *not impos-
> sible*, possible therefore in the bare or abstract
> sense.
>
> But most possibles are not bare, they are con-
> cretely grounded, or well grounded as we say.
> What does this mean pragmatically. It means
> not only that there are no preventative condi-
> tions present, but that some of the conditions
> of production of the possible thing are actually
> here. Thus a concretely possible chicken means:
> (1) that the idea of chicken contains no essen-
> tial self-contradiction; (2) that no boys, skunks,
> or other enemies are about; and (3) at least one
> actual egg exists. Possible chicken means actual
> egg--plus actual sitting hen, or incubator, or
> whatnot. As the actual conditions approach
> completeness the chicken becomes a better and
> better grounded possibility. When the conditions
> are entirely complete, it ceases to be a possi-
> bility, and turns into an actual fact.[96]

Now this is an undeniably rudimentary analysis of the
notion of possibility (to say the least). But the crucial

point about it is that it analyzes the notion in terms of
observable conditions, *without giving any ontological status
to them*: possibilities come into view depending on prevailing
conditions. When conditions are "entirely complete" what has
been construed as possible becomes "actual"--but this implies
nothing lasting, necessary, or inevitable about 'actualities.'

On the basis of this (admittedly crude) analysis of
possibility, James is able to make certain claims about
emergence. That is, given the plasticity of 'actualities,'
it becomes possible to picture things in the universe as
behaving in more and more complex ways as certain novel and
qualitatively unique properties become observable. With this
in mind, James says that

> we can imagine a world of things and of kinds in
> which the causal interactions with which we are
> familiar should not exist. Everything there might
> be inert towards everything else, and refuse to
> propagate its influence. Or gross mechanical
> influences might pass but no chemical action.
> Such worlds would be far less unified than ours.
> Again, there might be physico-chemical interaction,
> but no minds; or mind, but altogether private ones,
> with no social life; or social life limited to
> acquaintance, but no love; or love, but no customs
> or institutions that should systematize it. No
> one of these grades of universe would be abso-
> lutely irrational or disintegrated, inferior tho
> it might appear when looked at from the higher
> grades.[97]

The point (though stretched a bit here) is that it is possible
to describe the rules that govern phenomena as emerging on a
series of "grades" or levels, each of which is self-
sufficient, but none of which accounts for the sort of
behavior "above" it. Consider, for instance, the fact that
sensations "do not occur in the presence of matter generally;
only matter as it is in the living brain."[98] The rules that
govern the behavior of matter elsewhere (at 'lesser' levels)
break down when applied to brains. The 'exceptionless'
regulations governing the behavior of, say, hydrocarbon
molecules, potassium ions, free iron, and electromagnetic
fields applies to everything outside of brains, but "the flow
of electrons at the synaptic interfaces 'breaks the laws.'"[99]

But to claim that the behavior of things in the brain is

categorically different from the behavior of the same sorts of
things outside the brain does not generate lawlessness: it
calls for a differentiation and reformulation of theories.
Again, we have a situation in which certain events cannot be
predicted in terms of the laws or rules construed as governing
things (logically) prior to the occurrence: To reiterate
James's words, "What comes is determined only when it comes.
Ab extra, it appears only as a possible gift or graft."[100]

So the doctrine of emergence, as James deploys it, is
simply the application of the notion of novelty or 'chance-
event' at the level of theories and rules. It says, in other
of James's words (*pace* Bergson) that "not only . . . do terms
change, so that after a certain time the very elements of
things are no longer what they were, but relations also
change, so as no longer to obtain in the same identical ways
between the new things that have succeeded upon the old
ones."[101]

James's second principle of interpretation is that everything hangs together in a way that allows for the assimilation
of novel factors that can make a difference. Its importance
lies in the fact that when it is coupled with his first rule
--that each thing in the universe accommodates its behavior to
the environmental patterns of which it is a part--it not only
names change and historical development, but accounts for the
process or procedure in terms of which these phenomena come
about. By conceiving of the universe after a social analogy,
as a variety of populations each of which is subject to
mutation by constituent members, James avoids the derealiza-
tion of historical events *without* having to construe them
either as chaotic or irrational. Indeed, if his vision is
correct, novel and emergent factors may play a great part in
making the universe we live in more rational.

Activity

The third analogy that James advocates as holding between
a federal republic and the universe is the analogy of
activity. Federal republics are structured not only as
governments of the people and by the people, but also for the
people. It is not enough simply to say of a federal republic

that it is constituted by its members, who propose and ratify rules and changes in rules that govern everyone. For both regulation and innovation in a federal republic are generated and maintained *relative to* the common purposes or shared intentions of the entire group.

An analogous phenomenon may be evident in the universe, according to James. He does not only advocate that the universe is constituted by each thing in it; or that each thing in it is adapted to a variety of environments that govern, in part, its behavior; or that the universe hangs together in the concatenated sort of way that allows variant and emergent factors to generate changes in the way some things behave. He also advocates a vision of things in which both regulation and innovation are construed as relative to the purposes held in common by constituents of the universe-- and this is not unproblematic. For the only things, on James's own grounds, that we can look at in the universe that exhibit intentional behavior--the only things that not only serve but also bring purposes--are the things we call people.

Either James fell into the 'blunder of clumping' at this point, or this aspect of his social vision must be qualified. In support of the 'either' claim are the noises that he made from time to time about the possibility of advocating a kind of panpsychism.[102] But interpreters, like Flournoy, have pointed out that his espousal of the doctrine of pure experience militates against these noises, which were in fact only noises.[103] And interpreters of panpsychism, like Paul Edwards, have declared that even if James thought he might in some way advocate some sort of panpsychism, "James himself was *not* a panpsychist. He nowhere maintained that plants and inanimate objects have an inner psychic life."[104] Panpsychists, on the other hand, do maintain these things.

What James did maintain was that people (including possibly unseeable people, e.g., gods) may be "coconscious" or, roughly, may not only think alike, but actually share thoughts and intentions: they may be part of some "wider" epistemic pattern of behavior. But this tends to support the 'or' claim that the analogy of activity needs to be qualified.

To begin with, remember that James does not construe the
metaphysical task to be ontological in any strong sense of the
term. He is not attempting to tell us categorically what
there is. He is attempting to generate a stance from which to
view things generally: He wants to give us a background
(better:cinema) within which to place ourselves. And because
the motivation behind doing metaphysics is, for him at any
rate, the desire to feel at home in the universe, his chief
concern is to figure whether the background for our lives is
"foreign" and "brute" or "friendly" and "intimate." The
distinction is important from a pragmatic point of view
because, practically,

> the difference between living against a back-
> ground of foreignness and one of intimacy means
> the difference between a general habit of wari-
> ness and one of trust. One might call it a
> social difference, for after all, the common
> *socius* of us all is the great universe whose
> children we are. If materialistic, we must be
> suspicious of this socius, cautious, tense, on
> guard. If spiritualistic, we may give way,
> embrace, and keep no ultimate fear.[105]

But we have seen that James is too wary to be an out and
out spiritualist and too cognizant of the intentional behavior
of persons to be an out and out materialist. His universe is
one in which "something in every experience . . . escapes our
arbitrary control."[106] But it is also one in which we are
able to "make an *addition* to some sensible reality, and that
reality tolerates the addition." These "additions 'agree'
with the reality; they fit it, while they build it out."[107]
But no matter how 'wide' or inclusive the pattern(s) of
intentional behavior get, there are things that resist them:

> However much may be collected, however much may
> report itself as present at any effective center
> of consciousness or action, something else is
> self-governed and absent and unreduced to unity.[108]

James's universe is *functionally* dualistic, divided between
the purposive and nonpurposive. The "brute" nonpurposive
parts make life "serious" enough to question whether it is
worth living. The appearance of intentions makes the
strenuous life an option; so, on James's grounds

> it is . . . perfectly possible to accept sincerely
> a drastic kind of universe from which the element
> of "seriousness" is not to be expelled. Whoso
> does so is, it seems to me, a genuine pragmatist.
> He is willing to live on a scheme of uncertified
> possibilities which he trusts; willing to pay
> with his own person, if need be, for the realiza-
> tion of the ideals which he frames.[109]

And those "uncertified possibilities" do not go entirely
unspecified by James:

> What now actually *are* the other forces which he
> trusts to cooperate with him in a universe of
> such a type? *They are at least his fellow men,*
> in the stage of being which our actual universe
> has reached.[110]

There may also be "superhuman forces," "higher powers . . .
at work to save the world on ideal lines similar to our
own."[111] The forces that cooperate, i.e., behave in terms of
intentions that are shared or shareable are "at least" people
and maybe (unseen) agents that have intentions which are
similar to our own. But in any case the things that are able
to share intentions never comprise everything. Our activity
may be dictated in part or almost entirely by intentional
patterns more complex and inclusive than ourselves. This is,
in fact, the case inasmuch as most of our purposive behavior
is controlled by the intentions of our communities. But rocks
and trees, or generally physical things, do not share intentions because they do not intend at all. James never said
that they do.

So the analogy of activity does need to be qualified.
Either James could mean that the universe of cooperating
things is actually limited to those things called people (and
those things we call gods, if there are any). If this were
the case, then we could construe his "federal republic" as a
community of purposive beings set within an environment of
nonpurposive things. Or James could be specifying 'cooperation' in a rather loose sense and therefore be saying that,
while some of the things in the universe cooperate on purpose,
others do not: other things in the universe cooperate roughly
in the same way that clay may be said to cooperate (or not)
with a potter by not resisting his management, and thereby
suiting his intentions. But even on these grounds, it is hard

to construe many things, e.g., carcinogenic blood cells,
intentional behavior like murder, unsolvable epistemic
riddles, and so on, as cooperative (even though it is possible
that such things may become manageable enough not to hinder
the realization of our common purposes). If James meant, as
I think he did, to take 'cooperation' in the loose sense, then
we can construe his federal republic of cooperant things--some
of which bring purposes as well as serve them; others of which
only serve them--as set within an environment as yet untamed.

The fact that James's pluralistic universe is also
"melioristic" makes the latter vision clearer. James's
"meliorism" is constructed in response to environmental
factors that resist our shared intentions. It demands that
those things that contravene the realization of our common
purposes be somehow "overcome";[112] but it demands this with
full recognition that

> even though we do *our* best, the other factors
> will also have a voice in the result. If they
> refuse to conspire, our good will and labor may
> be thrown away. No insurance company can here
> cover us or save us from the risks we run in
> being part of such a world.[113]

With this third analogy, James's vision of a salvable
world is as complete as it ever gets. But if it lacks
specification, this is not because James was dumbfounded when
it came to filling it out. It is because the vision is self-
consciously vague. It is a vision not unlike the vision
behind his own government's constitution: a vision of the
possibility of developing a society that enables its members
to realize those values that they own, propose, and maintain
as social beings. Thus it is a vision of salvation *not* of the
individual--not of a being whose intentions are, in principle,
subjective. It is a vision of corporate salvation: a vision
of salvation that does not get finished until the shareable
intentions of each social being are realized.

One can imagine, says James, a fantastic world in which
every desire, every intention whether it be intersubjective
or not, is fulfilled willy-nilly. This is, says James, "the
Absolute's own world": "The world of wishing caps, the world
of telepathy, where every desire is fulfilled instanter,

without having to consider or placate surrounding or inter-
mediate powers."[114] But *in our world,*"

> the wishes of the individual are only one condi-
> tion. Other individuals are there with other
> wishes, and they must be propitiated first. So
> being grows under all sorts of resistances in this
> world of the many, and, from compromise to com-
> promise, only gets organized gradually into what
> may be called secondarily rational shape.[115]

Our world's salvation, in other words, must be *won* by the
process of isolating and instituting the purposes on which we
com-promise, i.e., the purposes that we come to share. James
can no more specify *what* salvation would bring than he can
determine which intentions people will both come to share and
be able to institute. But he can say that a saved world would
be a world that tolerated our shared intentions as agents and
patients of community and, indeed, funded them. James's
vision of the saved world, then, is a world that tolerates
government of, by, and for those of its constituents that
bring purpose to it. And it is within this soteric frame that
James claims that our activity creates "the world's salvation
so far as it makes room for itself . . . not the whole world's
salvation of course, but just so much of this as itself covers
of the world's extent."[116] It is with this vision that he
asserts:

> Our acts, our turning places, where we seem to
> ourselves to make ourselves and grow, are the
> parts of the world to which we are closest, the
> parts of which our knowledge is most intimate and
> complete. Why should we not take them at their
> face-value? Why may not they be the actual
> turning-places and growing places which they
> seem to be, of the world--why not the work-shop
> of being, where we catch fact in the making, so
> that nowhere may the world grow in any other
> kind than this?[117]

In other words, when we behave on purpose, we seem to make a
difference. "Our thoughts determine our acts, and our acts
redetermine the previous nature of the world";[118] inasmuch as
the world's "nature" is to be historical and inasmuch as our
behavior is a part of its history, the changes we bring are
changes in and of it as well. Why not take these changes at
face-value and assume that every change is brought about in

the same way?

It is with these questions generated from his vision that he turns to the task of justification, to the task of making reasonable the belief that our activity makes the only kind of difference that counts--historical difference. But to prepare for his defense of the efficacy of activity as well as for his defense of the historical reality of intersubjective behavior, he takes one logical step back to attack the notion of ontological categories head-on. He does this in his celebrated (and much debated) doctrine of radical empiricism or pure experience.

James's doctrine of radical empiricism or pure experience has generated more diverse interpretation than any other part of his work. Those interpreters who themselves have a stake in one sort of ontology or another, for instance, the phenomenologists Wild and Mathur and Wilshire and the phenomenalist Ayer, see James as attempting to reconstruct what is ontologically given.[119] In my opinion, these interpreters do not take James's metaphysical task seriously enough because they take his so-called 'ontological' claims too seriously. According to James,

> Radical empiricism consists first of a postulate, next of a statement of fact, and finally of a generalized conclusion.
>
> The postulate is that the only things that shall be debatable among philosophers shall be definable in terms drawn from experience. . . .
>
> The statement of fact is that the relations between things, conjunctive as well as disjunctive, are just as much matters of direct particular experience, neither more so nor less so, than the things themselves.
>
> The generalized conclusion is that therefore the parts of experience hold together from next to next by relations that are themselves parts of experience. The directly apprehended universe needs, in short, no extraneous trans-empirical connective support, but possesses in its own right a concatenated or continuous structure.[120]

In other words, philosophers should only debate things they can check out by observation; when they do observe things, they always find them in some context or other; the things-

in-context that they look at are self-supportive: philosophers
need no ontological principle(s) to back them up or make sense
of them. These claims rest on James's doctrine of pure
experience. The doctrine of pure experience is that

> primary reality is of a neutral nature. . . . I
> give it the name *pure experience*. Call this a
> monism, if you will; but it is an altogether
> rudimentary monism and absolutely opposed to
> the so-called bilateral monism of scientific
> positivism or that of the Spinozists.
>
> These pure experiences exist and succeed one
> another; they enter into infinitely varied
> relations; and these relations are themselves
> essential parts of the web of experiences. . . .
>
> The attributes "subject" and "object," "repre-
> sented" and "representative," "thing" and
> "thought" mean, then, a practical distinction
> of the utmost importance, but a distinction
> which is of a FUNCTIONAL order only, and not
> at all ontological as understood by classical
> dualism.[121]

On these grounds, data "*become* conscious in their entirety;
they *become* physical in their entirety":[122]

> in a certain context of associates one experience
> would be classed as a physical phenomenon, while
> in another setting it would figure as a fact of
> consciousness. . . .[123]

That is, they function that way for us; but they are ontolog-
ically neutral. Thus, as Thayer points out in regard to
James's historically startling essay, "Does Consciousness
Exist?"[124] James initiates

> a fundamental revision of the traditional con-
> cepts of object and subject (or *thing* and *thought*).
> He re-interprets these as "functional attributes,"
> or relations of a single postulated primal stuff:
> "pure experience." The specific argument does not
> concern us at the moment, but the procedure does.
> James nowhere claims that he has drawn a true
> representation of the facts. He does claim, how-
> ever, to have succeeded in avoiding the many
> notorious difficulties in the traditional concepts
> and their use while retaining what is useful in
> them. The effect is to preserve what is worth
> preserving of the older notions by providing them
> with their "pragmatic equivalents," while what does
> not need preservation, in this case 'consciousness'
> (not thought, but the un-thing like thing called
> "soul"), gets eliminated as a gratuitous obstacle

to knowledge. This essay of James's is a model of
his interpretation and use of the pragmatic method
of analysis.[125]

What Thayer does not point out is that James could just as
easily have answered negatively the question whether (physical) things exist. For James's focus is not just on
consciousness and physical things, subjects and objects, but
also on the term 'exist' when it is meant to give entitative
status to *either* thought *or* thing. Notice right away: James
does not want to *reduce* anything to anything. He wants to
replace talk about entities with talk about how things
function in specific contexts. As John E. Smith points out,
therefore,

> James's proposal is not, as has sometimes been
> thought, to eliminate the distinction between
> thought and thing by returning to an undiffer-
> entiated experience or feeling, but to re-
> interpret the traditional subject/object
> distinction in terms of contexts and func-
> tions.[126]

The point is that when we talk about thoughts and things,
we are engaging in what we might call anontological conversation: conversation that simply has no reference to ontological
sorts:

> subjectivity and objectivity are functional
> attributes solely, realized only when the
> experience is "taken," i.e., *talked-of*, twice,
> considering along with its two differing
> contexts respectively, by a new retrospective
> experience.[127]

On these lines, to perceive or conceive epistemically is to
perceive- or conceive-as, and to perceive- or conceive-as is
simply to have some sort of differential signal.

Now the first thing to notice is that James's specification of pure experience takes the traditional empiricistic
clout away from the term 'experience.' As Morris points out,
given the doctrine of pure experience, "to say that x is an
item of experience is no longer to say anything whatsoever
about it,"[128] except (I would add) that it is witnessable
within a particular theoretic context. In Martland's terms,
experience "is simply a general name for whatever we think or
feel."[129]

The second thing to notice is that 'experience' can no
longer be construed either as data or as interpretation where
those terms are meant to contradict each other. What James is
pointing to is the fact that the world we live in and talk
about is a world of subjects and objects: the moment we begin
to talk about *what* we perceive we are already perceiving-as;
we are already sorting our experiences into contexts that
function according to various norms. This is so obviously the
case that when we attempt to differentiate what is given in
experience from what is interpreted as experience, we fail:

> Sensations and apperceptive ideas fuse . . . so
> intimately that you can no more tell where one
> begins and the other ends, than you can tell, in
> those cunning circular panoramas that have been
> lately exhibited, where the real foreground and
> the painted canvas join together.[130]

James's advocacy of the *metaphysical* doctrine of pure
experience is *epistemologically* significant because it
eliminates all the problems in epistemology which stem from
construing people as ontologically discrete subjects who
must somehow mirror ontologically discrete objects. It is
phenomenologically significant because it provides one
category, behavior, in terms of which to describe things.
By replacing the ontological distinction between minds and
bodies with a functional one that is unpacked in terms of how
things behave under particular sorts of conditions, or in
particular normative contexts, James finally establishes the
metaphysical machinery to support his historiographic method
of analysis and his pragmatic maxim.

If there is a problem with James's doctrine, it has to do
with the fact that he never made clear just how the various
normative contexts in terms of which we report experiences are
themselves specifiable as experiences. He seems to leave us
wondering: given the fact that we can interpret the same (in
the transient sense of same) bit of behavior, e.g., in terms
of physical movement and in terms of intentions, how can we
generate the norms or rules of physical behavior on the one
hand and intentionality on the other from patterns of behavior
per se?[131] James is not clear. He says, roughly, that norms
can be extrapolated from the various sorts of history we take

of any particular phenomenon. But that begs the question.

If, however, one takes the *force* of James's doctrine to be functional and not phenomenal, as I think is appropriate, then it does not matter much whether or not he begs the question. James's *aim*, as we have seen, is not reductive. He does not, like some behaviorists, attempt to overcome ontological dualism with some sort of materialistic monism. Nor does he overcome ontological dualism by way of any transcendental phenomenological reduction, as Wilshire might insist.[132] To the contrary, his doctrine of pure experience is meant to be a metaphysical underpinning for normative pluralism, where anything we say about an event is colored by the context in which we place it. As Linschoten suggests, for James "the science of experience becomes the science of behavior (conduct)."[133] But unlike the behaviorism of, say, Watson, Linschoten suggests that James's science of behavior is governed by a "principle of complementarity." In Linschoten's words,

> it is only on the basis of a particular question-
> ing that an experience is construed either
> physically or epistemically. Phenomena can be
> questioned in their mutual connection, or in
> connection with the (experiencing) person. These
> two kinds of questioning are complementary, just
> like the resulting words.[134]

Such complementarity surely seems explicit in James's claim that "the same identical piece of 'pure experience' . . . can stand *alternatively* for a 'fact of consciousness' or a physical reality, according as it is taken in one context or the other."[135] Outside of context, experience as 'pure' is a virtual something about which nothing could be said, and in Wittgenstein's trenchant remark, "a nothing would serve just as well as a something about which nothing could be said."[136] If Linschoten is right, and I think he is, then it is not particularly James's task to give a genetic analysis of the rules that govern physical behavior on the one hand and purposive behavior on the other. It is more simply his task to point out that *whenever* we observe behavior we observe it as conjoined in a particular context. When we look at rocks, for instance, we don't first observe them and only later

construe them as governed by rules of physical behavior.
Rocks *look* physical. And when we look at people, we don't
first observe them, and then somehow infer that they are
governed by the rules of intentional behavior. They simply
look purposive. (Consider our response to some human that
appears as nonpurposive, e.g., a corpse. Are we not more
likely to say, 'That thing no longer behaves like a person,'
than we are to say 'That person no longer behaves intentionally?') It is in this sense that I think we ought to take
James's "statement of fact" that

> the relations between things, conjunctive as
> well as disjunctive, are just as much matters of
> direct particular experience, neither more so
> nor less so, than the things themselves.[137]

To say that the way we account for experience is context
(and, therefore, norm) dependent is not, however, to admit that
any context or set of norms will do. It is, first, just to
say that this is in fact the way things are. It is, second,
to admit the possibility that the way we talk about things may
change. James wants to admit a variety of complementary ways
to take experience, but he also wants to claim that the only
ways that should (or perhaps, simply will) prevail are those
that allow us to make appropriate transactions with our
environment.[138] This is why he insists that the "only
function that one experience can perform is to lead into
another experience, and the only fulfillment we can speak of
is the reaching of a certain experienced end."[139] Our
thoughts, in other words, *fail* us, just as other instruments
of behavior do, if they do not facilitate the adequate
management of our environment. They sustain us, on the other
hand, so long as they provide relevant norms of conduct and
better our ability to make environmental transactions.

By replacing the old ontological distinction between mind
and body with the new functional one, James advocates that we
construe people *not* as living within the medium of consciousness and not as living within the medium of physical movement,
but as living within the medium of behavior. He makes us
realize that we are able not only to dwell within conceptual
frames, but *use* them to enter into and exit from nonconceptual

or "sensible" experience over and over again. Not only do we
learn to respond, e.g., to physical smoke with the thought
(or:signal) 'Here is smoke' and therefore pass without a break
from the world of things to the world of thought. Not only do
we learn to move internally within conceptual frames from,
e.g., 'Here is smoke' to 'Near is fire' and therefore pass
fluidly from premise to conclusion. But we also learn to
construe 'Near is fire' (in appropriate circumstances) as a
motivating sign: we can move directly from sign to object;
i.e., we can take appropriate action. 'Smoke' and 'fire' are
construed here as 'thoughts,' there as 'things': what counts
is how these terms function as organizers of our conduct.

Now within the context of James's doctrine of pure
experience, the analysis of human behavior remains complex.
This is so because to say that we are conscious of our
behavior or that we know it still leaves open the question of
specification. We can observe our behavior (at least) both
physically and intentionally. *How* we observe our behavior
depends on the questions we ask, and the questions we ask
depend on the purpose behind the research. But already, this
raises an interesting thought. We say that either physical or
intentional specifications of behavior may do (despite the
fact that each is contrary to the other), depending on our
interests. If our aim is to establish kinesthiological
patterns of behavior, the way we analyze the waving of a hand
will differ *categorically* from the way we analyze the waving
of a hand when our aim is to establish social patterns of
behavior. The same data function in (at least) two different
ways. But the way we analyze their function seems to be
interest- and purpose-relative, which means, roughly, that the
same data can be tooled differently according to *intended*
usage.

The point is that, so long as we construe conceptual
frames to be interest-relative, and take (as James does)
'interest' as a primitive term, we employ a language with an
irreducibly intentional component. We use a language in which
we picture ourselves as doing things on purpose according to
socially constructed rules and norms. Thus, on James's
grounds, 'activity' (in the sense of purposive behavior) is

functionally (note well: not ontologically) irreducible (note
well: not irreplaceable).

James's doctrine of pure experience not only reconstructs
'activity' as a sort of behavior (avoiding problems generated
from the construal of 'activity' as the exhibition or realization of an ontological sort). It also provides a metaphysical
rule to sustain James's early insight that all the 'worlds' in
which people live are communities, or populations governed
according to shared norms. For once 'activity' is construed
functionally, once it is no longer tied to the notion of
'person' as a logically egocentric kind of *being*, it becomes
possible to construe other sorts of things than individuals as
active; e.g., communities may be construed as active. On
these grounds, indeed, it is possible to construe individuals
as *serving* the purposes of the communities to which they
belong; it is possible to picture them as instruments of
shared intentions. Thus, when James says that

> wider spans of consciousness are . . . quite in
> order, provided [we] distinguish the functional
> from the entitative point of view, and do not
> treat the minor consciousness under discussion
> as a kind of standing material of which the
> wider ones consist[140]

he is saying that, so long as we think in terms of patterns of
behavior, there is nothing in principle precluding us from
picturing ourselves as parts of more inclusive purposive acts
(some of which we may not even be aware of). And for James,
this opens the door wider for possible theological discourse,
inasmuch as he is left *able* to ask, "Why can't I have another
being own me and use me, just as I am, for its purposes,
without knowing any of those purposes myself?"[141]

In James's essay, "The Experience of Activity," he makes
it clear that he believes there is no pragmatic or radical
empiricistic reason for *precluding* theological discourse.
This essay represents James's most sustained effort to analyze
'activity' within the context of his doctrine of pure
experience. He says that

> by the principle of pure experience, either the
> word 'activity' must have no meaning at all, or
> else the original type and model of what it means
> must lie in some concrete kind of experience that

> can be definitely pointed out. Whatever ulterior
> judgments we may eventually come to make, *that*
> *sort* of thing will be what the judgments are
> about.[142]

Now James says that if we look at things generally, each
is active in the truncated sense that it exhibits "something
doing" or "the bare fact of event or change."[143] But this
sense is truncated because things generally (or without
further specification) exhibit "no definite direction, no
actor, and no aim."[144] If we look just at physical things,
their activity is truncated also. They may exhibit definite
direction and aim or goal, but they serve these things and in
no sense posit them. Activity in the full-blown sense, says
James, is the term we use to describe the behavior of persons.
It comes "in the dramatic shape of something sustaining a felt
purpose against felt obstacles and overcoming or being overcome."[145] In other words, activity in its most original sense
functions within the context of "biography" or our behavior as
social beings. It is an indelibly epistemic sort of behavior,
where "one thought in every developed activity-series is a
desire or thought of purpose, and all the other thoughts
acquire a feeling tone from their relation of harmony or
oppugnacy to this."[146] 'Activity' thus refers to the behavior
of people who are sustaining efficacious efforts against a
variety of resistant conditions. No matter what our ulterior
judgments about 'activity' are, no matter whether we say that
it is real or illusory, what we mean by it is the purposive
behavior exhibited by people.

But it is one thing to recognize that a certain sort of
situation is observed as an "activity-situation" and another
thing to specify the conditions that generate that sort of
situation. Our "ulterior judgments" are dependent on the
latter specification. "The *facts* of activity," says James,
"are something far more interstitial, so to speak, than what
my feelings record."[147] In other words, when we observe
activity, we are likely not to observe the history of reasons
and motivations behind it, and even less likely to observe the
neurological conditions supporting it. And in order to
account for these conditions that we do not observe when we
observe activity 'on its surface,' philosophers (says James)

have developed three typical theories of activity. Some take
the teleological aspect of activity to be primitive and "take
a consciousness of wider time span than ours to be the more
real activity. Its will is the agent and its purpose is the
action done."[148] Others simply underscore the habitual aspect
of activity and claim that "'ideas' struggling with one
another are the agents, and . . . the prevalence of one set of
them is the action."[149] And still others claim that "nerve
cells are the agents, that resultant motor discharges are the
acts achieved."[150]

Of these three theories, the only one that does not
reduce activity to some sort of behavior that is nonintentional is the first: it advocates that so-called individual
intentions must be construed as parts of more inclusive
patterns of purposive behavior. The second attempts to reduce
activity to a set of dispositions; and the third attempts to
reduce activity to a set of neurophysiological conditions.
But James points out that, while it is fine and proper to
construe activity dispositionally and correlate it with neurophysiological conditions, neither move accounts for the
distinction we ordinarily make between our purposive and nonpurposive behavior, inasmuch as *all* of our behavior is
dispositional and neurophysiologically conditioned. The
problem is that some dispositions are intentional and some
are not, and so on. Neither the philosophers of James's time
nor those of our own have established adequate rules of
reducibility or translation to dispose of James's *functional*
dualism. But for James, the first theory, the theory that our
intentions are governed by purposes "wider" than our own, has
merit inasmuch as it "does not de-realize my activities." It
"corroborates the reality of them."[151]

If the doctrine of pure experience is correct, if the
distinction between thoughts and things is functional, then
thoughts and things belong to two irreducible conceptual
frames. And if the doctrine of instrumentalism is correct, if
conceptual frames are generated relative to our interests and
in terms of norms that we share, then conceptual frames depend
on our behavior as purposive beings who *aim* to predict and
control our environment adequately enough to do what we

resolve to do. This is why James is convinced that

> Men of science and philosophy, the moment they
> forget their theoretic abstractions, live in
> their biographies as much as any one else, and
> believe as naively that fact even now is making,
> and that they themselves, by doing "original
> work," help to determine what the future shall
> become.[152]

In James's view the conceptual frame(s) in which things
are construed as behaving nonintentionally may very well
enable us to predict and control our environment in useful
ways. That frame, indeed, may better account for most
patterns of behavior than does an intentional frame. But to
say that much is, on James's grounds, to say that it enables
us to do better what we resolve to do. So, on James's
grounds, our vision of things needs be (at least) stereo-
scopic, inasmuch as the development of all conceptual frames
seems to depend on the interests and norms of the communities
that promulgate them.

The world of pure experience, in other words, corroborates the picture we have of ourselves as "sustaining,
persevering, striving, paying as we go, hanging on, and
finally achieving our intention."[153] And it makes possible
the picture James has of the universe in which 'activity' is
a cooperative enterprise. Just who and/or what cooperates is
another matter, to which we will shortly turn.

Reason and Faith

I opened this chapter by claiming that James's metaphysics is an example of the sort of "metaphysics without
ontology" articulated by Walsh in his book *Metaphysics*. I
believe that my exposition and analysis of James's vision of
a salvable world, conceived after the analogy of a federal
republic and justified on pragmatic grounds, supports that
claim. I believe that I have shown that James generates a
general esthetic stance, a place from which to view things
and a background in which to place them. By envisioning the
world as constituted by a "pluralism of independent powers"
some of which are friendly and some of which are brutal, he
aims to make possible an attitude towards things generally at

once strenuous and trusting. By envisioning the development of the world as promulgated by none other than its constituents--not least powerful of which are people, he aims to make possible an attitude at once responsible and risking: he aims to show that we cannot sustain our shareable intentions without actually *doing* what we resolve to do, despite great cost. By envisioning the world entire as more or less tolerant of those of its constituents who bring purpose to it, he aims to show that the eventual establishment of a "socius" adequate enough to satisfy our social claims is a real possibility. All in all, by envisioning the world as possibly and eventually governed of, by, and for those of us who are able to share intentions, he hopes to let loose in people the confidence they need to 'true' their deepest-felt desires, to achieve their most lasting goals, and to cash-out their most persistent claims.

The vision, I think, is brilliant and carefully constructed, articulating as it does the rather intricate relationships that hold among his three interpretive 'rules' of variety, novelty, and activity. Indeed, the vision is revolutionary in its time for a number of reasons. It is revolutionary in its head-on attack of essentialism. It is revolutionary in its ability not only to *name* historical process, but to *analyze* it. It is revolutionary in its insistence that science be identified not with any set of categorical claims but with a self-correcting method of investigation and discovery. It is revolutionary in its reconstruction of the mind-body distinction in terms of functions or sorts of behavior.

But the question arises, how can we ultimately judge the adequacy of James's vision and the reasoning that supports it? James is the first to admit that his metaphysical opponents may be more correct in their visions than he is (though less willing to admit that their reasoning is as adequate). He is the first to admit that his universe is hypothetical. How do we judge the adequacy of an esthetic stance or attitude from which to view things in the broadest sense of the term? What could constitute a telling argument for or against James's project? Walsh points to the difficulty here when he tells us

(*pace* Collingwood) that "the problem of establishing the
validity of a system of metaphysics is that of establishing
the validity of a set of principles of interpretation."[154]
The problem is that, in principle, such a set of rules "can be
grounded neither deductively nor inductively" because they are
posited as grounds for both argument and prediction. Walsh
suggests that we criticize metaphysical claims the way we
criticize literary critical ones, where we "look for qualities
like depth, penetration, insight."[155] There, "we expect a
good critic to reveal to us aspects of the writings under
review whose significance is commonly overlooked, and so
enable us to look at what we thought we knew well with fresh
eyes."[156] On these grounds

> the value of engaging in metaphysical inquiry can
> no longer be questioned. But the value is one
> which accrues to the individual, as commonly
> happens in the humanities; it is not, as is
> scientific or mathematical knowledge, the common
> possession of mankind as a whole.[157]

James's understanding of metaphysical inquiry is really
much the same. Where he differs explicitly from Walsh is his
insistence that metaphysical vision and practical behavior are
indissolubly linked. To envision things in a particular way
is to position oneself in an attitude, and to do that is to
dispose oneself in a particular way according to specifiable
norms. So, from James's point of view,

> in general it may be said that if a man's concep-
> tion of the world lets loose any action in him
> which is easy, or any faculty which he is fond
> of exercizing, he will deem it rational insofar-
> forth, be the faculty that of computing, fighting,
> lecturing, classifying, framing schematic, tabula-
> tions, getting the better end of a bargain,
> patiently waiting or enduring, preaching, joke-
> making, or what you like.[158]

If a metaphysical vision, in other words, facilitates your
transactions with things, you may deem it rational "insofar-
forth." There are so many sorts of transaction ("at least
. . . intellectual, aesthetical, moral, and practical
. . .")[159] that

> whatever demand for rationality we find satisfied
> by a philosophical hypothesis, we are liable to

> find some other demand for rationality unsatisfied
> by the same hypothesis. The rationality we gain
> in one coin we thus pay for in another; and the
> problem accordingly seems at first sight to resolve
> itself into that of getting a conception which
> will yield the largest *balance* of rationality
> rather than one which will yield perfect rational-
> ity of every description.[160]

What is important, again, is the extent to which a vision
corroborates your (educated) intentions.

At the most general levels, therefore, James reconstructs
rationality to suit a vision of inquiring men as agents, not
as spectators; to suit a vision of people as cooperative
agents attempting to domesticate the environments they
populate and depend on for maintenance. So for him, to be
rational no longer means to uncover and view an ordered world
that is already there; it means to make the environments in
which we live as ordered as possible by solving outstanding
problems that confront us (at least) intellectually,
esthetically, morally, and practically.

James's inquiry, therefore, not only calls essentialism
into question, but the sort of rationality that rides with it.
He challenges what he calls "vicious intellectualism" (and
what Toulmin has recently called 'the cult of systemati-
city')[161] that begins neither with absolute idealism nor
with scientific naturalism but

> began when Socrates and Plato taught that which a
> thing really is, is told to us by its *definition*.
> Ever since Socrates we have been told that reality
> consists of essences, not of appearances, and that
> the essences of things are known whenever we know
> their definitions. So first we identify the thing
> with a concept, and then we identify the concept
> with a definition, and only then, inasmuch as the
> thing *is* whatever the definition expresses, are we
> sure of apprehending the real essence of it or the
> full truth of it.

> So far no harm is done. The misuse of concepts
> begins with the habit of employing them privatively
> as well as positively, using them not merely to
> assign properties to things, but to deny the very
> properties with which the things sensibly present
> themselves. Logic can extract all the possible
> consequences from any definition, and the logician
> who is *unerbittlich konsequent* is often tempted,
> when he cannot extract a certain property from a
> definition, to deny that the concrete object to

> which the definition applies can possibly possess
> that property. The definition that fails to yield
> it must exclude or negate it. . . .
>
> It is but the old story, of a useful practice first
> becoming a method, then a habit, and finally a
> tyranny that defeats the end it was used for.
> Concepts, first employed to make things intel-
> ligible, are clung to even when they make them
> unintelligible.[162]

In other words, the entire mainline Western tradition from
Plato to (at least) nineteenth-century rationalism and
empiricism promulgates the belief that "our mind comes upon
a world complete in itself, and has the duty of ascertaining
its contents; but has no power of re-determining its character, for that is already given."[163]   But on James's reading
the given is simply a myth which *obstructs* our ability to act
rationally, i.e., to resolve contingent problems that undercut
our intentions as agents of community.

James is sometimes interpreted as an irrationalist
because of his claim that "life exceeds logic." He is not an
irrationalist. His attack on vicious intellectualism is an
attempt to return concepts to their useful place as instruments of arrangement by denying any of them ontological
status. It is an attempt to undercut the stilted distinction
between definitions and educated observations, or as Harman
has recently put it, between dictionary and encyclopedia
entries.[164]   In other words, he claims that concepts are
useful so long as they allow us to articulate what we observe
and predict what may occur. It is just that when someone
claims that we could not have observed what we claim to have
observed, because of the thing's *definition* or *identity*
(instead of, say, prevailing conditions), that concepts have
gone haywire, and myths of the given are born. Thus it is
that James confronts perhaps the most crucial dilemma of his
philosophical career:

> Can we, on the one hand, give up the logic of
> identity?--can we on the other, believe human
> experience to be fundamentally irrational?
> Neither is easy, yet it would seem that we
> must do one or the other.[165]

We must do one or the other, that is, on essentialist grounds.

For on essentialist ground rationality amounts to discovering
how numerically identical things relate systematically to one
another. But in James's view, "logic makes all things static.
As living, no *it* is a stark numerical unit. They all radiate
and coruscate in many directions; and the manyness is due to
the plurality round about them."[166] The historical, environmental relativity of facts, principles, and theories entire
force him to abandon the logic of identity as a *primitive* tool
for taking account of things. James feels "compelled to *give
up the logic*, fairly, squarely, and irrevocably."[167] But
notice, he does not give up logic entirely--only as "the only
usual test of rationality." He admits that the logic of
identity has significant uses:

> Each concept means a particular *kind* of thing,
> and as things seem once for all to have been
> created in kinds, a far more efficient handling
> of a given bit of experience begins as soon as
> we have classed the various parts of it. Once
> classed, a thing can be treated by the law of
> its class, and the advantages are endless. Both
> theoretically and practically this power of
> framing abstract concepts is one of the sublimest
> of our human prerogatives. We come back into
> the concrete from our journey into these abstrac-
> tions, with an increase both of vision and of
> power. It is no wonder that earlier thinkers,
> forgetting that concepts are only man-made
> extracts from the temporal flux, should have
> ended by treating them as a superior type of
> being, bright, changeless, true, divine, and
> utterly opposed in nature to the turbid, restless
> lower world. The latter then appears as but
> their corruption and falsification.[168]

But to be logical is not to be rational, inasmuch as logic
fails precisely where we need to be most rational, i.e., where
we need to transact with peculiar, novel, and extraordinary
conditions that force changes in our situations. It is in
this sense that James says that "reality ['where things
happen'], life, experience, concreteness, immediacy, use what
word you will, exceeds our logic, overflows and surrounds
it."[169] And it is for this reason that James emphatically
denies that rational behavior can be identified with logical
argument; and just as emphatically insists that rational
behavior should be construed as the admixture of reason and
faith which is evidenced in our ordinary decision-making

procedures.

Morton White has pointed to what he calls *the whole man strain* in James's work on rationality--a strain that appears as early as "The Sentiment of Rationality," and as late as *Some Problems in Philosophy*. He refers to a passage in the early essay that states:

> Pretend what we may, the whole man within us is at work when we form our philosophic opinions. Intellect, will, taste, and passion co-operate just as they do in practical affairs. . . .[170]

On the basis of this and like-meaning claims, White comments that

> The key phrase in the passage is "the whole man." When he spoke in this way, James did not wish to deny that intellectual considerations played some part in his abandonment of, say, determinism. When this strain comes to the fore in his thinking, he emphasizes that a decision to accept or reject a metaphysics is dictated by a blend of considerations that are logical, empirical, and emotional. When he is thinking along these lines, he is far from accepting the idea that a factual belief is tested by experience alone, a mathematico-logical belief by examining only the relationships between ideas, and a metaphysical belief by consulting only one's emotions.[171]

White goes on to consider relevant passages in *Pragmatism*[172] and summarizes his interpretation by saying that James was moving away

> from the notion that we test our beliefs individually in accordance with standards that are peculiar to the disciplines from which they come. He was leaning more and more towards the view that when we think we are testing an isolated belief whether metaphysical, scientific, or logical, we are really evaluating what he called a "stock of opinions" that is variously composed and subject to the demands of consistency, experience, and emotion.[173]

I agree with White's interpretation, particularly so far as metaphysical claims are concerned. I think that James's epistemology corroborates it. Further, I think James's articulation of what he called the "faith-ladder"--his last word on paradigmatic rationality--corroborates it even more emphatically. Given alternative metaphysical claims, says

James,

> One's general vision of the probable usually
> decides such alternatives. They illustrate what
> I once wrote of as the "will to believe." In
> some of my lectures at Harvard I have spoken of
> what I call the "faith-ladder," as something
> quite different from the *sorites* of the logic
> books, yet seeming to have an analogous form.
> I think you will quickly recognize in yourselves,
> as I describe it, the mental process to which I
> give this name.
>
> A conception of the world arises in you somehow,
> no matter how.
> Is it true or not? you ask.
> It *might* be true somewhere you say, for it is
> not self-contradictory.
> It *may* be true, you continue, even here and now.
> It is *fit* to be true, it would be *well if it were
> true*, it *ought* to be true, you presently feel.
> It *must* be true, something persuasive in you
> whispers in you next; and then--as a final result--
> It shall be *held for true*, you decide; it *shall be*
> as if true, for *you*.
> And your acting thus may in certain special cases
> be a means of making it securely true in the end.
> Not one step in this process is logical, yet it is
> the way that monists and pluralists alike espouse
> and hold fast to their visions. It is life
> exceeding logic, it is the practical reason for
> which the theoretic reason finds arguments after
> the conclusion is once there.[174]

Here we observe James being most self-consciously vague,
insisting that people, philosophers and all, choose to back
one set of metaphysical principles that competes with other
sets due to a "blending," as White says, of e.g., logical,
empirical, and emotional considerations: each time a person
really decides on this matter, his entire framework for
thought and action is at stake; any change at this level is
bound to rearrange and force revision in his whole "stock of
opinions." For surely *might* here has the force of logical
possibility, *may* the force of observable possibility, *fit* the
force of esthetic demand, *ought* the force of moral obligation,
must the force of pragmatic necessity--the blending of which
generates an imperative *decision*: It shall be held for true
for you.

The faith ladder is no argument in any strong sense of
the term. It does not lead from a specific set of premises

according to strict rules of inference to a conclusion that is valid relative to those premises. Its 'premises' are an indeterminate population of beliefs; its 'rules of inference' a mixture of reason (or:logic) and faith (or:conditional rules for behavior); and its 'conclusion' is, roughly, construed as the best view available for the guidance of my behavior as I attempt to interact successfully with my environments, as I view them and expect to view them. When such decisions better my ability to make environmental transactions of whatever sort, I crown myself rational. When they do not--and granting that I want to be rational--I feel compelled to review my total view, and revise it where needed.

It may be argued that James's faith-ladder admits the loosest kind of voluntarism complete with wishful thinking. It does. But the point is that it admits the most stringent sorts of criteria for belief as well. It all depends on the specification of criteria at every step. If the criteria by which we construe things as consistent, really possible, esthetically fit, emotionally compelling, and morally obligatory are rather loose criteria, then more perspicacious and strenuous thinkers are apt to call us wishful thinkers. But if, like James, we are perspicacious and strenuous in our thought, if our aim, like James's, is to preclude the sort of thought where "'you believe something that you know ain't true,'"[175] what is to keep us from developing the most puritanical ethics of belief that allow for the maintenance of only the sparest stock of opinions? Nothing.

The point is that James offers his faith-ladder as a phenomenological description of how inquiring people go about deciding what to believe and therefore how to behave: it is meant to account for the decisions of people who intend to maintain *any* degree of intellectual integrity (I do not believe it is meant to cover people who do not). James introduces this model of decision to force people to accept the conditionality of their claims, or, as he says, the ultimate inseparability of reason and faith. No matter how empirically justified or justifiable most of our beliefs are, they are bound up in the same stock or population with beliefs that "go beyond the evidence" and yet rule our behavior rather definitively. Therefore,

> In no complex matter can our conclusions be more
> than *probable*. We use our feelings, our good-
> will, in judging where the greater probability
> lies; and when our judgment is made, we practi-
> cally turn our back on the lesser probabilities
> as if they were not there. Probability, as you
> know, is mathematically expressed by a fraction.
> But seldom can we *act* fractionally--half action
> is no action (what is the use of only half killing
> your enemy?--better not touch him at all); so for
> purposes of action we equate the most probable
> view to 1 (or certainty) and other views we
> treat as not.[176]

This is not to say that the probable beliefs we transform into
certain actions need or will be maintained no matter what
conditions prevail or contingencies arise. As R. W. Beard has
pointed out, James does not divorce 'faith' from 'evidence.'[177] To the contrary, James says any of our so-called
"faith-tendencies"

> must remain a practical, and not a dogmatic
> attitude. It must go with toleration of other
> faiths, with the search for the most probable,
> and with the full consciousness of responsibil-
> ities and risks.[178]

Nonetheless, any such tendency

> may be regarded as a formative factor in the
> universe, if we be integral parts thereof, and
> co-determinants, by our behavior, of what its
> total character may be.[179]

Simply logical arguments result in *answers*. James's
faith-ladder results in *actions*. It is a thought process that
forces an exit from thought; a thought process that, to use
W. A. Clebsch's term, is *actionable* rather than *answerable*.[180]
When James insists on the part "good-will" plays in that
process, he is not aiming to allow people their wildest
fantasies; he is simply allowing people to enact their intentions. Thus it is that he says that

> the advocates of Reason's all-sufficiency can
> allow either of two courses, but not both.
> They can approve of the faith-ladder and adopt
> it, but at the same time call it an exercise of
> Reason. In this case they close the controversy
> by a verbal definition, which amounts to a mater-
> ial surrender to the opposite side.

> Or they can stick to Reason's more customary
> definition, and forbid us the faith-ladder, as
> something liable only to mislead. "Brace your-
> self against its fatal slope"; they can say;
> "wait for full evidence. Reason and facts must
> alone decide; rule good-will out; don't move
> until you're sure." But this advice is so
> obviously impossible to follow in any consid-
> erable practical or theoretical affair, and
> the rationalists themselves follow it so very
> little in their books and practice, fornicating
> as they do habitually with the unclean thing
> which they denounce, that I do not see how it
> can be seriously taken. Virtually it amounts
> to forbidding us to *live*.181

Consider each and any of your educated decisions, be it
theoretical or practical. It is James's bet that hardly one
of them was made with full understanding of its antecedent
conditions or its possible consequences. Most of the time we
"*cannot* wait but must act, somehow; so we act on the most
probable hypothesis, trusting that the event will prove us
wise."182

For these reasons James makes the claim that when we come
to judge the adequacy of a metaphysical inquiry like his own,
we must come to judge it 'on the whole' which 'whole' includes
the changes in our own behavior that would occur, were we to
accept it. To judge it on the whole means to judge it according to the faith-ladder. To accept it is to make it actionable or to elect it as a controlling set of rules for conduct.
To reject it is to behave some other way, deliberately or not.

Now James believes that there is no logical contradiction
in the notion of a salvable world, no logical contradiction in
the notion of a world that tolerates government of, by, and
for those of its constituents that are able to share intentions. And he believes that you will believe that this vision
is esthetically fit, emotionally satisfying, and ethically
appropriate. So what becomes rather crucial is that rung in
the ladder which reads, "It may be true . . . even here and
now." The sliding scale of observable possibilities--the
probability of historical actualization--becomes the controlling measure in James's project, and the focus of his attention. And as he sees it, the odds for making the salvable
world datable depend on the extent to which there *are*

constituents who could come to govern it of, by, and for
themselves. Indeed, he would like to espouse some sort of
theism because he believes that the odds for eventual salvation are pretty slim if humans are the only constituents in
the universe who are able to share intentions and therefore
forge communities. Strict humanism is *possible* on the grounds
of James's vision. It is just that if the "other factors"
"refuse to conspire, our good-will and labor may be thrown
away."[183] We humans can attempt to establish a kingdom of
ends on earth, but we do so at a risk 'no insurance company
would cover'[184] to the extent that there is nothing we can
look at which supports the belief that nonhuman people are
helping us. We must, says James,

> take one of four attitudes in regard to the
> other powers: either
> 1. Follow intellectualist advice: wait for
> evidence; and while waiting, do nothing; or
> 2. *Mistrust* the other powers and, sure that
> the universe will fail, let it fail; or
> 3. *Trust* them; and at any rate do *our* best, in
> spite of the *if*; or finally,
> 4. *Flounder*, spending one day in one attitude,
> another day in another.
> This 4th way is no systematic solution. The
> 2nd way spells faith in failure. The 1st way may
> in practice be indistinguishable from the 2d way.
> The 3d way seems the only wise way.

> "*If* we do *our* best, *and* the other powers do *their*
> best, the world will be perfected"--this propo-
> sition expresses no actual fact, but only the
> complexion of a fact thought of as eventually
> possible.[185]

A federal republic simply cannot run without presumptive faith
in its constituents *by* its constituents--without it active
cooperation dissembles. If the government of the universe is
like that of a federal republic, we humans must surely do our
best, in spite of the if, i.e., without certainty that there
are other (unseen, more powerful) agents that can do and are
doing theirs. We must provide, says James, *by our behavior*,
one of the 'premises' that would generate a salvable world.

But this is not to say that our trust needs be dogmatic.
Remember: our faith must remain practical and go with the
search for the most probable. For we can provide *only* one of
the premises; other powers must provide the rest. So James's

vision stands in need of *some* evidence, some phenomena that we
can look at, which will tend to support the claim that 'there
may be gods, even here and now.' He needs to be able to point
to some sort of phenomena that cannot be accounted for
strictly in terms of the "natural" physical and axiological
rules that govern our behavior--and that might be accounted
for in some theistic scheme. Thus he turns to chart the
phenomenology of religious belief and the varieties of
religious experience because his vision needs what he calls
distinctively "religious facts," if it is to be more plausible
than not. Without them, on his own grounds, any sort of
theism, at least, is a sham:

> *Do* the facts of natural experience force men's
> Reason, as it concretely exists, to religious
> conclusions? Certainly men having every other
> appearance of possessing Reason have been led to
> irreligious conclusions by the facts of the world.
> Men will always probably conclude diversely in
> this matter, as they have concluded diversely up
> to this hour. Some will see in moral facts a
> power that makes for righteousness, and in physical
> facts a power that geometrizes and is intellectual,
> that creates order and loves beauty. But along
> side of such facts there are contrary facts in
> abundance; and he who seeks *them* can equally well
> infer a power that defies righteousness, creates
> disorder, loves ugliness, and aims at death.
> It depends on which kind of fact you single out
> as the more essential. If your reason tries to
> be impartial, if she resorts to statistical com-
> parison and asks which class of facts tip the
> balance, and which way tends the drift, she must,
> it seems to me, conclude for irreligion, unless
> you give her more specific religious experiences
> to go by, for the last word everywhere, according
> to naturalistic science, is the word of Death,
> the death sentence passed by Nature on plant and
> beast, and man and tribe, and earth and sun, and
> everything that she has made.186

The chance of salvation therefore remains a problem which can
only be solved by examining and evaluating what people have
claimed to be distinctively religious experiences. And so it
is that James, a religious thinker, turns to a task that few
religious thinkers have attempted, the study of religion
itself.

NOTES

[1]See W. H. Walsh, *Metaphysics* (New York: Harcourt, Brace and World, Inc., 1963), especially chapters 5, 10, and 11.

[2]*Ibid.*, pp. 163-164.

[3]*Ibid.*, p. 163.

[4]*Ibid.*, p. 176.

[5]*Universe*, pp. 125-126. Cf. also *Radical Empiricism*, pp. 39-41.

[6]See *Pragmatism*, pp. 3-13; as well as *Universe*, pp. 10-11.

[7]*Pragmatism*, p. 4.

[8]*Will*, p. 118.

[9]*Radical Empiricism*, p. 170.

[10]*TC*II:469.

[11]*PP*II:661, f.n.

[12]*Universe*, p. 12.

[13]*Ibid.*, p. 13.

[14]*Ibid.*, p. 8.

[15]*Ibid.*

[16]*Problems*, p. 15. Cf. Sandra Rosenthal, "Pragmatism and Metaphysical Method," *Monist*, Vol. 52, No. 2 (April, 1973), p. 262.

[17]*Problems*, p. 142.

[18]*Pragmatism*, pp. 290-291

[19]Walsh, *op. cit.*, p. 71.

[20]*Pragmatism*, pp. 284-285.

[21]*Universe*, pp. 48-49.

[22]*Pragmatism*, pp. 286-287.

[23]*Problems*, pp. 228-229. Cf. also pp. 270-271 in *Will* for evidence that James's vision of the world was conceived after the analogy of a federal republic since his earliest writings.

[24]*Problems*, p. 229.

[25]*Pragmatism*, pp. 290-291.

[26]*Universe*, pp. 90-91. Cf. also *TC*II:763.

[27]*Pragmatism*, pp. 243-245, and *Universe*, pp. 321-322.

[28]Turner, *op. cit.*, has shown that some Victorian scientific naturalists never made any formal ontological claims at all. See, for instance, pp. 20-21.

[29]I do not know very much about Parmenides. I am approaching the problem this way because James approached the problem this way. For a brief, simple discussion of Parmenides and his problem, see W. K. C. Guthrie, *The Greek Philosophers From Thales to Aristotle* (New York: Harper and Row, 1960), pp. 46 ff.

[30]*Pragmatism*, p. 129.

[31]*Ibid.*

[32]*Universe*, p. 396.

[33]*Problems*, pp. 133-134.

[34]*Universe*, p. 48.

[35]*Pragmatism*, p. 138.

[36]*Ibid.*, p. 132.

[37]Cf. *Universe*, pp. 45-50; also, *Pragmatism*, pp. 132-149, *Problems*, pp. 115-134 and "Philosophical Conceptions," pp. 430-437 for James's specification of the sorts of unity or oneness.

[38] *Problems*, pp. 126-127.

[39] *Pragmatism*, p. 136.

[40] *Ibid.*, p. 138.

[41] *Ibid.*, p. 136.

[42] *Ibid.*, p. 141.

[43] *Ibid.*, pp. 141-142.

[44] *Ibid.*, p. 143.

[45] *Universe*, p. 396.

[46] See above, pp. 83-87.

[47] Gilbert Harman, *Thought* (Princeton: Princeton University Press, 1973), p. 105. I say "since the coming of Quine" for obvious reasons, though the point is surely debatable. In any case, see "Two Dogmas of Empiricism," in Quine's *From a Logical Point of View* (New York: Harper and Row, 1953), pp. 20-46. James *did* claim, by the way, that we can make *a priori* statements, by which he meant statements that are not generated from any *particular* experience and that cannot be assessed in terms of any particular experience. His metaphysical claims are, in this sense, *a priori*. But they are held for pragmatic reasons and can, in principle, be dropped for pragmatic reasons. Cf. L. U. Pancheri, "James, Lewis, and the Pragmatic A Priori," in *C. S. Peirce Society Transactions*, Vol. VII, No. 3, pp. 136-139, as well as Bernard P. Brennen, *The Ethics of William James* (New York: Bookman, 1961), p. 62. James's attitude toward *a priori* claims can be viewed in *Meaning*, pp. 83-84, where he says that invariant statements are simply those we *keep* invariant. We "make them 'timeless' by expressly decreeing that on *the things we mean* time shall exert no altering effect, that they are intentionally and it may be fictitiously abstracted from every corrupting real associate and condition."

[48] Harman, *op. cit.*, p. 105.

[49] *Ibid.*, p. 110.

[50] *Problems*, p. 138.

[51] *Ibid.*, p. 139.

[52] *Ibid.*, p. 138.

[53]*Universe*, p. 117.

[54]*Ibid.* Cf. also p. 194, where James says: "It is as if the characters in a novel were to get up from the pages, and walk away and transact business of their own outside of the author's story."

[55]*Ibid.*, p. 8.

[56]*Ibid.*, p. 263.

[57]*Ibid.*, p. 323.

[58]Toulmin, *op. cit.*, p. 356.

[59]*Universe*, pp. 257-258. My italics.

[60]*Pragmatism*, pp. 136-137; cf. *Radical Empiricism*, pp. 106-109.

[61]*Problems*, p. 131.

[62]Cf. *Problems*, pp. 147-152.

[63]*Pragmatism*, pp. 287-288.

[64]*Ibid.*

[65]*Problems*, p. 62. As I forewarned in my introduction, I must disclaim James's overly-simplistic summation of these views.

[66]*Will*, pp. 161-162. Notice that this is a rather dated sort of determinism. Most determinists are only committed to the thesis that investigation could, in principle, determine what occurrences have taken place. They are not committed to any theory of predetermination.

[67]*Problems*, p. 145.

[68]*Ibid.*, p. 140.

[69]Thayer, *op. cit.*, p. 427.

[70]*Ibid.*, particularly pp. 522-526.

[71]Nelson Goodman, *Fact, Fiction, and Forecast* (Indianapolis: Bobbs-Merrill, 1973).

[72] In *Will*, pp. 148-183.

[73] *Ibid.*, pp. 41-42 and pp. 51-52. Cf. also Arthur O. Lovejoy, "Pragmatism and Theology," in *The Thirteen Pragmatisms and Other Essays* (Baltimore: Johns Hopkins Press, 1963), especially pp. 72-73 for recognition of the part evil plays in James's work.

[74] *Will*, p. 147.

[75] *Ibid.*, p. 152.

[76] *Ibid.*

[77] *Ibid.*, p. 158.

[78] *Ibid.*, p. 159.

[79] *Ibid.*, p. 161.

[80] *Ibid.*

[81] *Ibid.*, p. 174.

[82] *Ibid.*, pp. 175-176.

[83] *Ibid.*, p. 158. My italics.

[84] *Ibid.*, pp. 150-151.

[85] *Ibid.*, pp. 153-154.

[86] *TC*II:748.

[87] *Will*, pp. 155-156.

[88] *Ibid.*, p. 157.

[89] *Ibid.*

[90] Some interpreters, e.g., Thayer, have not noticed this distinction, and have therefore differentiated an earlier 'tychism' from a later 'emergentism' in James's work. I believe this differentiation is incorrect.

[91] See Thayer, *op. cit.*, p. 427.

[92] *Pragmatism*, p. 282.

[93]*Ibid.*, p. 283.

[94]*Ibid.*

[95]*Ibid.*

[96]*Ibid.*, pp. 283-284.

[97]*Ibid.*, pp. 157-158.

[98]I am taking this example from Meehl and Sellars, "The Concept of Emergence," in *Minnesota Studies in the Philosophy of Science*, Vol. 1, eds. Feigl and Scriven (Minneapolis: The University of Minnesota Press, 1956), pp. 239-252.

[99]*Ibid.*

[100]See note 86 above.

[101]*Universe*, p. 397.

[102]Cf., e.g., affirmative references to panpsychism in *Radical Empiricism*, pp. 188-189; in *Universe*, Lectures V, VII, and VIII *in passim*; and *Problems*, pp. 118-119.

[103]Theodore Flournoy, *The Philosophy of William James* (New York: Henry Holt, 1917), p. 96.

[104]See Edwards's article, "Panpsychism," in the *Encyclopedia of Philosophy*, Vol. 6, pp. 22-31, especially p. 24.

[105]*Universe*, pp. 31-32.

[106]*Meaning*, p. 69.

[107]*Pragmatism*, pp. 252-253.

[108]*Universe*, p. 322.

[109]*Pragmatism*, pp. 297-298.

[110]*Ibid.*, p. 298. My italics except for "are."

[111]*Ibid.*, p. 300.

[112]Cf. *ibid.*, p. 297.

113*Problems*, p. 229.

114*Pragmatism*, p. 289.

115*Ibid.*

116*Ibid.*, p. 287.

117*Ibid.*, pp. 287-288.

118*Universe*, p. 317. James quotes an anonymous French philosopher as saying "Nous sommes du réel dans le réel."

119See Ayer's interpretation of James's radical empiricism as a reconstruction of what is phenomenally given, in *op. cit.*, pp. 310-317. D. C. Mathur interprets James as reconstructing the life-world, or the phenomenologically given world in *Naturalistic Philosophies of Experience* (St. Louis: Greer Publishing, 1971), pp. 13 ff. Wilshire claims that James was headed towards positing a transcendental reduction of phenomenological 'originals' in *op. cit., in passim*. Wild, another phenomenologist of a more existential stripe, points out that James rejected such a transcendental reduction. See *op. cit.*, pp. 159 ff.

120*Meaning*, pp. xxxvi-xxxvii.

121William James, "The Notion of Consciousness," in *The Writings of William James* (New York: Random House, 1968), ed. J. J. McDermott, pp. 191 and 194.

122*Ibid.*, p. 192.

123*Ibid.*

124*Radical Empiricism*, pp. 1-38.

125Thayer, *op. cit.*, pp. 349-350.

126John E. Smith, "Radical Empiricism," in *Themes in American Philosophy* (New York: Harper and Row, 1970), p. 31.

127*Radical Empiricism*, p. 23.

128Morris, *op. cit.*, p. 114.

129T. R. Martland, Jr., *The Metaphysics of William James and John Dewey* (New York: Philosophical Library, 1963), p. 80.

[130]*Radical Empiricism*, p. 30.

[131]J. E. Smith makes a criticism parallel to this one
when he says in *op. cit.* that James's "radical empiricism is
unable to account for triadic relations on the basis of pure
experience. These are relations in which two distinct terms,
A and B, are related to each other in virtue of the fact that
each is in turn related to the same third term C." See pp.
37-41. But this reading is based on the claim that "James
never seems to have broken away from some sort of copy-
correspondence theory." It seems to me that, if James's
radical empiricism is meant to do anything, it is meant to
construct a theory of knowledge, as James says, "without
representation"; i.e., a theory based on functional signs or
signals and not "mirror" copies.

[132]Wilshire, *op. cit.*, *in passim*.

[133]Hans Linschoten, *op. cit.*, p. 232. Cf. also R. W.
Sleeper, "Pragmatism, Religion, and 'Experienceable Difference,'" in Michael Novak, ed., *American Philosophy and the
Future* (New York: Scribner's, 1968), pp. 270-323; especially
p. 273.

[134]Linschoten, *op. cit.*, p. 248.

[135]*Radical Empiricism*, pp. 137-138.

[136]Ludwig Wittgenstein, *Philosophical Investigations*,
third English edition, eds. Anscombe and Rhees (New York:
Macmillan, 1958), p. 102e.

[137]*Meaning*, p. xxxvi.

[138]The notion of environmental transaction is usually
associated with Dewey; and Dewey does use the notion more
often than James. But see *TC*II:764 where James specifically
uses the term 'transaction' to account for epistemic behavior.

[139]*Radical Empiricism*, p. 63.

[140]*Ibid.*, p. 136.

[141]*TC*II:765.

[142]*Radical Empiricism*, p. 160.

[143]*Ibid.*, p. 161.

[144]*Ibid.*, p. 162.

[145] *Ibid.*, p. 168.

[146] *Ibid.*, p. 184 f.n.

[147] *Ibid.*, p. 175.

[148] *Ibid.*

[149] *Ibid.*

[150] *Ibid.*, p. 176

[151] *Ibid.*, p. 177.

[152] *Problems*, p. 152.

[153] *Radical Empiricism*, p. 183.

[154] Walsh, *op. cit.*, p. 169.

[155] *Ibid.*, p. 181.

[156] *Ibid.*

[157] *Ibid.*, p. 183.

[158] *Universe*, p. 113.

[159] *Ibid.*, p. 112.

[160] *Ibid.*, pp. 112-113.

[161] See Toulmin, *op. cit.*, pp. 52-85.

[162] *Universe*, pp. 218-219.

[163] *Problems*, p. 221.

[164] See Harman, *op. cit.*, p. 98.

[165] *Universe*, p. 211.

[166] *TC*II:764.

[167] *Universe*, p. 212.

[168]*Ibid.*, pp. 217-218.

[169]*Ibid.*, p. 212.

[170]Quoted in White, "Logical Positivism and the Pragmatism of William James," in White, *Pragmatism and the American Mind* (New York: Oxford University Press, 1973), pp. 117-118.

[171]*Ibid.*, p. 118.

[172]Cf., e.g., above, p. 51.

[173]White, *op. cit.*, pp. 118-119.

[174]*Universe*, pp. 328-329.

[175]*Will*, p. 29.

[176]James, "Reason and Faith," in *The Journal of Philosophy*, Vol. XXIV, No. 8 (April 14, 1927), p. 198. Hereafter cited as "Reason and Faith."

[177]See Beard's unpublished dissertation, "The Concept of Rationality in the Philosophy of William James," University of Michigan (Ann Arbor, 1972), p. 52.

[178]*Problems*, p. 225.

[179]*Ibid.*

[180]Private conversation with W. A. Clebsch.

[181]"Reason and Faith," pp. 198-199.

[182]*Problems*, p. 223.

[183]*Ibid.*, p. 229.

[184]Paraphrase of a statement in *ibid.*

[185]*Ibid.*, pp. 229-230.

[186]"Reason and Faith," p. 199.

CHAPTER IV
THE CHANCE OF SALVATION

The Science of Religions

The problem that remains outstanding for James at the end
of his metaphysical inquiry is what he calls the real possibility or "chance" of salvation. He thinks he has shown that
his salvable world meets all of the requirements of his faith-
ladder more or less adequately. The only question that
remains is just how probable salvability is, "here and now."
That depends, he thinks, on addressing the question whether
it is "probable that there is any superhuman consciousness at
all";[1] any "unseen" agents or forces or powers or conditions
cooperating with (conscious, deliberate) people here and now
to establish the sort of universal self-government that would
mean salvation. His answer concerning the probability of
"superhuman consciousness" is probably yes. "I think," he
says,

> it may be asserted that there are religious expe-
> riences of a specific nature, not deducible by
> analogy or psychological reasoning from other
> sorts of experiences. I think that they may
> point with reasonable probability to the con-
> tinuity of our consciousness with a wider
> spiritual environment from which the ordinary
> prudential man . . . is shut off.[2]

The force of "superhuman consciousness" needs, of course,
to be specified, and the key to that specification lies in the
claim that "superhuman consciousness" is a sort of consciousness "from which the ordinary prudential man . . . is shut
off." If the prudential man is the man who acts deliberately
according to prevailing norms, then "superhuman consciousness"
must be exhibited in people who do not so act. As a matter of
historical note, it should be remembered that when James
refers to "psychological reasoning," he is referring to
"psychology" as it was practiced before, say, Freud: he is
referring to *rational* psychology, or the investigation of
conscious, deliberate behavior. This is significant because,
as James sees it, "superhuman consciousness" *may* be specified

psychologically, but not on the grounds of rational psychology. "Superhuman consciousness" may be specified psychologically if psychology is meant to be the investigation of human
behavior however exhibited. In this regard, the force of
"super" is necessarily (though perhaps not sufficiently)
specified as nonrational: Again, superhuman consciousness is
exhibited in behavior which apparently is not rule-obedient.

Indeed, specifically religious experiences, according to
James, are "experiences of an unexpected life succeeding upon
death."[3] But the death and unexpected life which follows is
the death of deliberation and the unexpected fulfilment of
resolutions which comes in spite of that death. Thus James is
ready to qualify his heady claim by saying:

> By this I don't mean immortality, or the death
> of the body. I mean the deathlike termination
> of certain mental processes within the indi-
> vidual's experiences, processes that run to
> failure, and in some individuals, at least,
> eventuate in despair.[4]

These religious experiences, he says, "bring all our naturalistic standards to bankruptcy."[5] They suggest a world "wider
than either physics or philistine ethics can imagine," a
world where

> all is well, in *spite* of certain forms of death,
> indeed, *because* of certain forms of death--death
> of hope, death of strength, death of responsibil-
> ity, of fear and worry, competency and desert,
> death of everything that paganism, naturalism,
> and legalism pin their faith on and tie their
> trust to.[6]

One who has undergone such an experience, James continues, is
wont to confess that

> the tenderer parts of his personal life are con-
> tinuous with a more of the same quality which is
> operative in the universe outside of him and which
> he can keep in working touch with, and in a fash-
> ion get on board of and save himself, when all his
> lower being has gone to pieces in the wreck. In a
> word, the believer is continuous, to his own con-
> sciousness at any rate, with a wider self from
> which saving experiences flow in.[7]

Now, were it not for the fact that we have already examined
James's analysis of the self, it would be difficult to understand what sort of phenomenon James is trying to identify

here. But we have. We have seen that, as early as the
Principles, James claimed that the "self" is problematic in
that sort of circumstance where a person despairs over his
own ability to realize his intentions. It was there that
James claimed that, under these conditions, some people are
driven to pray, i.e., to effect some sort of transaction with
some unseen companion(s), which might bring about the fulfilment of their resolutions. In light of that "problem of the
self," it becomes clear what sort of experience James is
trying to identify when he talks about "religious experiences." He is trying to identify the sort of experience that
occurs when an individual 1) despairs over his own ability to
fulfil his own intentions, 2) is driven to pray, and 3)
construes himself as finding that his resolutions are being
fulfilled as a result of the transaction. *"To his own
consciousness at any rate*," a person under these conditions
believes he "is continuous . . . with a wider self from which
saving experiences flow in."[8] But notice: the force of
"wider" may be similar to that of "super." Quite simply, "to
his own consciousness" the religious experient believes that
someone else is realizing his intentions on his behalf. He
believes this to be the case because he knows that he must
consciously obey specific rules for behavior if he is to enact
relevant intentions; and he is not aware of having done so
under the circumstances. Apparently, the "self" that acts is
"wider" inasmuch as it eludes consciousness; and the "self"
that acts is "super" inasmuch as it accomplishes things which
ordinary rule-obedient behavior did not accomplish for the
person involved.

In sum, James is claiming that there is a sort of
specifically *religious* experience. He is claiming that there
is a kind of phenomenon in which people, who have actually
despaired over the possibility of satisfying their (shareable)
intentions, *find* their resolutions achieving satisfaction as a
result of operations not consciously performed by themselves.
He is claiming further that this religious kind of experience
establishes the real possibility of "co-operating forces"
existing here and now, at least for some people. He is
claiming further that, given this sort of experience, the

world is probably salvable here and now. Finally, he is
claiming that, given the probability of salvability, his
vision is plausible: Things behaving as they do, there may
be a chance of salvation.

The data for these claims--the varieties of religious
experience--were investigated, catalogued, characterized, and
evaluated about a decade before James's lectures on a pluralistic universe, in his Gifford Lectures delivered 1901-1902.
But what is chronologically prior need not be logically so;
and I suggest that *The Varieties of Religious Experience: A
Study in Human Nature* addresses a problem that only becomes
outstanding once James's psychological, epistemological, and
metaphysical positions are established. When James says (in
1906 and again in 1908) that "religious experience, strictly
and narrowly so-called, gives Reason an additional set of
facts to use. They show another possibility to Reason, and
Faith can then jump in,"[9] "Reason" refers to James and anyone
else who is attempting with him to address the question
whether there may be cooperant forces working with people to
establish a universe in which each of our resolutions might be
fulfilled; and therefore whether there might be a chance of
salvation. It is true that James's *Varieties* is an attempt to
establish--not a philosophy but--a science of religions; and
on these terms alone the work is of great significance. But
"the additional set of facts" that he wants to make available
are ones *required by his own vision*; ones that might permit us
to behave as though the world were salvable.

So in this last chapter I want to accomplish four things.
I want to examine the *method* that James uses to investigate
religious experiences, which he thinks is the method appropriate for a "Science of Religions." I want to consider the
claims that he makes about the *distinctiveness* of religious
experiences as one sort of phenomenon. I want to consider the
value he places on this sort of experience; in particular I
want to make clear how his "method" controls his evaluation
procedure. Finally, I want to reconsider the *plausibility* of
James's vision of a salvable world, once distinctively
religious experience has been added to his account of things
in the broadest sense of the term. I will do so by commenting

on the part the "will to believe" doctrine plays in James's
work.

First I must consider the matter of method. It is highly
significant, I believe, that James construed the *Varieties* as
a rudimentary work in the science of religions. We have seen
him attempting to accomplish scientific work before, and might
presume that here, as elsewhere, his "science" will be the
historiographic analysis of some distinct population or
species of phenomena. In fact, this is the case. Other
commentators have pointed out that James's method in the
Varieties is "empirical" and "phenomenological." Wild,
claiming to speak with a Jamesian tongue, says that

> if we are going to speak about religion, we must
> already have some direct acquaintance with it.
> Then, if our method is to be totally empirical,
> we must return to these original experiences,
> steep ourselves in them and find ways of verbally
> clarifying and describing them.[10]

For Wild, the force of "empiricism" is generated by "direct
acquaintance" with phenomena: He is saying that James profes-
ses to directly acquaint himself with religious experience,
become familiar with it, and find ways to articulate it. But
as Wild uses the term, "direct acquaintance" has an air of
mystery about it. We do not know whether he means some sort
of feeling or some sort of observation or what. In any case,
we might think, on Wild's interpretation, that James claimed
to feel or at least observe religious experiences. But James
does not claim anything of the sort in the *Varieties*. James
does not observe religious experiences in order to establish
his data base. He considers observation-reports about
religious experiences. And the difference is as great as the
difference in considering pain by observing people in pain and
considering pain by analyzing the reports about pain made
either by people who claim to have been in pain or by people
who claim to have witnessed others in pain. In point of fact,
James's data base is comprised of beliefs about experiences,
not of experiences pure and simple. So while his intention is
to be "scientific," his investigation labors under a condition
that might be considered rather unscientific: he trusts that
the documents under study are, in fact, phenomenologically

accurate. At least, the condition would be unscientific were
his intention to establish the characteristics of a sort of
experience by way of description alone. But again in point of
fact, James is aware of his limitation, and intends simply to
characterize what others have described as their own or still
again some other's religious experience. Thus Edie's interpretation of James's aim--"a study not of historical and
philological origins of religious symbols, but of the foundations of such meanings in consciousness itself"[11]--is not at
all helpful. Not only is it difficult to know what to make
of "foundations . . . in consciousness itself" on Jamesian
grounds; but also, the documents that James studies in the
Varieties are quite precisely historical documents. In fact,
what James does in the *Varieties* is to methodically consider
documents which report just those experiences in which
religious symbols seem to have originated. So perhaps Clebsch
comes closest to saying briefly what James is about in the
Varieties. Clebsch says that, there, James

> reached beyond simple curiosity about unusual
> religious behavior, beyond classifying or even
> typing spiritual phenomena. He charted human
> spirituality by the poles of extreme or abnormal
> behavior. Few case histories came out of his
> own empirical observation. He needed the
> starkest examples he could find in the liter-
> ature, because by mapping the extremes of their
> varied terrain he also was drawing the bound-
> aries of religiousness.[12]

I agree with Clebsch. If James's method is empirical, it is
so in the sense that he focusses on "those more developed
subjective phenomena recorded in literature produced by
articulate and fully self-conscious men, in works of piety
and autobiography,"[13] and *not* in the sense of any more direct
acquaintance. If James's method is phenomenological, it is
so in the sense (exemplified nowadays, say, by Wittgenstein,
not the so-called existential phenomenologists) that James's
primary goal is to picture the data presented in the literature, and not in the sense of establishing any "eidetic"
foundations beneath the data. In James's own words, his
lectures "are . . . a laborious attempt to extract from the
privacies [better: the published privacies] of religious

experience some general facts which can be defined in formulas upon which everybody may agree."[14]   To be able to state some general things about religious experiences based on observation-reports about them hardly establishes the "essence" of anything, at least in any strong sense of the term "essence."

So James's science of religions is not so much simply empirical or phenomenological as it is historical. He himself uses historical documents, and the procedures for study which he establishes are historiographic. James explicitly says that of two sorts of judgment that he *could* make about religious experience, "existential" and "spiritual" judgments, he is going to make mostly "existential" judgments. What are "existential" judgments according to James? They are judgments specifying "the constitution, origin, and history," of a thing.[15] Now in fact, James makes plenty of "spiritual" judgments or propositions of value concerning religious experiences as well. But the point is that the sort of phenomenon he is attempting to characterize is the sort one analyzes by way of making existential judgments: religious experiences are historical phenomena.

Why then are scholars like Edie led to claim that James is trying to establish a rather ahistorical phenomenology of religion? Well, James does say that, in terms of his method, it does no good to specify the causal origins of religious experience if one's aim is to characterize what is distinctive about religious experience and/or to evaluate religious experience. But James's interpreters have confused the problem of causal origins of religious experience with the problem of the historical origins of religions. The former problem obfuscates the characterization and evaluation of religions, on James's grounds, insofar as it entails category mistakes. The latter problem allows for the characterization and evaluation of religions, on James's grounds, insofar as religions are historical phenomena.

In fact, James applies the very same Darwinian method of analysis, employed in every other scientific investigation he has made, to the documents reporting a population of experiences people have claimed to be religious. Quite simply, he

focusses on the change and development that is reported as
having come about in the personalities of those most variant
people who claim to behave the way they do as a result of
their experiencing religious conversion. Why does he so
focus? Not because of any uneducated or educated predilection
for the "individual." Not because he simply has no interest
in "social" phenomena. But because, as he understands
religions, they are historical phenomena which, like any other
historical phenomena, are comprised through an interaction of
both innovative and selective factors. And, as he understands
religions, religious experiences make up the set of innovative
or mutant factors: they are the givens, the data, the facts
which may be either selected or neglected as fit resolutions
to a distinctively religious set of problems. He claims that
it is some religious experience(s) or another that is always
"selected," imitated, venerated, commemorated, or otherwise
socially funded, as an instance of salvation, an instance
which exhibits the possibility that each of our resolutions
might be fulfilled. The religions of ordinary religious
believers, says James, are "conventional." They have been
"made . . . by others, communicated . . . by tradition,
determined to fixed forms by imitation, and retained by
habit."[16] They are "second-hand." And,

> It would profit us little to study this second-
> hand religious life. We must make search rather
> for the original experiences which were the
> pattern-setters to all this mass of suggested
> feeling and imitated conduct.[17]

So he turns to documents reporting the experiences of religious "geniuses," people whose experiences are reported as
original and/or originative. But he does so for methodological reasons: He does so because, as he sees it, the *social*
phenomenon of religions is established when groups of people
select a variety of religious experience to imitate, or
venerate, or believe in, or whatnot. Whether James is correct
in specifying individual religious experiences as the
"spontaneous variations" of religions is an empirical matter
and somewhat besides the point, which is that James turns to
his study of "religious genius" for very specific methodological reasons.

His reasons for attacking various kinds of "reductions" of religious experience are just as specific. Remember: Darwin said that if we limit ourselves to looking at actual populations or species, we cannot specify how they are produced, for the causes of production are nonobservable. They are, he said, matters of internal molecular accident, and have no connection with the outer environment or with the historical development and/or preservation of species. We must characterize them as a population, and evaluate their ecological suitability without recourse to a specification of their molecular condition(s), because those conditions have no apparent connection with either species characteristics or ecological suitability. The same holds, according to James, for religious experiences. To "reduce" religious experience to some sort of psychological or physiological or sociological phenomenon does little to characterize or evaluate it-- particularly inasmuch as any describable human phenomenon is, on James's grounds, in some sense psychological, physiological, and sociological. To plead, for instance,

> the organic causation of a religious state of mind . . . in refutation of its claim to possess superior spiritual value, is quite illogical and arbitrary, unless one has already worked out in advance some psycho-physical theory connecting spiritual values in general with determinate sorts of physiological change. Otherwise none of our thoughts and feelings, not even our *dis*- beliefs, could retain any value as revelations of the truth, for every one of them without ex- ception flows from the state of its possessor's body at the time.[18]

To distinguish religious experience by reference to its psychological, physiological, and/or sociological origins is not to distinguish it at all. If it is to be distinguished, it will be distinguished as a pattern of (observable) behavior which is different from other such patterns.

This leads us to one last point in this section. James turns *away* from the intention to establish a *philosophy* of religion towards the intention to establish a *science* of religions because of his commitment to the nonessentialistic characterization of things made possible by Darwin's method of populational analysis. The subtitle to *Varieties* must be

underscored. It is a "study in human nature." But the nature
which is studied has, according to the student, no essence.
The nature which he studies exhibits variations, *some* of which
are distinctively religious in character. In turn, 'religion,' says James, "cannot stand for any single principle or
essence, but is rather a collective name."[19] We must, he
says, "freely admit at the outset that we may very likely find
no essence, but many characters which may alternately be
equally important to religion."[20] No matter what aspect of
religious phenomena he investigates, it appears composite.
Thus, for example, "religious sentiment" is a collective name
accounting for "a common storehouse of emotions upon which
religious objects may draw."[21] The same is the case for
religious objects and religious acts: there is "no specific
and essential kind."[22] In general:

> we are dealing with a field of experience where
> there is not a single conception that can be
> sharply drawn. The pretension, under such con-
> ditions, to be rigorously "scientific" or "exact"
> in our terms would only stamp us as lacking in
> understanding of our task. Things are more or
> less divine, states of mind are more or less
> religious, reactions are more or less total,
> but the boundaries are always misty, and it is
> everywhere a question of amount and degree.[23]

James's methodological attitude is, rather obviously,
similar to Wittgenstein's investigation of phenomena in terms
of "family resemblance."[24] As regards the question of definition, both point to a general lack of clear boundaries, both
construe things in terms of generic populations, both specify
those populations in functional terms. And for James, at
least, the *inexactness* of religions and the varieties of
religious experience is not an inexactness peculiar to those
phenomena alone; it is an inexactness that accompanies each
and every historical phenomenon, in particular, each and every
human phenomenon. For there is no "ideal type of human
character" that might be specified "apart from the utility of
his function, apart from economical considerations." To
search for something essential about human beings is as silly
as asking for a definition of the "ideal horse." Such a quest
is absurd

> so long as dragging drays and running races,
> bearing children, and jogging about with trades-
> men's packages all remain as indispensable dif-
> ferentiations of equine function. You may take
> what you call a general all-round animal as a
> compromise, but he will be inferior to any horse
> of a more specialized type, in some one particular
> direction.[25]

But just as the characteristics of equine functions *can* be determined, so the characteristics of religious phenomena can be differentiated. And the way to do that, on James's grounds, is to *look* at the phenomena people call religious, especially in its exaggerated, mutant types, to see what various functions religious experience plays in the lives of people. Those functions should become apparent, in James's view, if we focus on religious conversion, where specifically religious change and development can be witnessed, where specifically religious innovations are either selected or neglected as fitting responses to soteric problems.

Religious Facts

R. W. Sleeper has recently emphasized a point that, at this stage in our own inquiry, should be relatively obvious: either religious experiences exhibit some "experienceable difference," some distinguishable pattern of behavior, or religious experiences make no difference.[26] Equipped with Darwin's historiographic variables, James turns to documents reporting religions in the making--to documents reporting the varieties of religious experience--and attempts to character-ize them by specifying their consequences for human conduct.

"It is a good rule," James says,

> in physiology when we are studying the meaning of
> an organ to ask after its most peculiar and char-
> acteristic sort of performance, and to seek its
> office in that one of its functions which no other
> organ can possibly exert. Surely the same maxim
> holds good in our present quest. The essence of
> religious experiences, the thing by which we must
> finally judge them, must be that element which we
> can meet nowhere else. And such a quality will
> be of course most prominent and easy to notice in
> those religious experiences which are most one-
> sided, exaggerated, and intense.[27]

So we must turn to the second question that confronts us

in this last chapter: we must ask what James claims to be
distinctive about the varieties of religious experience so far
as (observable) human conduct is concerned. We must consider
what James distinguishes as the unique function(s) religious
experiences have for those who participate in them and/or
somehow take cognizance of them.

To do this, we must proceed carefully. Before we specify
"the thing by which we must finally judge" religious experience, we must "ask after its most peculiar and characteristic
sort of performance." And even before we do that, we must
remember that James is attempting to specify the difference
religious experiences makes for human conduct; and we must
call to mind the fact that James has already done a good deal
of analysis of human conduct. In particular, we must remember
that James has claimed, in *The Principles* and elsewhere, that
no analysis of human conduct is adequate which fails to
consider three distinguishable but not incompatible aspects
of 'selfhood.' In *The Principles*, James claimed that a
complete description of any person depends on the specification of his empirical, spiritual, and social selves. By that
he meant that the complete description of any instance of
human conduct must include physical, intentional, and social
specifications.

Indeed, James explicates the triadic structure of human
conduct in the *Varieties* itself. He says there that

> conduct is a relation between three terms: the
> actor, the objects for which he acts, and the
> recipients of the action. In order that conduct
> should be abstractly perfect, all these terms,
> intention, execution, and reception, should be
> suited to one another. The best intention will
> fail if it either work by false means or address
> itself to the wrong recipient. Thus no critic
> or estimator of the value of conduct can confine
> himself to the actor's animus alone, apart from
> the other elements of the performance.[28]

Quite simply, because religious experience is a kind of human
experience, it must have physical (or:physiological), intentional, and social specifications. This is significant so far
as interpretation of the *Varieties* is concerned. This is so,
because more often than not, James is criticized for focussing
on the religious behavior of individuals *at the expense* of

social religious behavior.[29]   But for James, the distinction
is false.   The religious behavior of individuals must be
social behavior (among other things), simply because the
individuals are people.

Now it *is* the case that James focusses on the conversion
experiences of individuals, and that therefore, he defines
'religion,' *"for the purposes of these lectures,"*[30] and
"arbitrarily," as *"the feelings, acts, and experiences of
individual men in their solitude, so far as they apprehend
themselves to stand in relation to whatever they may consider
the divine."*[31]   But he does so for the methodological reasons
we have reviewed.   Again, the "purpose" of the lectures is to
isolate religious facts or data; and the only way to do that
on James's grounds is to turn to the religious innovations
which set patterns of behavior for religious groups.

It is also the case that James claims that "religion" is
occupied with the questions and problems of "personal destiny."[32]   But, as we have seen now both in James's analysis of
the self and in his metaphysical inquiry, personal destinies
may be emphatically social in nature.   Indeed, as James sees
it, the entire question of destiny revolves around the problem
of the possible establishment of an adequate *socius* for my
resolutions.   It should be no surprise, then, when we come to
consider James's understanding of the social difference
religious experience makes, to find him claiming that "saints"
adapt their conduct "to the highest society conceivable,
whether that society ever be concretely possible or not."[33]

But again: it is not enough to say that the behavior of
characteristically religious people is triadic in structure.
That simply makes their behavior characteristically human.
What needs to be specified are the ways in which religious
experiences, and the patterns of behavior purportedly
generated by them, *differ* from other human experiences and
resultant patterns of behavior (which, likewise, are triadic
in structure).

The problem is that, in many ways, people who claim to
behave the way they do because they are religious or as a
result of having some religious experience or other, do not
always appear to behave differently than people who make no

religious claims at all. This problem is particularly inten-
sified when we focus on one aspect of a person's religious
profile without considering its relation to others. Thus, for
instance, James delineates three general emotional types of
religious personality (though most interpreters take note only
of the first two): Some religious individuals are "healthy-
minded";[34] some are "sick" or morbid-minded;[35] and some are
"saintly."[36] In other words, some religious people are
basically optimistic in temperament while others are basically
pessimistic while still others are basically melioristic. But
these sorts of temperament are witnessed in all sorts of
people, not just religious ones. It is only when these
temperaments are configured with other things, like certain
beliefs, certain observation-reports, certain intentions,
certain sorts of "execution," and certain "recipients" that we
are able adequately to distinguish a religious sort of behavioral pattern.

This configuration of things, according to James, is
given its most "exaggerated" testimony in documents reporting
religious conversions and conduct in the wake of those conversions. Methodologically, this should come as no surprise.
Religious conversions are the events in which religious
personalities develop, and are made or broken as pattern-
setters for social imitation, commemoration, and/or venera-
tion. But notice: According to James, not all people, not
even all religious people, are *subject* to conversion-
experiences. In particular, when a conversion occurs, the
convert must exhibit a peculiar temperament. When a conversion occurs, the convert must exhibit an emotional meliorism.
This is the case inasmuch as, characteristically, the convert
is said to experience "an uneasiness," and also "its solution":

> 1. The uneasiness, reduced to its simplest terms,
> is a sense that there is *something wrong about us*
> as we naturally stand.
>
> 2. The solution is a sense that *we are saved
> from the wrongness* by making proper connection
> with the higher powers.[37]

If the individual had a basically optimistic temperament, he might sense that some things, in some way or other, were "wrong." But he could hardly sense that "there is something wrong about us as we naturally stand," and be said to maintain his optimism. This is why James says that "the religion of healthy-mindedness," caricatured in the expressions, "I and my Father are One,"[38] and *"God is well, and so are you,"*[39] cannot represent the "completest religions," which are "essentially religions of deliverance: the man must die to an unreal life before he can be born into the real life."[40] The religious optimist is not subject to conversion as James specifies it, inasmuch as he construes his world as demanding no solution or salvation here and now.

On the other hand, if the individual had a basically pessimistic temperament, he might be said to sense some momentary satisfactions, and still maintain his outlook. But he would be in no position to sense that "we are saved" from the "wrong about us as we naturally stand." The simply sick-souled individual does not have any intention to better things, does not behave as if things could be bettered, and cannot conceive (much less try to establish) a *socius* in which his resolutions might be fulfilled. In fact, the extremely sick-souled individual, the utter "melancholiac," does not have any resolutions at all. As a person, he is a "failure."[41] Thus, James notes:

> As the healthy-minded enthusiast succeeds in
> ignoring evil's very existence, so the subject
> of melancholy is forced in spite of himself to
> ignore that of all good whatever: for him it
> may no longer have the least reality.[42]

Were you able to observe yourself as sick-souled, you would find yourself "suddenly stripped of all the emotion with which your world now inspires you":[43]

> It will be almost impossible for you to realize
> such a condition of negativity and deadness. No
> portion of the universe would then have import-
> ance beyond another; and the whole collection of
> its things and series of its events would be
> without significance, character, expression, or
> perspective.[44]

So neither pessimist nor optimist can participate in religion's "most peculiar and characteristic sort of

performance." Indeed, that performance is possible for just
one temperamental type, which James calls the "divided self"
in the *Varieties*. Now according to James, most people exhibit
divided selves. That is, most people have certain intentions
which, somehow, never seem to get realized. They know they
have those intentions, they believe it should be possible to
execute them, and yet they behave to the contrary, and they
know that they do. In the extreme, they do not do what they
think they ought to do, and do what they think they ought not
do. They are not utterly pessimistic, inasmuch as they try to
do what they ought. But they are not utterly optimistic,
inasmuch as they repeatedly fail to do what they should.
These are the people, says James, who may be led to sense
that there is something wrong about their situation, in
principle. These are the people who may be led to make
religious demands, i.e., ask (better:pray) for solution or
salvation; and these demands make sense only in case they
believe their situation is meliorable.

But again: Nonreligious people also experience "heterogeneous personalities."[45] Nonreligious people may also demand
unification or integration of their divided selves. Indeed,
nonreligious people may experience some solution or other
which effects the integration of selves they pursue. Conversion, says James,[46] is simply one sort of process of self-
unification. But it is a peculiar sort; and its peculiarity
is marked by certain beliefs or observation-reports about it,
as well as by certain psychological traits effected by it.

Based on his analysis of literature reporting religious
conversions, James believes he can "formulate the essence of
. . . religious experience in terms like these:--"

> The individual, so far as he suffers from his
> wrongness and criticizes it, is to that extent
> consciously beyond it, and in at least possible
> touch with something higher, if anything higher
> exist. Along with the wrong part there is thus
> a better part of him, even though it may be but
> a most helpless germ. With which part he should
> identify his real being is by no means obvious
> at this stage; but when stage 2 (the stage of
> solution or salvation) arrives, the man identi-
> fies his real being with the germinal higher
> part of himself; and does so in the following

way. *He becomes conscious that this higher part*
is conterminous and continuous with a more of
the same quality, which is operative in the
world outside of him, and which he can keep in
working touch with, and in a fashion get on
board of and save himself when all his lower
being has gone to pieces in the wreck.

It seems to me that all the phenomena are accurately describable in these very simple general
terms. They allow for the divided self and the
struggle; they involve the change in personal
centre and the surrender of the lower self; they
express the appearance of exteriority of the
helping power and yet account for our sense of
union with it; and they fully justify our feelings of security and joy. There is probably no
autobiographic document, among all those which
I have quoted, to which the description will not
well apply.[47]

James's language, however--and James to the contrary--is
hardly "simple." In fact, it is ambiguous enough to allow
some interpreters, most recently Strug,[48] to claim that it
belies an "underbelly" of metaphysical and epistemological
dualism. For James may be construed as saying that, in
religious conversion, the minds of heterogeneous personalities
become unified as a result of some connection with some mental
power outside of the physical part of people but continuous
with the mental part of people. To construe him so, of
course, is wrong. It is wrong, not because what he says may
not admit to this interpretation (though it may not). It is
wrong inasmuch as the construction is based on the conflation
of first-order description and analysis of the observation-
reports of others. James is saying that his "terms"
adequately describe what is reported in "autobiographical"
documents. He is not saying anything whatever about the case
itself.

James underscores his critical, second-hand role in
coming to grips with religious conversion when he comes to
summarize his "conclusions." He says:

Summing up in the broadest possible way the
characteristics of the religious life, as we
have found them, it includes the following
beliefs: --

1. That the visible world is part of a more
spiritual universe from which it draws its

chief significance;
2. That union or harmonious relation with that
higher universe is our true end;
3. That prayer or inner communion with the
spirit thereof--be that spirit "God" or "law"--
is a process wherein work is really done, and
spiritual energy flows in and produces effects,
psychological or material, within the phenomenal
world.

Religion includes also the following psychological
characteristics: --

4. A new zest which adds itself like a gift to
life, and takes the form either of lyrical en-
chantment or of appeal to earnestness and heroism.
5. An assurance of safety and a temper of peace,
and in relation to others, a preponderance of
loving affections.[49]

These are the beliefs that religious people report themselves
as holding and the psychological characteristics they are
reported as exhibiting *when* (not: because) they claim to have
experienced conversion and the solution(s) which it effects.

Lots of people may have divided selves and lots of people
may experience self-integration, but religious conversion
generates an "additional set of facts" inasmuch as these
beliefs and psychological characteristics emerge *together* only
in its condition. But this "additional set of facts" is
rather empty within further specification.

First of all, it is crucial to keep in mind that once-
divided selves, not just anybody, are said to confess these
beliefs and behave this way. In fact, some of those divided
selves are said to be extremely strenuous--making every effort
to realize their intentions which they deliberately can make--
and extremely serious--criticizing as best they can the
mistakes they have made.

Second, it is important to emphasize that these strenuous
(or: deliberate) and serious (or: critical) people are said to
find their personalities integrated *when* if not *because* they
give up deliberation and self-responsibility. Conversion
differs from many other processes of self-unification (if not
all of them) inasmuch as its "turning-point" is a kind of
"self-surrender." In fact, the "self-surrender" generated in
religious conversion distinguishes a peculiar *social*
character, a *religious* character, a pattern of social behavior

which is simply not observable under any other condition we
know of: Where the religious conversion of serious, strenuous
people is witnessed,

> Passivity, not activity; relaxation, not intent-
> ness, should now be the rule. Give up the feeling
> of responsibility, let go your hold, resign the
> care of your destiny to higher powers, be genu-
> inely indifferent as to what becomes of it all,
> and you will find not only that you gain a perfect
> inward relief, but often also, in addition, the
> particular goods you sincerely thought you were
> renouncing. This is the salvation through self-
> despair, the dying to be truly born, of Lutheran
> theology, the passage into *nothing* of which Jacob
> Behmen writes. To get it, a critical point must
> usually be passed, a corner turned within one.
> Something must give way, a native hardness must
> break down and liquefy; and this event . . . is
> frequently sudden and automatic, and leaves on
> the Subject an impression that he has been wrought
> on by an external power.

> Whatever its ultimate significance may prove to
> be, this is certainly one fundamental form of
> religious experience.[50]

James's point is that, however we evaluate such experiences,
whether it be psychologically, sociologically, theologically,
etc., documents report these distinctively religious experiences in which people behave the way they do under these
conditions of "self-surrender."

> "Man's extremity is God's opportunity" is the
> theological way of putting the fact of the need
> of self-surrender, whilst the physiological way
> of stating it would be, "Let one do all in one's
> power, and one's nervous system will do the rest."
> Both statements acknowledge the same fact.[51]

Indeed, both (physiological) psychology and (Christian)
theology

> admit that there are forces seemingly outside of
> the conscious individual that bring redemption to
> his life. Nevertheless, psychology, defining
> these forces as "subconscious," and speaking of
> these effects as due to "cerebration" or "incu-
> bation," implies that they do not transcend the
> individual's personality; and herein she diverges
> from Christian theology. . . .[52]

And no matter which account is more adequate, the converted
individual is more likely than not to express *certainty* that

the forces are indeed "other," at least cooperating with him
to realize things he was never able to realize by himself
before.

This leads us to one final qualification. James claims
that, according to the documents he has studied, the self-
surrender of serious and strenuous people in religious conversion apparently generates a sense of "well-being" on the part
of the individual in question. This sense of well-being is
purportedly unavailable to (serious and strenuous) people
under other conditions.[53] According to James, this emotional
sense of well-being disposes the religious individual to
behave at his "highest centre of energy."[54] And while he
admits that there simply are no invariant criteria in terms
of which we might verify the claim that a person is behaving
at his "highest centre of energy" (and so verify the claim
that he is exhibiting that sense of well-being), he says this
epistemic insufficiency

> must not leave us blind to the extraordinary
> momentousness of the fact of his conversion to
> the individual himself who gets converted.
> There are higher and lower limits of possibility
> set to each personal life. If a flood but goes
> above one's head, its absolute elevation becomes
> a matter of small importance; and when we touch
> our own upper limit and live in our own highest
> centre of energy, we may call ourselves saved, no
> matter how much higher someone else's centre may
> be. A small man's salvation will always be a
> great salvation and the greatest of all facts *for
> him*.[55]

This sense of well-being, where the individual construes
his conduct as "perfect" inasmuch as his intentions, executions, and recipients seem suited to one another, is the
"practically important *differentia* of religion for purposes,"
according to James. It is an emotion that has consequences
for every aspect of human conduct: physiological, psychological, and social. For the serious and strenuous individual
who both claims to feel it and exhibits it is observably
different than his unconverted counterpart. The difference,
says James, is the difference between "well-being" and "well-
doing" which can be characterized by comparing "the Christian"
and "the stoic" (note well: two *social* sorts of character):

"A life," says James,

> is manly, stoical, moral, or philosophical . . .
> in proportion as it is less swayed by paltry per-
> sonal considerations and more by objective ends
> that call for energy, even though that energy
> bring personal loss and pain. This is the good
> side of war, insofar as it calls for volunteers.
> And for morality life is a war, and the service
> of the highest is a sort of cosmic patriotism
> which also calls for volunteers. Even a sick man,
> unable to be militant outwardly, can carry on the
> moral warfare. He can willfully turn his attention
> away from his own future. . . . He can train himself
> to indifference to his present drawbacks. . . . He
> can follow public news and sympathize with other
> people's affairs. He can cultivate cheerful man-
> ners. . . . He can contemplate whatever ideal
> aspects of existence his philosophy is able to
> present to him, and practice whatever duties . . .
> his ethical system requires. . . . And yet he lacks
> something which the Christian *par excellence* . . .
> has in abundant measure, and which makes of him a
> human being of an altogether different denomination.
>
> The Christian also spurns the pinched and mumping
> sick-room attitude. . . . But whereas the merely
> moralistic spurning takes an effort of volition,
> the Christian spurning is a result of a higher kind
> of emotion, in the presence of which no exertion
> of volition is required. The moralist must hold
> his breath and keep his muscles tense; and so long
> as this athletic attitude is possible all goes
> well--morality suffices. But the athletic attitude
> tends ever to break down, and it inevitably does
> break down even in the most stalwart when the organ-
> ism begins to decay, or when morbid fears invade the
> mind. To suggest personal will and effort to one
> all sicklied o'er with the sense of irremediable
> impotence is to suggest the most impossible of things.
> What he craves is to be consoled in his very power-
> lessness, to feel that the spirit of the universe
> recognizes and secures him, all decaying and failing
> as he is. Well, we are all such helpless failures
> in the last resort. The sanest and best of us are
> of one clay with lunatics and prison inmates, and
> death finally runs the robustest of us down. And
> whenever we feel this, such a sense of the vanity
> and provisionality of our voluntary career comes
> over us that all our morality appears but a plaster
> hiding a sore it can never cure, and all our well-
> doing as the hollowest substitute for that well-
> *being* that our lives ought to be grounded in, but,
> alas, are not![56]

No matter how we specify the *causes* of religious conversion, says James, the documents catalogued in *Varieties* give

testimony to the effect that, *when* religious conversion
occurs, the convert finds his depleted sense of well-doing
displaced by a sense of well-being. And while the "moralist"
and the "religious genius" may appear to behave the same way,
the former feels exhausted as a result of his efforts and the
latter feels transported through cooperation with powers, or
forces or conditions not his own. These are the religious
facts which the documents in *Varieties* make available. Just
how to evaluate them is another question.

The Survival of the Humanly Fittest

If conversion is religion's "most peculiar and characteristic sort of performance," the peculiar sense of "well-being"
which seems to follow conversion is "that element which we can
meet nowhere else." It is "the thing we must finally judge"
religious experience by.[57] The problem confronting James is
to specify the consequences for human conduct of this emotional profile which is (purportedly) distinctively religious.
For on his grounds, the way to evaluate a distinctive pattern
of human behavior is to consider its functions and uses.

Were we able to isolate some essential characteristic of
personhood, were we able to picture the complete person,
things might be different. We would then have an invariant
standard in terms of which to measure distinctively religious
behavior. But there simply is no essential characteristic of
personhood. So we are precluded from descending "upon our
subject like Catholic theologians, with our fixed definitions
of man and man's perfection and our positive dogmas about god.
. . ."[58] As regards the evaluation of religious experience,
therefore, James says that "we"--those of us who are willing
to investigate and evaluate things on the pragmatic, historiographic lines that James suggests--

> *We* cannot divide man sharply into an animal and
> a rational part. *We* cannot distinguish natural
> from supernatural effects; nor among the latter
> know which are favors of God, and which are
> counterfeit operations of the demon. We have
> merely to collect things together without any
> special *a priori* theological system, and out of
> an aggregate of piecemeal judgments as to the
> value of this and that experience--judgments in
> which our general philosophic prejudices, our

> instincts, and our common sense are our only
> guides--decide that *on the whole* one type of
> religion is approved by its fruits, and another
> type condemned. "On the whole"--I fear we shall
> never escape complicity with that qualification,
> so dear to your practical man, so repugnant to
> your systematizer.[59]

The "whole man strain" in James is nowhere more evident.
He thinks there simply is no way to judge religious experience
save in terms of the web of belief in which he lives (and
presumably shares with his cultural fellows). In particular,
he is wary of attempts to distinguish the epistemic "truth"
of claims about religious experiences from the part those
claims play as axiological norms or guides for conduct. For

> nothing is more striking than the secular alter-
> ation that goes on in the moral and religious
> tone of men, as their insight into nature and
> their social arrangements progressively develop.
> After an interval of a few generations the mental
> climate proves unfavorable to notions of the
> deity which at an earlier date were perfectly
> satisfactory: the older gods have fallen below
> the common secular level, and can no longer be
> believed in.[60]

James is prepared to admit that his own critical stance
--roughly "the voice of human experience"[61] as *he* speaks it--
is anything but presuppositionless. Indeed, "If disbeliefs
can be said to constitute a theology, then the prejudices,
instincts, and common sense which I chose as our guides make
theological partisans of us whenever we make certain beliefs
abhorrent."[62] Quite simply, according to James,

> the gods we stand by are the gods we need and can
> use, the gods whose demands on us are reinforce-
> ments of our demands on ourselves and on one
> another. What I propose to do is, briefly stated,
> to test saintliness by common sense, to use human
> standards to help us decide how far the religious
> life commends itself as an ideal kind of human
> activity. If it commends itself, then any theo-
> logical beliefs that may inspire it in so far forth
> will stand accredited. If not, then they will be
> discredited, and all without reference to anything
> but human working principles. It is but the
> elimination of the humanly unfit, and the survival
> of the humanly fittest, applied to religious
> beliefs; and if we look at history candidly and
> without prejudice, we have to admit that no
> religion has ever in the long run established or

proved itself in any other way. Religions have
approved themselves; they have ministered to sundry
vital needs which they found reigning. When they
violated other needs too strongly, or when other
faiths came which served the same needs better,
the first religions were supplanted.[63]

Notice: it is saintliness, religious conduct in its
social aspect, which James is going to evaluate in order to
judge the fruits of religious experience. And notice as well:
his evaluation procedure is controlled by the very same
criteria he has used in other investigations. He will attempt
to isolate those religious beliefs, those religious rules for
conduct, which adequately respond to various human problems,
and most particularly, religious problems.

This "method of appreciation" should not be confused
with the "survival theory of religion" advocated by some of
James's contemporaries, who construed religious belief as "an
atavistic relapse into a mode of thought which humanity in its
more enlightened examples has outgrown."[64] For the method is
predicated, in part, on distinguishing a peculiar *religious*
problem in terms of which religious beliefs might be selected
as fitting or neglected as unsuitable. I say "in part,"
because, obviously, religious beliefs can be evaluated in
terms of a variety of standards: James realizes this. In
fact, he queries: "How is success to be absolutely measured
when there are so many environments and so many ways of
looking at the adaptation? It cannot be measured absolutely,
the verdict will vary according to the point of view
adopted."[65] For example, James says with force if amusingly
that

> from the biological point of view Saint Paul was
> a failure, because he was beheaded. Yet he was
> magnificently adapted to the larger environment
> of history; and so far as any saint's example is
> a leaven of righteousness in the world, and draws
> it in the direction of more prevalent habits of
> saintliness, he is a success, no matter what his
> immediate bad fortune may be.[66]

From the biological point of view the saints, like all of us,
fail. But from a soteric point of view, they are successful
inasmuch as they adapt their conduct "to the highest society
conceivable."[67]

Besides viewing the beliefs and concomitant activity of
religious individuals biologically and soterically, James
views them four other ways: physiologically, psychologically,
sociologically, and epistemologically. St. Paul may have been
a biological failure, because probably he could have lived
longer than he did. But characteristically, James observes,
the sense of well-being which follows religious conversion
makes for physiological success, or as Lovejoy disparagingly
put it, "biological serviceability."[68] In other words,
according to the observation-reports available to James, the
behavioral 'face' of that sense of well-being is a sort of
sensory-motor facility, an ability to do whatever is being
done with ease. The sort of thing James has in mind is well
known to many athletes. *Ad hominem*: I think the sort of ease
that James says is observed following religious conversion is
like the sort of ease I find myself exhibiting sometimes when
I am mountain-hiking. Sometimes when I hike up mountain
trails, I clench my teeth, place one foot in front of the
other, and deliberately sweat myself up the path. Other
times, I suddenly find myself halfway up an equivalent slope,
having paid no attention to my own exertion. These latter
times do not occur very often, but when they do, I am
surprised by the ease, the apparent absence of effort and
deliberation, with which I made my ascent. When I clench my
teeth, and deliberately place one foot in front of the other,
I feel resigned. I do it, because accomplishing it is my
goal. If I do it well, I have a sense of well-doing. But I
am aware of the tension between my effort and the land about
me. When I find myself somehow transported up the slope,
however, the more usual sense of well-doing is displaced by a
sense of well-being. Quite simply, my conduct seems to have
fit its environment. In each case I may end up roughly in the
same place. But I am exhausted when I think I have done well;
and I am elated when I feel as though I have been transported.
This is not to say that my backpacking experience is "religious." It is to say that, as far as I can tell, the
behavioral face of the "sense of well-being" described by
James is *like* that peculiar sort of athletic ease. And if,
says James, religious experiences generate this sort of

fitness, it may become "an essential organ of our life, performing a function which no other portion of our nature can so successfully fulfill."[69]

The psychological counterpart to this sensori-motor fitness is, according to James, a kind of happiness. Almost every document that he reads that reports religious conversion gives testimony to an extraordinary level of emotional integration, a "passionate happiness."

But if religious experiences or conversions simply generated a kind of psychophysiological integration, if they merely transformed divided selves into united ones, and were evaluated in these terms alone, their "experienceable difference" might be called into question. Other sorts of experience seem to make us happy, calm, stable, and/or fit. To go backpacking, and to experience that sense of elated transportation, is to exhibit a sort of psychophysical integrity. But it is hardly to report transactions with any divinity. And in any case, happiness, calmness, stability, physical fitness are not always construed as valuable. As James says, "What immediately feels 'good' is not always most 'true' when measured by the verdict of the rest of experience."[70] Some fanatics are apparently happy people, and from particular physiological and psychological points of view, they may be construed as 'homogeneous' personalities, but it is questionable how valuable fanatics are as social types. Naive people may also exhibit integrated personalities. But if the only kind of happiness bred in religious experience were the kind that led Marx to condemn religions as the opiate of the masses--lulling people to sleep while their social worlds disintegrated--then so much the worse for religious experience, from the standpoint of social criteria.

This, again, is why it is crucial to remember that James insists that religious conduct, as a sort of human conduct, be specified socially and evaluated as such. If we are to evaluate the sense of well-being that follows religious conversion, we must isolate the social difference which it makes. And, indeed, that is just what James does.

To begin with, the "happiness" following religious conversion is not the "relief" "occasioned by our momentary

escapes from evils either experienced or threatened."[71] It is
"no mere feeling of escape. It cares no longer to escape."[72]
It is happiness "parted off from all mere animal happiness,
all mere enjoyment of the present," by an "element of
solemnity."[73] It is happiness accompanied by the ability to
"live with energy, though energy bring pain."[74] In other
words, it is the sort of happiness found in that peculiar
social type James characterizes as the saint.

This is why James distinguishes religious experience and
its consequences from moral experience and its consequences.
Both are sorts of social performance. Both are triadic in
structure, involving intentions, executions, and recipients
(that find articulation through specific normative claims on
the actor). Indeed, both moral and religious behavior, says
James, may exhibit "solemnity" or "seriousness" or "earnestness." Both the moral agent and the religious convert can be
strenuous. But morality, says James,

> accepts the law of the whole which it finds
> reigning, so far as to acknowledge and obey it,
> but it may obey it with the heaviest and coldest
> heart, and never cease to feel it as a yoke.
> But for religion, in its strong and fully
> developed manifestations, the service of the
> highest is never felt as a yoke. Dull submission
> is left far behind, and a mood of welcome, which
> may fill any place on the scale between cheerful
> serenity and enthusiastic gladness, has taken its
> place.[75]

The difference, as we have already pointed out, is as emotionally and practically great as the difference between the
"stoic resignation to necessity" and the "passionate happiness
of Christian saints." It is as great as that "between
passivity and activity," i.e., as that between heteronomous
and autonomous behavior. But notice what James says the
documents reporting religious experiences claim: they claim
that religious experiences, in which people "let go," or stop
behaving deliberately, generate apparently autonomous
behavior, i.e., socially adequate behavior that requires no
social reinforcement. The documents claim that, as a result
of religious experiences, saints tend to do what they think
they ought "automatically," i.e., without effort. What is
more, James produces an impressively diverse catalogue of

documents reporting saintly behavior.

Following his nonessentialistic program, of course, he insists that there is no "saint-in-general." There is, rather, a population of people whose behavioral character-istics are more or less the same. Saintliness is "the collec-tive name for the ripe fruits of religion in a character."[76] A saint is characteristically described or describes himself as accommodating his conduct to the rules of an unseen, yet to be realized society; and as in transaction of some sort with some nonobservable force, or power, or condition, or agent:

> In Christian saintliness this power is always personified as God; but abstract moral ideals, civic or patriotic utopias, or inner versions of holiness or right may also be felt as the true lords and enlargers of our life. . . .[77]

A saint construes that "ideal power" as "friendly" and sur-renders "to its control." And characteristically, this transaction or condition of "prayer" results in the "mood of welcome" described above "as the outlines of confining self-hood melt down."[78] Far from being egocentric, a saint is said to experience "a shifting of the emotional centre towards loving and harmonious affections, towards 'yes! yes!' and away from 'no,' where the claims of the non-ego are concerned."[79]

In particular, a saint is likely to be rather ascetic, anonymous, self-sacrificing, and charitable. In sum and at best, they behave as though they were agents and patients of "the highest society conceivable," no matter what historical characterization such a vision takes. In general, when the loved one of such an individual dies, or when he becomes aware of how immanent his own death is, he has the capacity to keep on living and to take death as a fact of life. When he finds that events out of his control can and do disrupt his inten-tions, he has the capacity to keep on intending, and to take disruption and contingency as facts of necessity. When he is struck with the absurdity of his life, he has the capacity to keep on searching for meaning, and to make the experience of meaninglessness meaningful. When he catches himself breaking the obligations that he has as a member of his communities, he has the capacity to keep on trying to act ethically and to take his broken intentions as a fact of the ethical life. In each and all, he has the capacity to live with energy though energy bring pain--and the capacity he has he is reported as *finding*, not willing or making.

This does not mean that religious experiences only generate good fruit. Middling and bad fruit have also resulted from religious experiences. Indeed, as Clebsch paraphrases James,

> Too much devoutness produces fanaticism and intolerance and persecution. Purity unbalanced with social responsibility leads to selfish withdrawal from useful life. Excessive charity makes beggars and parasites. Extreme asceticism yields egotism and morbidity instead of the heroism which is "the moral equivalent of war."[80]

But in any case, the saint is evaluated by James as a social type. They are best or middling or bad as paradigms or exemplars of a particular sort of community action and passion. It is the saint's function in "social evolution" that is "vital and essential." It is in "social relations" that his "serviceability is exemplary." He participates in an "imaginary society," i.e., is disposed to behave as if there were "no aggressiveness, but only sympathy and fairness," on the part of each and every other person that he meets.[81] He disposes himself to others as he would to any of his "true friends." He adapts his conduct to "a millenial society," in which "his peaceful modes of appeal would be efficacious over his companions, and there would be no one extant to take advantage of his non-resistance."[82]

Such behavior may make the saint ill-adapted to the world as his nonreligious, unsaintly fellows see it. In terms of any number of standards, the saint may appear to fail. But what tends to distinguish him from his *morally* strenuous counterpart is his apparently effortless trust in the other agents and patients of community who *could* forge the kingdom of heaven on earth which he envisions. So James is convinced that

> were the world confined to . . . hard-headed, hard-hearted, and hard-fisted methods exclusively, were there no one prompt to help a brother first, and find out afterwards whether he were worthy; no one

> willing to drown his private wrongs in pity for
> the wronger's person; no one ready to be duped
> many a time rather than live always on suspicion;
> no one glad to treat individuals passionately and
> impulsively rather than by general rules of pru-
> dence; the world would be an infinitely worse place
> than it is now to live in. The tender grace, not
> of a day that is dead, but of a day yet to be born
> somehow, with the golden rule grown natural, would
> be cut out from the perspective of our imagination.[83]

If religious experience has brought in its wake naive happiness
and brutal fanaticism, it has also brought this. So, again,
while religious experience may have engendered some pretty
awful social fruit, according to James, its best fruits "are
the best things that history has to show."[84] Saints, strenuous livers with religious intentions, religious executions,
and religious recipients, have engendered "a creative social
force, tending to make real a degree of virtue" which their
vision of things alone "is ready to assume as possible."[85]
And for that, at least, religious experience makes a difference, indeed, a valuable difference.

 Notice: James has isolated a pattern of behavior which
apparently suits his own vision of a salvable world. He
thinks that the documents reporting saintly behavior may give
rise to the *presumption* (obviously, not the certainty) that
other than human forces cooperate with humans to bring about
"the better order," the "millennial society," the "federal
republic" of universal self-government, by tolerating valuable
human activity at its "highest centre of energy."

But how forceful is the presumption? Even James is not
certain. For what he needs to do is to convince other veracious people--people committed to the search for truth--of the
possibility that, here and now, there may be gods cooperating
with us in our effort to solve our outstanding problems. What
he is able to do in this respect is to offer an impressive
array of documents reporting incidents and patterns of behavior supporting the claim. He has argued that the sort of
behavior reported is of physiological, psychological, and
social value. Based on *those* sorts of value, he thinks he
has warrant to claim that

> In a general way, then, and "on the whole," our
> abandonment of theological criteria and our

> testing of religion by practical common sense
> and the empirical method, leave it in possession
> of its towering place in history. Economically,
> the saintly group of qualities is indispensable
> to the world's welfare.[86]

But there are all sorts of value. And to claim that
religious experience is valuable religiously, so far as it
responds adequately to the soteric demand that an adequate
socius be realized, valuable physiologically insofar as it
tends to make the experiencer physically fit, valuable psychologically insofar as it integrates otherwise divided personalities, and valuable sociologically insofar as it generates
one kind of exemplary behavior, *does not* make religious experience valuable in each and every respect. Indeed, the
observation-reports of religious experiences that James
analyzes may be of little value epistemologically. And it is
precisely epistemological values that must concern James if
he aims to convince veracious people that his own vision is
plausible. James knows this, and confronts the issue head-on:

> How, you say, can religion, which believes in two
> worlds and an invisible order, be estimated by
> the adaptation of its fruits to this world's order
> alone? It is its *truth*, not its utility, you
> insist, upon which our verdict ought to depend.
> If religion is true, its fruits are good fruits,
> even though in this world they should prove
> uniformly ill-adapted and full of not but pathos.
> It goes back then after all, to the question of
> the truth of theology. The plot inevitably
> thickens upon us; we cannot escape theoretical
> considerations. I propose, then, that to some
> degree we face the responsibility.[87]

By "theoretical considerations," James means, of course,
epistemological ones. He must face the responsibility of
evaluating on epistemological grounds the claims made by
religious people about their conversion experiences as well
as the philosophical claims which support the conditions that
make conversion experience a real possibility. He must do so,
that is, if he is to convince others that his own vision is
plausible.

Now the first thing that James does in this effort is to
issue a cautionary note: not every individual who reports
undergoing religion experiences claims to *know* anything

extraordinary as a result. But many do: "Religious persons
have often, though not uniformily, professed to see truth in
a special manner. That manner is known as mysticism."[88] Note
well that it is the "manner," the epistemological *how*, that is
at issue. For mystics claim to undergo experiences in which
they make, in principle, private transactions with some sort
of deity or other, which *transaction* is revelatory of the
truth. Mystics claim that these transactions are *ineffable*,
that is, not describable in words or pictures or any other
sort of sign, symbol, or signal.[89] They claim that these
experiences are "*noetic*,"[90] i.e., epistemic (but again, "of
truth unplumbed by the discursive intellect").[91] They claim
that these experiences are *transient*, i.e., that they do not
last very long. And finally, they claim that their transactions are *ecstatic*: "The mystic feels as if his own will were
in abeyance, and indeed sometimes as if he were grasped and
held by a superior power."[92] There are, of course, degrees of
mysticism and variants of mysticism--and, as usual, James
gives voice to these varieties in great detail. But the
composite picture that he develops is of a variety of religious experience that is distinctive because it is reportedly
epistemic. Every religious experience that James reads about
is to some degree or other reported as ineffable, transient,
and ecstatic. But only mystical religious experiences give
rise to truth claims.

For as a result of his or her ineffable, transient,
ecstatic experience, the mystic claims to know certain things.
Just *what* he claims to know and how he specifies what he
claims to know seem to a large extent dependent on his particular experience. In fact, mystical claims to truth are as
varied and contradictory as the decrees issued by a Polish
Diet. Even so, there seems to be a "pretty distinct theoretic
drift" to the claims; and it is the "cognitive aspects of
them, their value in the way of revelation,"[93] that James has
an interest in criticizing.

Perusing the literature, James notes that

> the kinds of truth communicable in mystical ways,
> whether these be sensible or supersensible, are
> various. Some of them relate to this world--
> visions of the future, the reading of hearts,

the sudden understanding of texts, the knowledge
of distant events, for example; but the most
important revelations are theological or meta-
physical.94

And while there is really no end to the kinds of claims that
have been made by mystics, many of those claims are

on the whole pantheistic and optimistic, or at
least the opposite of pessimistic. It is anti-
naturalistic and harmonizes best with twice-
bornness and so-called other worldly states of
mind.95

In other words, many mystics are liable to claim that there
are cooperant but nonhuman forces permeating the world; that
these forces are friendly, insuring good results; and that one
must die to this world (however "die" is specified) if one is
to be born again in the real world of cooperant forces
(however the event of new birth and however these forces are
specified).

But the question is whether mystical experience furnishes
"any warrant for the truth of the twice-bornness and super-
naturality and pantheism which it favors."96 And James's
answer is an unqualified no. It does not provide any warrant
for the *truth* of its claims. Yet it may play a certain role
as regards revisions in our total view of things. Consider
what James says:

(1) Mystical states, when well-developed, usually are, and have the right to be, absolutely
authoritative over the individuals to whom
they come.

(2) No authority emanates from them which should
make it a duty for those who stand outside of
them to accept their revelations uncritically.

(3) They break down the authority of the non-
mystical or rationalistic consciousness, based
on the understanding and the senses alone. They
show it to be only one kind of consciousness.
They open out the possibility of other orders of
truth, in which, so far as anything in us vitally
responds to them, we may freely continue to have
faith.97

Now this is a complex if well thought out answer that
needs analysis. (1) In some sense, the beliefs generated in
mystical experiences are warranted, but that sense is

psychological, not epistemological. In this respect, mystical experiences have certain parallels with pain experiences. If Mrs. Smith shrieks with pain, and tells the doctor that she is in pain, what does it matter if, in turn, the doctor tells her that he can find no pain-inducing symptoms and that her pain may be psychosomatic or illusory? It does not matter one whit. Mrs. Smith's pain may or may not be psychosomatic or illusory. It does not matter at all so far as her pain is concerned. (Obviously, it may matter as regards therapy for her pain.) It still hurts. Mrs. Smith and she alone is the final authority when it comes to feeling her own pain, because feelings are not simply a matter subject to public witness. The same is the case with mystical experience. As reported by mystics, in any case, mystical experiences are private in principle. This is why James says that

> as a matter of *psychological* fact, mystical
> states of a well-pronounced and emphatic sort
> are usually authoritative over those who have
> them. They have been "there" and know. It is
> vain for rationalism to grumble about this. If
> the mystical truth that comes to a man proves
> to be a force that he can live by, what mandate
> have we of the majority to order him to live in
> any other way? We can throw him into a prison
> or a madhouse, but we cannot change his mind--we
> commonly attach it only the more stubbornly to
> its beliefs. It mocks our utmost efforts, as a
> matter of fact, and in point of logic it abso-
> lutely escapes our jurisdiction.[98]

Mystical experiences escape our jurisdiction, that is, as people living in an epistemic community governed by the logic of *reasons*. For the mystic simply does not claim that his experience is governed by that logic. Mystical experiences are said to be "absolutely sensational in their epistemolog-ical quality--they are face to face presentations of what seems immediately to exist."[99] For the mystic, they are the experiences around which webs of belief are spun. And just because he or she does not submit to the rules of our episte-mic community does not give us cause to challenge those claims, which may be intended as *confessional*. Indeed, so far as the mystic's beliefs are confessional--so far as the mystic simply cannot help believing what he does--he is "invulnerable," just as Mrs. Smith, who cannot help feeling her own pain, is invulnerable.

(2) But that is simply another way of saying that mystical claims are *not* epistemically warranted per se; and that, as articulated in the confessional mode, they are not epistemically warranted *at all*. Epistemic warrants simply play no role in confession. Epistemic warrants--reasons-- have a role in cases where we *can* help believing one thing or another, where we are trying to decide what to believe among a population of competing beliefs. Mystics do not deal in reasons: they do not try to convince themselves or others that their beliefs are more adequate than competing ones according to normal rules of inference. So

> mystics have no right to claim that we ought to accept the deliverances of their peculiar experi- ences, if we are ourselves outsiders, and feel no private call thereto. The utmost they can ever ask of us in this life is to admit that they establish a presumption. They form a consensus and have an unequivocal outcome; and it would be odd, mystics might say, if such a unanimous type of experience should prove to be wrong altogether. At bottom, however, this would only be an appeal to numbers, like the appeal of rationalism the other way; and the appeal to numbers has no logical force. If we acknowledge it, it is for "suggestive," not for logical reasons: we follow the majority because to do so suits our life.[100]

The mystic cannot play the knowledge game if, from his point of view, there are no reasons that could change his mind about his beliefs concerning men, gods, and worlds. If we accept the mystic's claims, it is not from force of argument but from force of some other sort of persuasion. Whether the mystic claims that his experience has the epistemological status of a "sensation" or the psychological status of a subconscious conviction, he presents "no infallible credential."

(3) But this is not to say that his claims should be dismissed in principle. His claims, like any other, may be "sifted and tested, and run the gauntlet of confrontation with the total context of experience. . . . Its value must be ascertained by empirical methods so long as we are not mystics ourselves."[101] The mystic does not provide arguments that might warrant his claims which he says are generated from his transaction with some deity or other. But this neither

implies that his claims were not so generated nor implies that
his claims are necessarily false. It implies that he does not
reason. It implies that he (deliberately or not) does not
subject himself to reasonable criticism with respect to those
beliefs he is convinced he cannot help having. In fact,
mystical experiences may generate evidence of an ability to
signal events unconsciously and/or nonepistemically. In any
case, many of the claims purported to result from religious
experiences "point in directions to which the religious
sentiments of non-mystical men incline."[102]   And, if we are
not mystics ourselves, but veracious people committed to the
open search for truth, the mystics may still

> offer us *hypotheses*, hypotheses which we may
> voluntarily ignore, but which as thinkers we
> cannot possibly upset. The supernaturalism
> and optimism to which they would persuade us
> may, interpreted in one way or another, be after
> all the truest of insights into the meaning of
> life.[103]

Mystical experiences may have the force of self-evidence
for those who purportedly undergo them. But that itself is an
admission that mystics find no reason to compel others to
assent to their claims. On the other hand, there is nothing
in principle which prohibits mystics from believing what they
do or from acting accordingly. They may have the right to
believe what they do (if their beliefs are, in fact, confessional). They may believe that they have the duty to believe
what they do (if, as is characteristically the case, they
construe their mystical revelation as authoritative). And
they may ask us to try or will to believe what they do. But
their dialogue with us simply does not take place within the
logical space of reasons.

If, however, the 'self-evidence' generated in mystical
experience is worth no more than presumption so far as we
veracious people are concerned, the "necessary truths"
established by the varieties of religious philosophy are
worth less. Philosophy, says James,

> publishes results which claim to be universally
> valid if they are valid at all, so we now turn
> with our question to philosophy. Can philosophy
> stamp a warrant of veracity upon the religious

man's sense of the divine?[104]

James's answer--again, at this point in our inquiry--should
be obvious: religious philosophy cannot stamp a warrant of
veracity on its claims in any way that is "objectively
convincing."[105] For as James has argued over and over again,
the notion of necessary or essential truth is itself bankrupt,
based as it is on one variety of myth of the given or another.
Religious philosophers--who do not confess but profess truth,
or claim it with impunity--are as 'unscientific' or as
counter-investigatory as mystics. Like every other sort of
essentialist program, religious philosophy, says James,

> finds arguments for our convictions, for indeed
> it *has* to find them. It amplifies and defines
> our faith, and dignifies it and lends it words
> and plausibility. It hardly ever engenders it;
> it cannot now secure it.[106]

Indeed, the reason James turned to the varieties of religious
experience in the first place was to consider whether religious visions--particularly his own--had any basis in fact.
For

> what religion reports, you must remember, always
> purports to be a fact of experience: the divine
> is actually present, religion says, and between
> it and ourselves relations of give and take are
> actual. If definite perceptions of fact like
> this cannot stand on their own feet, surely
> abstract reasoning cannot give them the support
> they are in need of. Conceptual processes can
> class facts, define them, interpret their indi-
> viduality. There is always a *plus*, a *thisness*,
> which feeling alone can answer for. Philosophy
> in this sphere is thus a secondary function,
> unable to warrant faith's veracity, and so I
> revert to the thesis which I announced at the
> beginning of this lecture.
>
> In all sad sincerity I think we must conclude
> that the attempt to demonstrate by purely intel-
> lectual processes the truth of the deliverance
> of direct religious experience is absolutely
> hopeless.[107]

Mysticism gives rise to psychological certainty and to a
presumption of some specifiable religious observation or
other, on the part of some people, but does not give rise to
any sort of *epistemic* compulsion or authority. Religious

philosophies (or natural theologies) "only corroborate our pre-existent partialities,"[108] i.e., attempt to find reasons and theoretical supports for the beliefs generated as a result of religious experiences. So, *prima facie*, James's quest for a new set of facts seems to be rather like a wild goose chase. First he says that *without* distinctively religious facts, intellectually honest people will be epistemically compelled to assent to "irreligious" beliefs, i.e., account for what goes on in the world without reference to any kind of cooperant force or forces which might better enable people to fulfil their intentions as agents and patients of community. Then he argues that there *are* distinctively religious facts, experiences in which people are described or describe themselves as realizing certain intentions as a result of powers apparently not their own. Then he argues that these experiences may be valuable physiologically, psychologically, and sociologically, inasmuch as they tend to integrate bodies, personalities, and societies. But finally he argues that the claims made by or about religiously experienced people carry no more epistemic weight than presumption. Whatever the practical significance of these claims, they are, roughly, parallel to claims like 'I just saw a black swan': there is nothing logically impossible about them; they are conceivable given certain real conditions; if corroborated, they would force revision in our total view of things. They are presumptive: offered as something worth investigating. But they hardly convince us of their veracity *in se*. That conviction comes from "sifting and testing and running the gauntlet of confrontation with the total context of experience." If "Reason" must "conclude for irreligion, unless we give her more specific religious experiences to go by,"[109] she seems hardly bound to conclude *for* religion once she has looked at those more specific religious experiences.

But the point is that James never thought nor claimed that reason would be bound to conclude for religion once she had looked at the varieties of religious experience. To the contrary, he said:

> religious experience, strictly and narrowly so-
> called, gives Reason an additional set of facts

> to use. They show another possibility to Reason,
> and Faith then can jump in.110

Faith can then jump in, not epistemic authority or "compulsion." Religious experiences do not tip the balance for
"Reason" one way or the other. People, attending to all sorts
of fact with all sorts of reasons, motives, purposes, and
desires do that. But what the varieties of religious experience do provide is a large set of reports around which a
religious web of belief might be spun. Quite simply, a
totally religious view of things is as truncated without them
as a totally physicalistic view of things would be without
reports of physical objects. They give ballast to second-
order religious claims which, without them, come across like
"news from nowhere."

But if we are veracious people, whether we choose to
account for things in terms of some religious framework to
the exclusion of some other kind, or vice versa, or if we
choose to view some things one way, and some another, we must
indeed be sure that the claims we make are epistemically
permissible. That is what veraciousness is all about.

And according to James, religious experiences give us
epistemic permission of a sort: they offer us hypotheses that
we can investigate or "try on." For as he sees it, there is
a chance that some sort(s) of cooperant power(s) exist,
because as far as his investigations have led him, a) there
is nothing that we know for sure that precludes the possibility, and b) religious experiences may give us cause to accept
the possibility (not as fact, but as hypothesis).

Indeed, he says that "it may be that possibility and
permission of this sort are all that our religious consciousness requires to live on."111 For practical purposes--so far
as conduct is at stake--"the chance of salvation is
enough."112 For as long as we have no information that
precludes the possibility of some sort of deity, and indeed
have some kind of information that may presume it, we may
live as if there might be cooperant forces, and still be
veracious people. On James's grounds, if an individual is
intellectually honest, he may maintain his faith that there
is some sort of deity or other, so long as he does not pretend

to know that this is the case, and so long as he remains open
to the possibility that it is not the case. There is no
intellectually honest way to escape this last risk, according
to James. But then as he remarks, "no fact in human nature is
more characteristic than its willingness to live on a
chance."[113] And, indeed, James is religious enough to insist
that "the existence of the chance makes the difference . . .
between a life of which the keynote is resignation and a life
of which the keynote is hope."[114]

Possibility and Permission

Suppose, at least momentarily, that we grant James two
things. Suppose we grant him that, in light of the varieties
of religious experience, (1) it is possible to spin a religious web of belief about a distinctive set of observations
reporting deity-experiences; and (2) that, because such a web
of belief is about as coherent, practical, explanatory,
esthetically fit and morally appropriate as the others with
which it competes, it is permissible for us--as veracious
people--to adopt it as normative for our behavior. The
question may still recur: how plausible is James's own vision
of a salvable world? How plausible is James's vision of a
world that may come to be governed of, by, and for those of
its constituents who are able to share intentions?

Let me simply suggest that James's vision is about as
plausible as his vision of epistemological reality. What do
I mean? Well, in our study of James's epistemological work,
we saw that he correctly construed himself as a realist. But
his pragmatic critique of epistemic foundations made both
naive or direct and perspectival realism unacceptable,
inasmuch as the former construes things directly perceived as
given, and the latter construes things perspectively perceived as given. Nothing is given, in any strong epistemic
sense, so far as James is concerned. For him, there is no
reality that epistemologically precedes inquiry. He is (what
has come to be known as) an end-of-inquiry realist: reality is
accounted for in the corrected doxastic system of a veracious
person who finds each of his epistemic questions answered
satisfactorily and is therefore faced with no verific

alternatives. In other words, reality is simply that account
of things that would be left standing were inquiry to end due
to complete epistemic satisfaction.

Now I suggest that James's vision of a *saved* world parallels his vision of the end of inquiry, and not coincidentally
either.[115] We know from our own look at James's metaphysical
inquiries that, on his account, the world would be saved,
were our intentions as agents and patients of communities
adequately fulfilled. The parallel is not coincidental
because, again on James's account, *there is no difference so
far as behavior is concerned* between the person who has
achieved the truth and the person who adapts his behavior to
the highest society conceivable. Both would exhibit the
"perfect conduct" triadically structured by actors, intentions, and recipients. And that ultimately adequate transaction might be realized only in case the saint is serious and
the inquirer is courageous. The saint who makes demands that
his actual environments will not tolerate or who has not
adequately domesticated his surroundings is bound to inquiry.
He is bound to ask what it is in his account of things that
precludes him from successful environmental transaction. But
on James's grounds, the veracious person is no different,
inasmuch as he is committed to modifying his conduct (including his assertions) so long as verific alternatives avail.
To be serious, he must behave in ways that are guided by
norms meant to secure the sort of integration of persons and
environments that would solve his outstanding problems and
therefore save him. To be serious is to be strenuous and
vice versa, if only because to know is to have a justified
true belief based on no false suppositions; and to have that
sort of belief is to be able to behave correctly according to
rules meant to govern conduct that is simply fitting.

I suggest as well that, *like* the plausibility of James's
end-of-inquiry realism, the plausibility of what might be
called his end-of-effort soteriology depends rather heavily
on how we interpret James's understanding of "the long run of
experience," for that is the space in which he places both
epistemics and soterics. Finally, I suggest that James's
vision of salvability is melioristic in the extreme: it

depends on the assumption that things may ultimately be just
as wreckable as they are salvable. Indeed, it depends on the
assumption that we might come to know that things will
probably "shipwreck."

But before I reiterate my interpretation of James's
understanding of "the long run of experience," and before I
underscore the radical meliorism exhibited in James's vision,
let me return to the prior task abandoned momentarily. Let
me return to the questions about the possibility of spinning
religious webs of belief and about the permissibility of
adopting such webs as normative for our behavior. Let me do
so by way of interpreting James's essay, "The Will to
Believe," in the context of his work and vision as I have
presented them.

"The Will to Believe" amplifies our understanding of
James's "faith-ladder," particularly in those "certain special
cases" where acting as if a certain vision adequately
accounted for things is "a means of making it more securely
true in the end."[116] This is important with regard to the
problem of plausibility because, in fact, James construes his
own vision as one of these "certain special cases."

Stylistically, "The Will to Believe" is perhaps the most
highly orchestrated essay that James ever wrote. This is to
say that its audience, intent, and execution are all narrowly
specified. In it James addresses (young, Protestant-reared,
Ivy League) people who *could* believe certain religious hypotheses, *do not* believe those hypotheses, but can *try* to
believe them (because of their psychological condition and
the logical condition of the hypotheses). James's intent is
to defend "our right to adopt a believing attitude in religious matters, in spite of the fact that our merely logical
intellect may not have been coerced."[117] His strategy is to
argue from the procedure of scientific investigation.

Almost uniformly, critics go about interpreting "The
Will to Believe" by focussing on the specific conditions
enumerated by James as warranting "a believing attitude in
religious matters" despite a lack of logical coercion.[118]
Among these critics, some attempt to defend James's intent
and execution by pointing out how rigorous those specific

conditions are.[119]   Others attack his intent and execution by
arguing that the conditions are really never applicable.[120]
Each and every one of these critics construes James as
claiming a categorical distinction between beliefs that are
either analytically true or empirically verifiable on the one
hand and will-to-believe-beliefs on the other. This is simply
wrong; and the mistake is probably made as a result of the
focus. If any of James's essays must be analyzed entire,
"The Will to Believe" is foremost among them.

The most blatant mistake that critics make--the one that
governs the shape of "Will to Believe" criticism generally--
is to assume that when James says he is interested in defending a believing attitude that is not logically coercive, he
is simultaneously supporting the notion of (simply) logically
coercive beliefs. But both his psychology and epistemology
preclude the notion of logically or epistemologically *coercive*
belief. And even if James speaks with a kind of Kantian
tongue in this early essay,[121] the force of his argument is
as pragmatistic as any he ever delivered.

After establishing the intent of his essay, James
executes his argument in ten sections. That argument runs
as follows:

1. Certain conditions hold whenever we are in the process
of deciding which of two competing beliefs to hold. Whenever
we decide between competing beliefs, each belief is a "live
hypothesis"; each belief appeals "as a real possibility to
him to whom it is proposed."[122] The reality or "liveness"
of any such belief is relative, measured by our "willingness
to act" as if it were true. *Beliefs* are live insofar as they
guide our conduct. *Decisions* are live insofar as the options
involved *could* guide our conduct. If one or another belief
could not guide our conduct in any supposed option, then the
decision would be "dead": it would be no decision.

Decisions are "forced" if the options comprise a
"complete logical disjunction."[123] Decisions cannot be
forced unless they are live, because both options in a forced
decision must be possible choices. What distinguishes forced
live decisions from other live ones is that there is "no
possibility of not choosing" one of the two options

presented.[124] This is the case whenever not choosing either
to believe x or to believe not x is equivalent to choosing to
believe not x so far as our conduct is concerned. Thus, for
instance, "Either accept this truth or go without it,"[125] is
a forced option. All other sorts of decision are "avoidable."

Decisions are "momentous" insofar as they generate some
sort of experienceable difference. They are "trivial" insofar
as they do not. Momentous decisions are obviously live ones,
but they need not be forced. The same holds for trivial
decisions. "Momentous" and "trivial" are employed by James
as terms of relative significance or importance.[126] "Genuine"
decisions, says James, are live, forced, and momentous.[127]

2. But it is not enough to point out that our decisions
between competing beliefs are either live or dead, forced or
avoidable, momentous or trivial. Other conditions hold whenever we are deciding between beliefs. Most importantly, our
decisions are never presuppositionless: they are always made
with reference to a population of beliefs that we hold at any
given time. While our decisions may modify that population
of beliefs, the innovations which they generate do not disturb
its more durable members. If no belief is sacrosanct, many
are compelling enough to inhibit our attempts not to believe
them:

> Can we, by just willing it, believe that Abraham
> Lincoln's existence is a myth, and that the por-
> traits of him in McClure's Magazine are all of
> someone else? Can we, by any effort of our will,
> or by any strength of wish that it were true,
> believe ourselves well and about when we are
> roaring with rheumatism in bed, or feel certain
> that the sum of two one dollar-bills in our
> pocket must be a hundred dollars? We can *say*
> any of these things, but we are obviously impotent
> to believe them; and of just such things is the
> whole fabric of the truths that we do believe in
> made up,--matters of fact, immediate or remote,
> as Hume said, and relations between ideas, *which
> are either there or not there for us if we see
> them so*,[128] and which cannot be put there by any
> action of our own.[129]

Indeed, these "matters of fact" and "relations between ideas"
comprise the *live* beliefs without which *live* decisions cannot
be made: they generate the "pre-existing tendency to
believe"[130] necessary for live decisions to occur.

"The talk of believing by our volition seems, then, from one point of view, simply silly. From another point of view it is worse than silly, it is vile."[131] It is silly to try to believe something that contradicts what you take as evident. And if--like empirical scientists--you conceive of attendance to evidence as a duty, then "wishful thinking" or trying to believe something that contradicts what you take as evident may be vile. This is the reason, says James, why Clifford claims "It is wrong always, everywhere, and for everyone, to believe anything upon insufficient evidence."[132]

3. But to say that wishful thinking is at least silly and even vile according to the paramount norm of the scientific community is hardly to admit that "pure reason" settles our opinions. "Our willing nature"--"all such factors of belief as fear and hope, prejudice and passion, imitation and partisanship, the circumpressure of our caste and set"[133]-- always plays a part in our decisions between competing beliefs. Normally, "we find ourselves believing, we hardly know how or why"; and "all for no reasons worthy of the name."[134] A "mixed-up state of affairs" conditions our total views. In particular, the decision to try to believe something instead of its competition may be made, in part, in light of our belief that even trying to believe it is more valuable than trying to believe otherwise. *Pace* Pascal, an hypothesis can be construed as so potentially valuable (if, in fact, it is true) that its competition holds little interest.

4. Quite simply, it is phenomenologically the case that "our non-intellectual nature does influence our convictions."[135] And in a certain sort of instance, *if* we are to decide between competing beliefs, we must allow our willing or "passional" nature to *govern* our decision:

> The thesis I defend is, briefly stated, this:
> Our passional nature not only lawfully may, but
> must, decide an option between propositions,
> whenever it is a genuine option that cannot by
> its nature be decided on intellectual grounds;
> for to say, under such circumstances, "Do not
> decide, but leave the question open," is itself
> a passional decision,--just like deciding yes or
> no,--and is attended with the same risk of losing
> the truth.136

5. Why and for whom is this the case? It is never the case for the epistemological "absolutist" (either the absolute methodist or the absolute particularist)[137] who claims some sort of epistemic foundation or other. It may be the case for the "empiricist" who thinks that although we may attain the truth "we cannot infallibly know when."[138] The empiricist measures the epistemic value of beliefs in terms of their consequences for our conduct as veracious people--people *interested* in and desirous of searching for the truth. They admit the axiological character of their behavior *as* epistemologists.

6. Absolutists labor under the fact that "no concrete test of what is really true has ever been agreed upon."[139] Empiricists are in accord with scientific procedure and with historical fact by maintaining that each and every opinion is, in principle, "reinterpretable or corrigible."[140] While Absolutists contrive epistemic foundations to warrant our opinions,

> It matters not to an empiricist from what quarter
> an hypothesis may come to him: he may have
> acquired it by fair means or by foul; passion
> may have whispered or accident suggested it; but
> if the total drift of thinking continues to con-
> firm it, that is what he means by its being true.[141]

Thus, on empirical grounds, our passional nature may play a part in generating the truth.

7. This is not to say that empiricists go about their business without obeying specific rules of investigation or without obeying specific epistemic norms. Broadly, some construe it a duty to know the truth; whereas others construe it a duty to avoid error:

> We may regard the chase for truth as paramount,
> and the avoidance of error as secondary; or we may,
> on the other hand, treat the avoidance of error as
> more imperative, and let truth take its chance.[142]

Thinkers like Clifford[143] take the latter course. But in either case, "these feelings of our duty about either truth or error are in any case only expressions of our passional life."[144] There is no Archimedean epistemic point from which either is chosen.

8. Both commands to avoid error at any price and to know the truth at any price are undeniably axiological. But it may be that, once one or the other is established, no other "passional step" needs to be taken. In fact, says James, "In scientific questions, this is almost always the case; and even in human affairs in general, the need of acting is seldom so urgent that a false belief to act on is better than no belief at all."[145] But the "scientific questions" which ought not be answered in any way or part by our passional nature are questions addressed by "the purely judging mind,"[146] or the spectator. The questions of the scientific investigator, to the contrary, are ones that involve live, forced, and momentous options: Interest and desire inevitably play a part in the decisions of such an individual:

> The most useful investigator, because the most sensitive observer, is always he whose eager interest in one side of the question is balanced by an equally keen nervousness lest he become deceived. Science has organized this nervousness into a regular *technique*, her so-called method of verification.[147]

So James does not offer philosophical opponents very much by being willing to agree that "Wherever there is no forced option, the dispassionately judicial intellect with no pet hypothesis, saving us, as it does, from dupery at any rate, ought to be our ideal."[148]

9. Like the questions confronting the empirical investigator, "*Moral questions* immediately present themselves as questions whose solution cannot wait for sensible proof."[149] Like the investigator, the moral agent provides, by his conduct, some of the evidence that will either support or infirm the opinion he is trying to believe. The same is the case with some beliefs concerning the intentions of other people. Suppose I am trying to decide whether to believe that you like me or not. My *trying* to believe one way or the other, i.e., my behaving as though you did (or as though you did not) may influence the outcome of your behavior and therefore may influence the veracity of the options confronting me. Indeed, there are "cases where a fact cannot come at all unless a preliminary faith exists in its coming."[150] "A social organism," for instance,

> is what it is because each member proceeds to
> his own duty with a trust that the other members
> will simultaneously do theirs. Wherever a
> desired result is achieved by the co-operation
> of many independent persons, its existence as a
> fact is a pure consequence of the precursive
> faith in one another of those immediately
> concerned.151

Any hypothesis that depends on "our personal action" for
confirmation demands that we act--try to believe it, try to
behave as though it were the case--before we are sure that it
is or is not the case, even before we are reasonably sure.

10. "The religious hypothesis" depends on our personal
action for confirmation. That hypothesis says a) "that the
best things are the more eternal things";152 and b) "that we
are better off even now if we believe her first affirmation
to be true."153 Now *if* this hypothesis is live, it is forced
and momentous. It is forced inasmuch as not deciding to
assent to it is tantamount to deciding not to assent to it:

> We cannot escape the issue by remaining sceptical
> and waiting for more light, because, although we
> do avoid error in that way *if religion be untrue*,
> we lose the good, *if it be true*, just as certainly
> as if we positively chose to disbelieve. It is
> as if a man should hesitate indefinitely to ask
> a certain woman to marry him because he was not
> perfectly sure that she would prove an angel after
> he brought her home.154

The hypothesis is momentous inasmuch as even trying to believe
it may generate a distinguishable pattern of behavior (e.g.,
characteristic saintliness).

Whether to believe the religious hypothesis or not is,
then, a "living option which the intellect of the individual
cannot by itself resolve."155 It is a living option that can
only be decided by trying to believe *as well* as by not trying
to believe or trying not to believe: "In either case we *act*,
taking our life in our hands."156 The establishment of
evidence one way or the other depends on our own experiment,
so we must obviously act before the evidence is in. "Each
must act as he thinks best; and if he is wrong, so much the
worse for him."157

So runs James's "defence of our right to adopt a believing attitude in religious matters, in spite of the fact that

our merely logical intellect may not have been coerced."[158]
On this reading, at least, William James Earle is correct in
his overall assessment of the essay:

> James was making a general statement in support
> of the method of empirical science, with special
> emphasis upon the initially unwarranted character
> of every scientific hypothesis. We must at least
> believe our hypotheses sufficiently to bestir
> ourselves to test them; without our active inter-
> est in and partisanship of belief the enterprise
> of science would come to a silent, ghostly end.
> It is the theoretical daring of science which
> inspired James. His doctrine of the will to
> believe is no fuzzy *ad hoc* concession to self-
> indulgent piety but an integral part of his
> general theory of belief.[159]

And if this is the case, then many of the criticisms of
the essay are simply misplaced. Some criticisms have long
been known to be shallow. In particular, those criticisms
exemplified by Kaufmann's,[160] that construe the essay as
supportive of wishful thinking, display "a fundamental
misunderstanding of James's position."[161] As we have seen,
a simply wishful thought--"something that you know ain't
true"[162]--is, in James's terms, not even a live hypothesis.
But this criticism, precisely because it is so shallow, is
hardly noteworthy. Others are.

Ayer's interpretation and criticism of "The Will to
Believe" is significant if only because it articulates so
well what many have tried to insist: James's will-to-believe
doctrine issues criteria solely to warrant ethical or moral
claims. The doctrine, on this account, is generated from
James's "tender-mindedness,"[163] and must be distinguished
from "tough-minded" criteria which he issues to warrant
empirical and logical claims. This trichotomizing of James's
theory of belief results in equivocation:

> The fact is that James's own attitude to his assump-
> tion is equivocal. His purpose in maintaining
> that such questions as that of the existence of
> God or the objectivity of morals are not decidable
> on purely intellectual grounds is to ensure that
> certain propositions which he strongly wishes to
> believe are not put out of court by *a priori* argu-
> ment. He is determined to protect them from being
> summarily disqualified either by scientific posi-
> tivism or Hegelian dialectic. It does not appear,

> however, that he really wants to hold that these
> propositions are not susceptible to evidence. On
> the contrary, the position towards which he is
> moving is that they are subject to experimental
> tests, but that these tests are of a special
> kind. What verifies or falsifies them is their
> agreement or disagreement not with our perceptual
> but what may be broadly called our moral experi-
> ence.164

But this equivocation is read into James, not out of him. On
our reading of the essay (and of James generally), no proposition is put out of court by *a priori* arguments; any proposition either admits to evidential checks or means nothing;
each proposition is a member of a population of propositions
and competes with every other for survival.

True: For the will-to-believe doctrine to take effect, a
hypothesis must be live, and part of a forced, momentous
decision that is *ambiguous* with respect to evidence. But
Ayer displaces the ambiguity condition with a noncognitivity
condition, which makes evidence irrelevant. This seems rather
odd, given that the will-to-believe is effected in order to
generate possible evidence.

Ayer's confusion between ambiguity and noncognitivity
leads to the recognition of a more general mistake that
occurs in criticism of the will-to-believe: Many assume that
James is attempting to warrant *beliefs* under the conditions
of a genuine option. That simply is not the case: He is
attempting to warrant a *believing attitude*. He is attempting
to specify the conditions under which people who do not
believe x, but could believe x, can try to believe x, by
acting as though x were the case. Whether x is the case is
another matter. James becomes equivocal for Ayer, if only
because Ayer construes his doctrine as developed to warrant
beliefs--not believing attitudes. But that is Ayer's problem.

If Ayer misconstrues the essay because of his desire to
picture James as a classical empiricist with a tender heart,
Matson misconstrues it as an argument for the existence of
God, because of his desire to undercut James's pragmatic
theory of truth.165 Matson claims that "The Will to Believe"
argues to the thesis that theism should be accepted. But on
our reading, James argues to the thesis that whenever two

hypotheses participate in a genuine option, a veracious individual can try to believe either one. James underscores this in his preface to *The Will to Believe* where he says that, had his audience been dogmatically religious, he could and might have emphasized the other side of the option concerning the religious hypothesis.[166]

Matson claims that James's argument "is vitiated by failure to distinguish *believing what is true* from *knowing the truth*, and by a confusion of believing with deciding what to do."[167] In other words, he points out that guessing right is not the same as knowing; and that making a claim is not the same as disposing oneself in a particular way under certain conditions according to specific norms. But (a) James never supports the notion that one can know that x is the case if he only guesses that x is the case. Familiarity with his epistemological work should lead to this realization. But even in the essay under consideration, James specifically says that no hypothesis is live which is not grounded in some pre-existing tendency to believe, and by that he means, not ultimately grounded on what we take to be matters of fact. If the will-to-believe involves guessing, it is the radically educated sort of guessing that is part and parcel of scientific method. Then (b) James specifies believing in terms of behavior. Here the burden of proof is on Matson's shoulders, and he fails to carry it. He might give effective counter-examples to the contrary, but he does not. He says: "If my house is burning, my rushing into it does not by any means prove that I believe my family is inside; all it shows is that I am aware of the possibility."[168] But, on James's grounds, to be aware of a possibility is to have a kind of belief. The point is that James gives us a means to warrant the adequacy of beliefs in terms of possible dispositions. He does not even intend to give us a method by which to read out intentions or beliefs from behavior--as Matson's example suggests.

More generally, Oakes has pointed out that James presents no "argument" for the religious hypothesis.[169] Decision procedures are not arguments. Faith-ladders are explicitly not syllogisms. To infer from my current population of

beliefs to the best pragmatic stance is to deduce nothing.
The will-to-believe doctrine certifies nothing as true; it
commits individuals to test hypotheses they think may be
satisfactory in some sense--based on how they see things.
The "abstractionist," says James, "accuses the believer of
reasoning by the following syllogism":

> All good desires must be fulfilled;
> The desire to believe this proposition is a
> good desire;
> *Ergo*, this proposition must be believed.

> He substitutes this abstraction for the concrete
> state of mind of the believer, pins the naked
> absurdity of it upon him; and easily proves that
> anyone who defends him must be the greatest fool
> on earth. As if any real believer thought in
> this preposterous way, or as if any defender
> of the legitimacy of man's concrete ways of
> concluding ever used the abstract and general
> premise, "All good desires must be fulfilled."[170]

James is just such a defender, and his subject is the person
whose

> situation is as particular as that of an actress
> who resolves that it is best for her to marry
> and leave the stage, or of a priest who becomes
> secular, of a politician who abandons public
> life. What sensible man would seek to refute
> the concrete decisions of such a person by trac-
> ing them to abstract premises, such as that "all
> actresses must marry," "all clergymen must be
> laymen," "all politicians should resign their
> posts." . . . For men's real probabilities [the
> abstractionist] gives a skeletonized abstraction
> which no man was ever tempted to believe.[171]

So much for Matson's resumé of James's "argument" that

> 1. It is expedient to believe that there is a
> Deity.
> 2. But expedient belief is identical with true
> belief.
> 3. Therefore belief in a Deity is true belief.[172]

There simply is no such argument. The will-to-believe doctrine has to do with the procedures we use when we make
important decisions in the face of ambiguous evidence.

But this leads us to consider the criticisms presented
by Ferré.[173] Ferré discounts the 'wishful thinking' criticisms of the will-to-believe doctrine, does not trichotomize

James's theory of belief, and does not claim that James argues
for the existence of god. He correctly construes the essay as
a defense of a particular kind of method for a particular kind
of decision. He claims that, on James's grounds, the issue
between believers and nonbelievers--people who believe that
"the supremely valuable may be actual" and those who do not--
presents a genuine option. The evidence is ambiguous. The
option, if it is worth disputing, is living. The option is
momentous because our choice will dispose us to behave in a
distinctive way. It is forced because not to choose the
religious hypothesis is to act as if it were voided.

Indeed, Ferré goes on to point out that--again on James's
grounds--if either hypothesis is dead, or if either hypothesis
is discounted as less adequate than another, or if either
hypothesis is confirmed or infirmed sufficiently to discount
the other, then the method, the attempt to believe, cannot be
effected.[174] I think Ferré is correct in claiming that James
would have to abandon not only a hypothesis but the procedure
as well. In fact, I think the three situations articulated by
Ferré reduce to one: if either hypothesis is construed by the
individual making the decision as more adequately evident than
its competition, then either no "genuine" decision will have
to be made or--if such a decision has already been made--the
'test' effected by the attempt to believe will have become
sufficiently complete. This is only common sense. The kind
of decision that James is coming to grips with is the sort of
decision that has to be made by one who, in light of the
evidence, still finds no clear warrant to believe and behave
one way or the other. His decision affects a commitment to
behave one way and not the other. It is not an irrevocable
decision. It is not simply a mouthed assent. The one who
makes it votes with his feet, but he goes on "experiencing
and thinking [his] experience, for only thus can [his]
opinions grow more true. . . ."[175] This is the case because
he construes his decision as "reinterpretable or corrigible."[176] One vote, itself irrevocable, hardly precludes a
switch in party.

Now how in particular does "The Will to Believe" throw
light on the question of the real possibility of deity-

experiences? Well, James explicitly says that

> Since belief is measured by action, he who for-
> bids us to believe religion to be true also
> forbids us to act as we should if we did believe
> it to be true. The whole defence of religious
> faith hinges upon action. If the action required
> or inspired by the religious hypothesis is in no
> way different from that dictated by the natural-
> istic hypothesis, then religious faith is a pure
> superfluity, better pruned away, and controversy
> about its legitimacy is a piece of idle trifling,
> unworthy of serious minds.[177]

Religious hypotheses are peculiar ones to put to the test,
because of their generality, but no more nor less so than the
hypotheses which govern other interpretive schemes; e.g., the
principles of causation and uniformity which undergird
physical explanation. And just as it is possible to maintain
a coherent set of observation-reports based on these latter
rules of interpretation, so it is on the former. But no
hypothesis of whatever sort is noninfirmable. As Earle
reminds us:

> For James all genuine belief, including religious
> belief, must address itself to the tribunal of
> experiment. If all possible procedures of verifi-
> cation are irrelevant to some religious doctrine,
> then that doctrine cannot rightly be the object
> of any belief; such a doctrine, having no positive
> content, would be meaningless.[178]

The problem is that there is complexity, if not irony, in
James's assertion that the things we cannot will to believe,
the things we either *do* or *do not* believe, are those that are
"either there or not there for us if we see them so, and which
cannot be put there by any action of our own."[179] There is
complexity because on James's grounds, conceptual frames are
relative. Certainly some things we intend to be the case are
not the case and may never be the case. And certainly to say
that a thing or act or event may be described in different
ways does not imply that each way is correct. But if I *see*
that a man is demonically possessed, or if I *see* that an event
is deity-inspired, and my sight coheres suitably with everything else I believe, what method of confirmation external to
my web of belief is going to make a difference? If every
experience is experience-as, as James says it is in his essays

in radical empiricism;[180] if every experience is sorted,
e.g., observed *as* physical or *as* intentional; if experience
as *pure* is more like nothing than something, then methods of
confirmation are always internal to conceptual frames.[181]
And if this is so, it may be, as for instance, Hick claims,
"as rational for the religious man to treat his experience
of God as veridical as it is for him and others to treat their
experience of the physical world as veridical."[182]

James knows exactly what he is saying, then, when he
claims that religious hypotheses give

> to the world an expression which specifically
> determines our reactions, and makes them in a
> large part unlike what they might be on a purely
> naturalistic scheme of belief.[183]

For the religious man, the *world*--the facts of the matter,
not some interpretation of the facts nor some symbol for the
matter--looks different than does the world of the non-
believer. The rock-bottom, the sorts of things he believes
he *reacts* to, his stimuli, include unseen people or conditions
or powers or forces that do not stimulate his nonbelieving
counterpart in any way. And this is no less the case for
veracious religious people than it is for fanatics and wishful
thinkers. What separates the former from the latter so far as
the question of belief is concerned is that the former commit
themselves to search for verific alternatives; the latter do
not.

The point is that neither James's faith-ladder generally
nor that sort of faith-ladder articulated in "The Will to
Believe" *provide* real deity-experiences; they *assume* the
possibility of real deity-experiences. On James's grounds,
if the possibility is not assumable, the religious hypothesis
is dead, and there is neither motivation nor reason to try to
believe it.

Time and again I have pointed to the crucial role that
the real possibility of deity-experiences plays in James's own
vision. We have seen that, for the religiously experienced
person, gods are not taken as possibilities, but as "quasi-
sensible" realities. The task for this sort of person is to
elaborate an adequate interpretation of things in general that

will corroborate religious experiences and can compete with
other visions of things in general. The task is different
for thinkers like James who profess religious visions while
(publicly)[184] admitting no religious experience of their own.
Unlike the religiously experienced, their task is to find
experiences that support normative claims about how things in
general ought to be taken. They must isolate religious experiences that could be noticed as such by any serious-minded
person. To do that they must distinguish some pattern of
experience that *could* support religious interpretation; indeed
support religious interpretation adequately enough to infirm
the adequacy of other sorts of interpretation.

For example, James asserts that the varieties of religious experience corroborate the belief that there may be
gods, even here and now. These experiences provoke declara-
tions of religious belief including reports of divine transaction. They generate moot religious questions. They
generally fit James's own vision of the universe as a republic
of independent powers. Such experiences may and might be
accounted for in various ways: physiologically, psychologically, sociologically, and soterically. They are ambiguous
with respect to specification. But their ambiguity is not
indeterminable. They are ambiguous because they may be
accounted for in rather specific ways. And since "belief is
measured by action," so long as some veracious person is
prepared to say that one would not behave that way unless one
construed things in the broadest sense of the term as including a sort of thing that is unseen but cooperates with us as
agents and patients of communities, religious hypotheses take
part in the ambiguity. So long, for instance, as one veracious person claims that the lives of the saints catalogued by
James in *Varieties* are distinctively religious in character,
they may (but might not) be taken to support the real possibility of the deity-experiences on which they are purportedly
based.

So the questions of possibility and permission are
conceptually inseparable for James. The only people who are
asking permission to try to believe are those, like himself,
whose religious hypotheses compete with others in a genuine

option--an option in which evidence is ambiguous *because* real
possibilities are apparent both pro and con; an option where
differences in patterns of behavior are at stake; an option
where not deciding one way or the other is still decisive by
way of disposition.

Just how ambiguous does evidence have to be for a genuine
option to occur? Davis has recently suggested a specification
of the conditions of ambiguity implied by James that would
support critical lines of thought taken by Ayer and Matson.
He claims that James implies that a person has the right to
believe (note well: not try to believe) any hypothesis p,
where

> (1) No evidence is now available or ever will be
> available relative to the truth or falsity of p.
> (2) No evidence is now available relative to the
> truth or falsity of p and there will probably
> never be any.
> (3) No evidence is now available relative to the
> truth or falsity of p but at some time in the
> future evidence will probably be available.
> (4) No sufficient, adequate, coercive evidence
> is now available relative to the truth or falsity
> of p. There is only a slight preponderance of
> evidence for p over not-p (or vice-versa).
> (5) The evidence for p and against not-p is evenly
> balanced with the evidence for not-p and against
> p, i.e., the evidence for p and against not-p is
> neither stronger nor weaker than the evidence for
> not-p and against p.[185]

Davis claims that James's right to believe doctrine is correct
in all five situations. He claims that the only problematic
situation with respect to permissibility occurs in (4). He
reasons that in (1) and (5) evidence plays no part; therefore,
the intention that something be the case is sufficient. He
reasons further that in (2) and (3) evidence merely *may* play
a role; until it does, at least, the intention that something
be the case is sufficient. He qualifies (4) by suggesting
that

> the will or the passions can justifiably deter-
> mine one's choice in a situation 4-kind of forced
> option where the preponderance of evidence in
> favor of one alternative or the other is so
> slight that choosing on the basis of evidence
> gives us no better chance of making what will
> turn out to be the correct choice than choosing
> on the basis of the will or passions. . . . The

> critic is supposing that the rule 'In situation
> 4-type cases always act on the basis of whatever
> evidence you have' will in the long run lead to
> fewer errors than the rule 'In situation 4-type
> cases you may justifiably act on the basis of
> your will.' This may or may not be true.[186]

Now I suggest that Davis's interpretation is wrong. To
begin with, (1) and (2) would preclude the generation of a
genuine option, inasmuch as a hypothesis is live only in case
it is a real possibility; and inasmuch as a hypothesis is a
real possibility only in case there is evidence of some sort
to support it. The same is the case with (3), which on
James's grounds is simply an impossible situation. For there
simply is no way to forecast evidence in the future except on
the basis of evidence available in the present. (5) would not
preclude the generation of a genuine option, but is highly
implausible as stated. On James's grounds, in any case,
evidence is framework-dependent. James would need to say that
the evidence for each hypothesis is balanced where the
evidence for each is judged according to relevant criteria
for each and found to be equally compelling as a way of
construing things. How one could ever establish this is
important, but not specified by James himself.

Finally, (4) allows for a genuine option. But James's
position is (typically) misconstrued as holding that *either*
we decide on the basis of evidence *or* we decide on the basis
of will. Again, the point is that (a) no genuine option can
occur without evidence supportive of each hypothesis; and (b)
that no "intellectual" option is really ever decided without
willful support--intentions, obligations, and/or desires of
one sort or another. The "whole man" decides, based on his
total view of things--reports of observation, principles,
intentions, motivations and all.

What serves, then, as the key to both the will-to-believe
doctrine and the question of permission as it applies to that
doctrine, is James's assertion that the religious hypothesis
as he (loosely) specifies it is the sort of hypothesis that
can be confirmed solely by 'trying it out.' We are permitted
to try to believe any doctrine whose veracity depends on our
effort. We have the right to will to believe that x, when x

could only possibly be confirmed or infirmed on the basis of
our acting as if it were the case. This is as true of religious hypotheses as it is for any other sort of experimental
one, and, roughly, in the same way. And in particular, it is
true of James's own vision. For how could we ascertain
whether or not the world were salvable unless we tried to
believe that it is, and behaved accordingly? We would have
to try to believe it if, as James claims, we are among the
only constituents of the universe that could do that sort of
thing. Here, permission is not only generated from 'real
possibility' but may itself allow for increased probability,
when hypothesis is transformed into deed. This is why James
insists that a rule precluding the will to believe under the
conditions he specifies is "a rule of thinking which would
absolutely prevent me from acknowledging certain kinds of
truth if those kinds of truth were really there": in other
words, "an irrational rule."[187]

Thus, Kauber and Hare are correct when they claim that,
on James's grounds, (1) the right or permission to believe
something even in light of insufficient (but relevant)
evidence is upheld under certain conditions; that (2) the
will or attempt to believe is upheld under certain conditions;
and that, indeed, (3) the *duty* to try to believe is upheld
under certain conditions.[188] If, for instance, an individual
agrees with James that the imperative,

> We should seek incessantly, with fear and trem-
> bling, so to vote and to act as to bring about
> the very largest total universe of good that we
> can see,[189]

is an "unconditional commandment," he must agree that any
belief which tends to support that commandment must also be
upheld: As Kauber and Hare put it,

> To the extent to which we are obliged to act in
> such and such a fashion, we are similarly obliged
> to generate, if possible, the conditions which
> will enable or re-inforce the primary morally
> required act. Under the dispositional analysis,
> we have a duty, to try to believe those proposi-
> tions which will enable, or re-inforce us in our
> moral responsibilities.[190]

The same is the case for any sort of rule-obedient condition.

Thus, for instance, the scientific investigator who conceives
it his duty to seek the truth despite risk of error, may be
obliged to try to believe hypotheses which are insufficiently
warranted by evidence. He will dispose himself to specific
test conditions for those hypotheses to establish their
adequacy.

With respect to James's vision in particular, the same
may also hold. If an individual conceives of "the very
largest total universe of good" as a federal republic,
governed of, by, and for those of its constituents who are
able to share intentions, and if he conceives of himself as
committed to the realization of that universe, then he will
have a duty to try to believe any proposition which will
enable or reinforce that realization. And if, like James,
that individual intends to be veracious, he will qualify his
duty to attempt to believe by precluding any attempt that will
render him "incapable either of desiring to apprehend or of in
fact apprehending further evidence, either on the issue in
question or any other issue."[191] But note well: trying to
believe that something is the case does not in principle
preclude attendance to evidence. In fact, trying to believe
that something is the case may be among the necessary conditions supporting the attendance to evidence. Trying to
believe does not inevitably generate belief or the dispositions entailed by it; trying to believe that x may result in
recognition of the inadequacy of belief that x.

Kauber and Hare therefore point out that the issues
presented in "The Will to Believe" boil down to possible
conflicts between James's two claims, (1) that as truth
seekers we have a duty to attend to evidence, and (2) that
as agents of communities we have a right to try to believe
hypotheses which enable or reinforce the obedience to rules
that govern our behavior as community members.[192] And with
this possible conflict we come face to face with problems
concerning the relationship between epistemic welfare and
welfare in general.

The problem is that there is nothing in principle which
precludes conflict between social and epistemic norms, much
less conflict between a person's *commitment* to social rules

and regulations and a person's commitment to search for verific alternatives. In particular, there is nothing in principle which precludes conflict between attempting to realize James's "total universe of good" and trying to know what is true. And if there are times when James assumes that to live strenuously is to think seriously and vice versa, it is right to wonder whether he then slips into the sort of unguarded optimism exhibited by some of his post-Hegelian contemporaries.[193]

The point, however, is to remember just how logarithmic the conditionality of James's vision is. Certainly, James's *paradigmatic* truth-achiever and his *paradigmatic* citizen of the universe behave the same way, inasmuch as the former exhibits the most active thought conceivable and the latter exhibits the most thoughtful action conceivable: both behave in ways that are simply fitting. But whether anybody is actually choosing verific alternatives each time they become available is always a possibility and never a certainty on James's grounds. And whether anybody is behaving according to simply fitting norms is just as possible and just as uncertain. Indeed, on James's grounds, we *may* come to know that it makes more sense to think of our communities of shared intention as ending in shipwreck than it does to think of the universe as approaching salvation. For the conditions which support James's vision of a salvable world also support a vision of a wreckable one. On James's grounds, what *may* be bettered, *may* also be worsened. In other words, part and parcel of his vision, as van Buren has pointed out, is the "metaphysical risk" of failure.[194] This sort of risk is neither the risk of individuals failing to make good on their resolutions nor the risk of individuals failing to exchange false beliefs for truer ones. It is the risk that our epistemic welfare and our welfare in general may be simply at odds with one another.

For as we saw early on, there is nothing inevitable about the "long run of experience" so far as James is concerned. In order to know whether our resolutions *could* be fulfilled, we would have to establish their adequacy as guides for environmental transaction, and though we might know this, "we cannot

infallibly know when," for "no bell in us tolls to let us know
for certain when truth is in our grasp."[195]

Indeed, James's attitude towards his own vision is
characteristically tentative. For him, there is a chance that
truth might be attained; there is a chance that each constituent who is able to share intentions might dispose himself to
that truth, so there is a chance of salvation, but only a
chance.

How plausible is James's vision? It still depends on
whether you, as a veracious person attending and adhering to
evidence, construe yourself as *permitted* to try to believe
that, even here and now, there may be unseen powers or conditions or forces or persons that tolerate if not satisfy your
resolutions as an agent and patient of various communities.
If you construe that hypothesis as no real possibility, it is
dead for you, and James's vision is no option. If, like
James, you have investigated the varieties of religious experience and find it *possible* to construe some events as
instances of divine transaction, then *ipso facto*, James's
vision is live and holds some plausibility for you. If, then,
you accept James's claim that the evidence supporting his
vision is incomplete unless and until each of us tries to act
as though it were true, you must "trust [the other powers];
and at any rate do [your] best, in spite of the *if*." You must
deal with James's claims "as hypotheses, testing them in all
the same manners, whether negative or positive, by which
hypotheses are ever tested."[196] You must keep "religion in
connection with the rest of science," and "renounce the
ambition to be coercive" in your arguments.[197] If you follow
James's lead, you may try to believe his hypothesis so long as
it remains "something that may fit the facts so easily that
your scientific logic will find no plausible pretext for
vetoing your impulse."[198] When and if it no longer fits those
facts with ease, your experiment will have come to an end: you
will be bound to try to believe other options.

As far as James himself was concerned, the documents
exhibited in *Varieties* were persuasive enough to generate the
presumption that divine transactions may occur. However the
conditions supporting religious experiences are specified,

those experiences are "literally and objectively true as far
as it goes": some people who have lost the ability to deliberately realize their intentions find those intentions realized
anyway. However the conditions for this sort of phenomena are
specified, they are *effectively* cooperative, if only in the
loose sense in which clay may be said to cooperate with a
potter, by suiting his intentions.

On the presumption that divine transactions may occur,
James himself tries or wills to believe that, indeed, there
are gods who cooperate with us somehow on purpose. He commits
himself to this over-belief or hypothesis. Whether his
attempt to believe is successful, whether he not only tries to
behave as if there were gods, but actually is able to behave
that way is something that he never admits. For on his
grounds, the admission could only occur when the hypothesis
became sufficiently warranted as evident which, on his
grounds, it is not. The hypothesis could only become sufficiently warranted were enough people to dispose themselves to
it successfully. And the only measure of success would be the
extent to which our resolutions were fulfilled, despite or
even in light of our own inability to fulfil them.

In the end, therefore, the question of the plausibility
of James's vision becomes utterly empirical: the evidence
relating to apparently religious experiences must admit to
some interpretation(s) which corroborate the hypothesis that
things in general support our best efforts. If that hypothesis has evidential support, there is nothing prohibiting a
veracious person from trying to believe it, for there is
nothing in principle about the hypothesis that precludes our
adherence to evidence. Whether or not the hypothesis has
evidential support is, however, a matter of observation which
I, in my office as philosopher, simply cannot answer.

[1] *Universe*, p. 295.

[2] *Ibid.*, pp. 299-300.

[3] *Ibid.*, p. 303.

[4] *Ibid.*

[5] *Ibid.*, p. 304.

[6] *Ibid.*, pp. 305-306.

[7] *Ibid.*, p. 307.

[8] *Ibid.*

[9] "Reason and Faith," p. 200; cf. *Universe*, pp. 306-330.

[10] Wild, *op. cit.*, p. 294.

[11] James M. Edie, "William James and the Phenomenology of Religious Experience," in Novak, ed., *op. cit.*, p. 250.

[12] William A. Clebsch, *op. cit.*, p. 151.

[13] *Varieties*, p. 4.

[14] *Ibid.*, p. 423.

[15] *Ibid.*, p. 6.

[16] *Ibid.*, p. 8.

[17] *Ibid.*

[18] *Ibid.*, pp. 15-16.

[19] *Ibid.*, p. 27.

[20] *Ibid.*

[21] *Ibid.*, p. 29.

[22]*Ibid.*

[23]*Ibid.*, p. 39.

[24]Cf. Wittgenstein, *op. cit.*, pp. 31e-34e.

[25]*Varieties*, pp. 365-366.

[26]Cf. R. W. Sleeper in Novak, *op. cit.*, pp. 270-323.

[27]*Varieties*, p. 45.

[28]*Ibid.*, p. 347.

[29]Cf., for instance, the influential claims to that effect made by Royce in his essay, "William James and the Philosophy of Life," in *William James and Other Essays*, pp. 1-45; as well as the claim made by Perry, *TC*II:322-327.

[30]*Varieties*, p. 29.

[31]*Ibid.*, pp. 31-32.

[32]*Ibid.*, p. 493.

[33]*Ibid.*, p. 366.

[34]*Ibid.*, cf. Lectures IV and V.

[35]*Ibid.*, cf. Lectures VI and VII.

[36]*Ibid.*, cf. Lectures XI, XII, and XIII.

[37]*Ibid.*, p. 498.

[38]*Ibid.*, p. 100.

[39]*Ibid.*, p. 106.

[40]*Ibid.*, p. 162.

[41]*Ibid.*, p. 135.

[42]*Ibid.*, p. 142.

[43]*Ibid.*, p. 147.

44 *Ibid.*

45 *Ibid.*, p. 166.

46 *Ibid.*, cf. p. 172.

47 *Ibid.*, pp. 498-499.

48 See Cordell Strug, "Seraph, Snake, and Saint: The Subconscious Mind in James's *Varieties*," in *The Journal of the American Academy of Religion*, Vol. XLII, No. 3 (Sept., 1974), pp. 505-515.

49 *Varieties*, pp. 475-476.

50 *Ibid.*, p. 108.

51 *Ibid.*, p. 206.

52 *Ibid.*, p. 207.

53 James makes the distinction between well-being and well-doing elsewhere and prior to the *Varieties*. Cf., in particular, his introduction to *The Literary Remains of the Late Henry James*, intro. William James (1884; rpt. 1970, Upper Saddle River, N.J.), pp. 117-119.

54 *Varieties*, p. 234.

55 *Ibid.*

56 *Ibid.*, pp. 45-47.

57 *Varieties*, p. 45.

58 *Ibid.*, p. 320.

59 *Ibid.*, p. 321.

60 *Ibid.*, p. 322.

61 *Ibid.*, p. 324.

62 *Ibid.*, p. 322.

63 *Ibid.*, pp. 324-325.

64 *Ibid.*, p. 488.

[65]*Ibid.*, p. 367.

[66]*Ibid.*

[67]*Ibid.*, p. 366.

[68]Lovejoy, *op. cit.*, p. 27.

[69]*Varieties*, p. 51.

[70]*Ibid.*, p. 17.

[71]*Ibid.*, p. 48.

[72]*Ibid.*

[73]*Ibid.*

[74]*Ibid.*, p. 258.

[75]*Ibid.*, p. 41.

[76]*Ibid.*, p. 266.

[77]*Ibid.*, pp. 266-267.

[78]*Ibid.*, *inter alia*, Lectures XIV and XV.

[79]*Ibid.*

[80]Clebsch, *op. cit.*, p. 156.

[81]*Varieties*, p. 350 and pp. 361-362.

[82]*Ibid.*, pp. 361-362.

[83]*Ibid.*, p. 348.

[84]*Ibid.*, p. 254.

[85]*Ibid.*, p. 349.

[86]*Ibid.*, p. 368.

[87]*Ibid.*, pp. 368-369.

[88]*Ibid.*, p. 369.

[89]*Ibid.*, p. 371.

[90]*Ibid.*

[91]*Ibid.*

[92]*Ibid.*, p. 372.

[93]*Ibid.*, p. 399.

[94]*Ibid.*, p. 401.

[95]*Ibid.*, p. 413.

[96]*Ibid.*

[97]*Ibid.*, p. 414.

[98]*Ibid.*, pp. 414-415. My italics.

[99]*Ibid.*, p. 415.

[100]*Ibid.*

[101]*Ibid.*, pp. 417-418.

[102]*Ibid.*, p. 419.

[103]*Ibid.*, pp. 419-420.

[104]*Ibid.*, p. 421.

[105]*Ibid.*, p. 426.

[106]*Ibid.*, p. 427.

[107]*Ibid.*, p. 445.

[108]*Ibid.*, p. 423.

[109]"Reason and Faith," p. 199.

[110]*Ibid.*, p. 200.

[111]*Varieties*, p. 420.

[112]*Ibid.*, p. 516.

[113]*Ibid.*

[114]*Ibid.*

[115]Bixler claims that there is a conflict in James's religious thought. He says that both "auto-soteric" and "hetero-soteric" strains can be distinguished, where the former is "humanistic, seeking salvation through its own effort," and the latter is "more mystical, reaching out for help from a higher Power. . . ." To generate this "conflict," a critic would have to assume that James maintains the sort of metaphysical dualism in his religious thought that I argue he does not. On my reading, salvation would occur--for James-- were certain conditions satisfied, only some of which *could* be satisfied by human effort. Cf. J. S. Bixler, *Religion in the Philosophy of William James* (Boston: Marshall Jones Co., 1926), p. 16 f.

[116]*Universe*, p. 329.

[117]*Will*, pp. 1-2.

[118]There is probably no more celebrated--and no more criticized--essay written by an American philosopher. The references that follow are those I consider helpful and/or representative criticisms.

[119]Perhaps the classic statement of this strategy occurs in Perry, *Spirit*, pp. 170-208. But see also Frederick Ferré, *Basic Modern Philosophy of Religion* (New York: Scribner's, 1967), pp. 284-291; Patrick K. Dooley, "The Nature of Belief: The Proper Context for James' 'The Will to Believe,'" *C. S. Peirce Society Transactions*, Vol. 8, No. 2 (1972); Stephen T. Davis, "Wishful Thinking and 'The Will to Believe,'" *C. S. Peirce Society Transactions*, Vol. 8, No. 4 (1972); James L. Muyskens (who construes the essay as a defense of "justified hope"), "James' Defense of a Believing Attitude in Religion," *C. S. Peirce Society Transactions*, Vol. 10, No. 1 (1974), and C. J. Ducasse, *A Philosophical Scrutiny of Religion* (New York: Ronald Press, 1953), pp. 161-167.

[120]The classic statement of this strategy occurs in the Dickenson Miller correspondence with James on the essay. Cf. Hare and Madden, "William James, Dickenson Miller and C. J. Ducasse on the Ethics of Belief," *C. S. Peirce Society Transactions*, Vol. 4, No. 1 (1968), for a bibliography of Miller's essays on the matter, pp. 128-129.

[121]See Charles Stephen Evans, *Subjective Justification of*

Religious Belief: a Comparative Study of Kant, Kierkegaard, and James, unpublished diss. (New Haven, 1974). Evans makes the provocative claim (which he attributes in turn to John E. Smith) that the sort of strategy employed by James in "The Will to Believe" and elsewhere in the defense of religious faith closely parallels Kant's discussion of the sorts of tribunal before which conflicts of reason are decided in the third section of the Antinomies of *The Critique of Pure Reason*. See Evans, p. 169.

[122]*Will*, p. 2.

[123]*Ibid.*, p. 3.

[124]*Ibid.*

[125]*Ibid.*

[126]*Ibid.*, pp. 3-4.

[127]*Ibid.*, p. 3.

[128]My italics. The importance of this qualification will be considered below, p. 232 f.

[129]*Will*, pp. 4-5.

[130]*Ibid.*, p. 6.

[131]*Ibid.*, p. 7.

[132]*Ibid.*, p. 8.

[133]*Ibid.*, p. 9.

[134]*Ibid.*

[135]*Ibid.*

[136]*Ibid.*

[137]Cf. my discussion of methodists and particularists above, pp. 50-53.

[138]*Will*, p. 12.

[139]*Ibid.*, p. 15.

[140]*Ibid.*, p. 14.

[141] *Ibid.*, p. 17.

[142] *Ibid.*, p. 18.

[143] Cf. note 132 above.

[144] *Will*, p. 18.

[145] *Ibid.*, p. 20.

[146] *Ibid.*, p. 21.

[147] *Ibid.*

[148] *Ibid.*, pp. 21-22.

[149] *Ibid.*, p. 22.

[150] *Ibid.*, p. 25.

[151] *Ibid.*, p. 24.

[152] *Ibid.*, p. 25.

[153] *Ibid.*, p. 26.

[154] *Ibid.*

[155] *Ibid.*, p. 29.

[156] *Ibid.*, p. 30.

[157] Quoted by James in *Will*, p. 31, from Fitz James Stephen, *Liberty, Equality, Fraternity* (London, 1874), second ed., p. 353.

[158] *Will*, pp. 1-2.

[159] William James Earle, in *op. cit.*, p. 245.

[160] Walter Kaufmann, *Critique of Religion and Philosophy* (New York: Harper & Brothers, 1958), pp. 82-86.

[161] Ferré, *op. cit.*, p. 297.

[162] *Will*, p. 29.

[163]Ayer, *op. cit.*, p. 182.

[164]*Ibid.*, pp. 184-185.

[165]Wallace Matson, *The Existence of God* (Ithaca: Cornell University Press, 1965), pp. 212-213.

[166]See the preface to *Will*, p. x.

[167]Matson, *op. cit.*, p. 206.

[168]*Ibid.*, p. 207.

[169]Robert A. Oakes, "Pragmatism, God, and Professor Matson: Some Confusions," in *Philosophy and Phenomenological Research*, Vol. 32 (1972), pp. 397-402.

[170]*Meaning*, pp. 258-259.

[171]*Ibid.*, p. 261.

[172]Matson, *op. cit.*, p. 189.

[173]See Ferré, *op. cit.*, pp. 284-298.

[174]*Ibid.*, particularly pp. 291-298.

[175]*Will*, p. 14.

[176]*Ibid.*

[177]*Ibid.*, pp. 29-30.

[178]Earle, *op. cit.*, p. 245.

[179]*Will*, p. 5

[180]See above, pp.

[181]John Hick makes this point as it relates to the question of religious faith in "Religious Faith as Experiencing-As," *Royal Institute of Philosophy Lectures: Talk of God*, ed. G. N. A. Vesey (London: St. Martin's, 1969), pp. 20-35.

[182]*Ibid.*, p. 35.

[183]*Will*, p. 30.

[184]Biographical information indicates that James privately admitted religious experiences of his own. See his letter to his wife written after his "Walpurgis Nacht" experience, *Letters*, 2:76-77.

[185]Davis, *op. cit.*, pp. 240-241.

[186]*Ibid.*, p. 243.

[187]*Will*, p. 28.

[188]Peter Kauber and Peter Hare, "The Right and Duty to Will to Believe," *Canadian Journal of Philosophy*, Vol. 4, No. 2 (1974), pp. 327-343.

[189]*Will*, p. 209.

[190]Kauber and Hare, *op. cit.*, p. 330.

[191]*Ibid.*, p. 339.

[192]*Ibid.*, pp. 337-339.

[193]E.g., Peirce. Cf. Wilfrid Sellars's criticism of Peirce's assumption that the intersubjective intention to promote epistemic welfare implies the intersubjective intention to promote "*welfare sans phrase*," in Sellars, *Science and Metaphysics* (London, 1968), p. 225.

[194]See Paul M. van Buren, "William James and Metaphysical Risk," in Novak, *op. cit.*, pp. 87-106.

[195]*Will*, p. 30.

[196]*Varieties*, p. 446.

[197]*Ibid.*, p. 501.

[198]*Ibid.*

LIST OF WORKS CITED

Ayer, A. J. *The Origins of Pragmatism*. San Francisco: Freeman, Cooper and Co., 1968.

Beard, Robert W. "The Concept of Rationality in the Philosophy of William James," Diss. University of Michigan, 1972.

Bennett, Jonathan. *Rationality: An Essay Towards Analysis*. London: Routledge & Kegan Paul, 1964.

Berger, Peter L. and Luckmann, Thomas. *The Social Construction of Reality*. Garden City: Doubleday & Co., 1966.

Bixler, J. S. *Religion in the Philosophy of William James*. Boston: Marshall Jones Co., 1926.

Brennen, Barnard P. *The Ethics of William James*. New York: Bookman, 1961.

Buren, Paul M., van. "William James and Metaphysical Risk," in *American Philosophy and the Future*, ed. Michael Novak. New York: Scribner's, 1968.

Capek, Milec. "The Reappearance of the Self in the Last Philosophy of William James," in *Philosophical Review*, 62 (1953), 526-544.

Chisholm, Roderick. *The Problem of the Criterion*. Milwaukee: Marquette University Press, 1973.

Clebsch, William A. *American Religious Thought*. Chicago: University of Chicago Press, 1973.

Davis, Stephen T. "Wishful Thinking and 'The Will to Believe.'" *C. S. Peirce Society Transactions*, 8, No. 4 (1972), 231-245.

Dewey, John. *The Problems of Men*. New York: Philosophical Library, 1946.

Dooley, Patrick K. "The Nature of Belief: The Proper Context for James' 'The Will to Believe.'" *C. S. Peirce Society Transactions*, 8, No. 3 (1972), 141-151.

---. *Pragmatism as Humanism: The Philosophy of William James*. Chicago: Nelson Hall, 1974.

Ducasse, C. J. *A Philosophical Scrutiny of Religion*. New York: Ronald Press, 1953.

Duncan-Jones, Austin. "Further Questions about 'Know' and 'Think.'" *Philosophy and Analysis*, ed. Margaret MacDonald. Oxford: Basil Blackwell, 1966.

253

Earle, William James. "William James," *The Encyclopedia of Philosophy*. New York: Collier-Macmillan, 1967, 4, 240-249.

Edie, James M. "William James and the Phenomenology of Religious Experience," in *American Philosophy and the Future*, ed. Michael Novak. New York: Scribner's, 1968.

Edwards, Paul. "Panpsychism," *The Encyclopedia of Philosophy*. New York: Collier-Macmillan, 1967, 6, 22-31.

Evans, Charles Stephen. "Subjective Justification of Religious Belief: A Comparative Study of Kant, Kierkegaard, and James," Diss. Yale University, 1974.

Ferré, Frederick. *Basic Modern Philosophy of Religion*. New York: Scribner's, 1967.

Flournoy, Theodore. *The Philosophy of William James*. New York: Henry Holt, 1917.

Goodman, Nelson. *Fact, Fiction, and Forecast*. Indianapolis: Bobbs-Merrill, 1973.

Guthrie, W. K. C. *The Greek Philosophers from Thales to Aristotle*. New York: Harper and Row, 1960.

Hare, Peter H. and Madden, Edward H. "William James, Dickenson Miller and C. J. Ducasse on the Ethics of Belief." *C. S. Peirce Society Transactions*, 4, No. 1 (1968), 115-129.

Harman, Gilbert. *Thought*. Princeton: Princeton University Press, 1973.

Hegel, G. W. F. *The Phenomenology of Mind*, trans. J. B. Baillie. New York: Harper and Row, 1967.

Hick, John. "Religious Faith as Experiencing-As," in *Royal Institute of Philosophy Lectures: Talk of God*, ed. G. N. A. Vesey. London: St. Martin's, 1969, 20-35.

James, William. "Are We Automata?" *Mind*, 4, No. 13 (Jan., 1879).

----. *Essays in Radical Empiricism*, ed. Ralph Barton Perry. New York: Longmans, Green, and Co., 1943.

----. "The Hidden Self." *Scribner's Magazine*, VII (1890), 361-373.

----. *The Letters of William James*, ed. Henry James. 2 vols. Boston: The Atlantic Monthly Press, 1920.

----. *The Meaning of Truth*. Ann Arbor: The University of Michigan Press, 1970.

----. "Philosophical Conceptions and Practical Results," in

Collected Essays and Reviews, ed. Ralph Barton Perry. New York: Longmans, Green and Co., 1920, 406-437.

---. *A Pluralistic Universe*. New York: Longmans, Green and Co., 1909.

---. *Pragmatism: A New Name for Some Old Ways of Thinking*. New York: Longmans, Green and Co., 1907.

---. *The Principles of Psychology*. 2 vols. New York: Dover Publications, Inc., 1950.

---. "Reason and Faith." *The Journal of Philosophy*, XXIV, No. 8 (April, 1927), 197-203.

---. *Some Problems of Philosophy*. New York: Longmans, Green and Co., 1911.

---. "Spencer's Definition of Mind as Correspondence," in *Collected Essays and Reviews*, 43-68.

---. *Talks to Teachers on Psychology; and to Students on Some of Life's Ideals*. New York: W. W. Norton & Co., Inc., 1958.

---. *The Varieties of Religious Experience: A Study in Human Nature*. New York: The Modern Library, n.d.

---. *The Will to Believe and Other Essays*. New York: Dover Publications, 1956.

---. *The Writings of William James*, ed. J. J. McDermott. New York: Random House, 1968.

Kant, Immanuel. *Critique of Pure Reason*, trans. Norman Kemp Smith. New York: St. Martin's, 1965.

Kauber, Peter and Hare, Peter H. "The Right and Duty to Will to Believe." *Canadian Journal of Philosophy*, 4, No. 2 (1974), 327-343.

Kaufmann, Walter. *Critique of Religion and Philosophy*. New York: Harper and Bros., 1958.

Lehrer, Keith. *Knowledge*. Oxford: Clarendon Press, 1974.

Linschoten, Hans. *On the Way Toward a Phenomenological Psychology: The Psychology of William James*, trans. and ed. Amedeo Giorgi. Pittsburgh: Duquesne University Press, 1968.

The Literary Remains of the Late Henry James. Ed. and intro. William James. Boston: Houghton Mifflin, 1884.

Lovejoy, Arthur O. *The Thirteen Pragmatisms and Other Essays*. Baltimore: Johns Hopkins Press, 1963.

Martland, T. R., Jr. *The Metaphysics of William James and John Dewey*. New York: Philosophical Library, 1963.

Mathur, D. C. *Naturalistic Philosophies of Experience*. St. Louis: Greer Publishing, 1971.

Matson, Wallace. *The Existence of God*. Ithaca: Cornell University Press, 1965.

Meehl, P. E. and Sellars, Wilfrid. "The Concept of Emergence." *Minnesota Studies in the Philosophy of Science*, ed. Herbert Feigl and Michael Scriven. Minneapolis: The University of Minnesota Press, 1956, 1, 239-252.

Moore, G. E. *Philosophical Studies*. London: K. Paul, Trench, Trubner, and Co., 1922.

Morris, Charles. *The Pragmatic Movement in American Philosophy*. New York: George Braziller, 1970.

Murphey, Murray G. "Kant's Children: The Cambridge Pragma-tists." *C. S. Peirce Society Transactions*, 4, No. 4 (1968), 3-33.

Muyskens, James L. "James' Defense of a Believing Attitude in Religion." *C. S. Peirce Society Transactions*, 10, No. 1 (1974), 44-54.

Neurath, Otto. "Protokollsatze." *Erkenntnis*, 3 (1932), 204-214.

Oakes, Robert A. "Pragmatism, God, and Professor Matson: Some Confusions." *Philosophy and Phenomenological Research*, 32 (1972), 397-402.

Pancheri, L. U. "James, Lewis, and the Pragmatic A Priori." *C. S. Peirce Society Transactions*, 7, No. 3 (1971), 136-149.

Peirce, C. S. *Collected Papers*, ed. Hartshorne and Weiss. 6 vols. Cambridge: Belknap Press, Harvard, 1931-1935.

Penelhum, Terence. "Personal Identity," *The Encyclopedia of Philosophy*. New York: Collier-Macmillan, 1967, 6, 95-107.

Perry, Ralph Barton. *In the Spirit of William James*. Bloomington: Indiana University Press, 1958.

- - - . *The Thought and Character of William James*. 2 vols. Boston: Little, Brown and Co., 1935.

Quine, W. V. O. *From a Logical Point of View*. New York: Harper and Row, 1953.

Quine, W. V. O. and Ullian, J. *The Web of Belief*. New York: Random House, 1970.

Rosenthal, Sandra. "Pragmatism and Metaphysical Method."
     Monist, 52, No. 2 (April, 1973), 252-264.

Roth, John K. *Freedom and the Moral Life: The Ethics of
     William James.* Philadelphia: Westminster Press, 1969.

Royce, Josiah. "The Problem of Truth in the Light of Recent
     Discussion," in *Royce's Logical Essays*, ed. Daniel S.
     Robinson. Dubuque: William C. Brown Co., 1951, 63-97.

---. *William James and Other Essays on the Philosophy of
     Life.* New York: Macmillan, 1912.

Russell, Bertrand. *Philosophical Essays.* New York: Simon
     and Schuster, 1966.

Scheffler, Israel. *Four Pragmatists.* New York: Humanities
     Press, 1974.

Schutz, Alfred. *Collected Papers: The Problem of Social
     Reality.* The Hague: Martinus Nijhoff, 1962.

Sellars, Wilfrid. *Science and Metaphysics.* London: Routledge
     & Kegan Paul, 1968.

---. *Science, Perception, and Reality.* London: Routledge &
     Kegan Paul, 1963.

Sleeper, R. W. "Pragmatism, Religion, and 'Experienceable
     Difference,'" in *American Philosophy and the Future,*
     ed. Michael Novak. New York: Scribner's, 1968.

Smith, John E. *Themes in American Philosophy.* New York:
     Harper and Row, 1970.

Strug, Cordell. "Seraph, Snake, and Saint: The Subconscious
     Mind in James' *Varieties.*" *The Journal of the American
     Academy of Religion*, XLII, No. 3 (Spring 1974), 505-515.

Thayer, H. S. *Meaning and Action: A Critical History of
     Pragmatism.* Indianapolis: The Bobbs-Merrill Co., 1968.

Toulmin, Stephen. *Human Understanding.* Princeton: Princeton
     University Press, 1972.

Toulmin, Stephen et al. *Metaphysical Beliefs.* London: SCM
     Press, 1957.

Turner, Frank Miller. *Between Science and Religion: The
     Reaction to Scientific Naturalism in Late Victorian
     England.* New Haven: Yale University Press, 1974.

Wahl, Jean. *Les Philosophies Pluralistes d'Angleterre et
     d'Amérique.* Paris: Librairie Félix Alcan, 1920.

Walsh, W. H. *Metaphysics.* New York: Harcourt, Brace and
     World, Inc., 1963.

Ward, James. *Naturalism and Agnosticism*. 2 vols. London: Macmillan Co., 1899.

White, Morton. *Pragmatism and the American Mind*. New York: Oxford University Press, 1973.

Wiener, Philip. *Evolution and the Founders of Pragmatism*. Philadelphia: University of Pennsylvania Press, 1972.

Wild, John. *The Radical Empiricism of William James*. Garden City: Doubleday & Co., 1969.

Wilshire, Bruce. *William James and Phenomenology*. Bloomington: Indiana University Press, 1968.

Wittgenstein, Ludwig. *Philosophical Investigations*, ed. Anscombe and Rhees, 3rd English ed. New York: Macmillan, 1958.

Woozley, A. D. "Knowing and Not Knowing," in *Knowledge and Belief*, ed. A. Phillips Griffiths. Oxford: Oxford University Press, 1967, 82-99.